T0244269

Litcomix

Litcomix

Literary Theory and the Graphic Novel

ADAM GECZY AND JONATHAN McBURNIE

Rutgers University Press

New Brunswick, Camden, and Newark, New Jersey; and London and Oxford, UK

Rutgers University Press is a department of Rutgers, The State University of New Jersey, one of the leading public research universities in the nation. By publishing worldwide, it furthers the University's mission of dedication to excellence in teaching, scholarship, research, and clinical care.

Library of Congress Cataloging-in-Publication Data

Names: Geczy, Adam, author. | McBurnie, Jonathan, author.
Title: Litcomix: literary theory and the graphic novel / Adam Geczy and Jonathan McBurnie.
Description: New Brunswick: Rutgers University Press, [2023] | Includes bibliographical references and index.
Identifiers: LCCN 2022019249 | ISBN 9781978828650 (paperback) | ISBN 9781978828667 (cloth) | ISBN 9781978828674 (epub) | ISBN 9781978828681 (pdf)
Subjects: LCSH: Graphic novels—History and criticism. | Graphic novels—Social aspects. | Comic books, strips, etc.—History and criticism. | Comic books, strips, etc.—Social aspects. | Popular culture and literature. | LCGFT: Literary criticism.
Classification: LCC PN6710 .G396 2023 | DDC 741.5/9—dc23/eng/20220421
LC record available at https://lccn.loc.gov/2022019249

A British Cataloging-in-Publication record for this book is available from the British Library.

References to internet websites (URLs) were accurate at the time of writing. Neither the author nor Rutgers University Press is responsible for URLs that may have expired or changed since the manuscript was prepared.

♾ The paper used in this publication meets the requirements of the American National Standard for Information Sciences—Permanence of Paper for Printed Library Materials, ANSI Z39.48-1992.

rutgersuniversitypress.org

Manufactured in the United States of America

To Marcel, comix demon,
and
Suzi, for being the folio edition complete works of Ursula K. Le Guin
to my ratty piles of coverless, moldering Jack Kirby comics

Contents

Introduction

. . . .

In the era of newsprint, they used to be called the funnies: these were what you removed from an insert in the newspaper on weekends. As a child, you may have been given a floppy, medium-format, folio-like book with the adventures of your favorite superhero: Batman, Superman, Wonder Woman. You may have remembered the smell of the paper and the clean glossiness of the cover that would slowly deteriorate as it passed through many hands. Later, in high school, you may have found, against your parents' wishes, an illustrated storybook of a few famous works of Edgar Allan Poe or Charles Dickens. You may have been chastised, "Read the real thing." If you are of a more recent generation, you may have not received the same reproach. And even if your English teacher may not have admired them, you had enough friends who agreed on the value of comics and their postmodern offshoot, the graphic novel. While you could see the inherent value of great literature, some of the best graphic novels spoke to you with a depth and sophistication that prompted reflection and wonder. In the hallowed halls of academia, it would have been unthinkable even twenty years ago to have in a literature faculty an expert in graphic novels, no less than in the 1970s an expert on jazz in a music conservatorium. Now the prospect has become a lot less unthinkable and perhaps, indeed, a pressing question. Can there be a theory of the graphic novel that is commensurate with literary theory? This book answers with a resounding yes.

1

It is a question that needs to be addressed for several reasons. One is the decline in the reading of "proper" literature and the decline in reading, period—or rather, a rise in a different kind of reading practiced before the age of the internet and digital devices. Related to this is the seismic rise in visual culture, visual imagery, and the moving image. Further, the last twenty years have seen an expansion in the production, experience, and reception of modes of popular culture such that popular culture has become something of a redundancy, since it permeates all things. This change occurred first in the visual arts in the late nineteenth century, when the avant-garde turned to the subject matter of the everyday, which in the next century would regularly involve introducing collage and montage into its visual syntax. The phenomenon of pop art has now become its own historic entity, for contemporary art no longer can distinguish content between high and low culture. In music, the division between "classical" and "pop" still pertains but is so rough and vernacular that its authority is suspect. Most classically trained musicians today will engage with the alternative forms as much as the traditional repertoire. In literature, there is still a creditable line to be drawn between "real" literature and "comix," the latter in its phonetic spelling denoting forms of narrative using image and text, usually when the image is manually drawn or looks that way. But the difference, we contend, has to be seen along more formal and less qualitative grounds. We are not in any way arguing that graphic novels have taken over from literature—although they are beginning to do so quantitively for newer generations just as pop music immeasurably supersedes classical music—only that they need to be taken seriously as a form of literature. As having their accompanying theory, graphic novels are subjected to serious evaluative judgments set against a history that is made by eminent agents and proponents in the field. First coined in 1964 by an early scholar of fandom, Richard Kyle, the graphic novel now has an undisputed place in literary culture, getting reviews in venerated journals such as the *New York Review of Books* and serious histories and analyses from respectable university presses such as this one. These publications are willing to publish comment and criticism in recognition of a serious endeavor and field of experience.

The phenomenon of the graphic novel—not just sui generis but as literature—is a component part of a much larger change in cultural awareness and production that we call "Gaga aesthetics" and that, a little earlier, David Carrier and Joachim Pissarro called "wild art."[1] Gaga aesthetics contends that there are still aesthetic value judgments—standards of good and bad, however fluid and subjective—that we need to uphold, only that the mainstream art world has become increasingly impoverished to be the main place to make them. With contemporary art resembling the world of fashion,² it is in sites of creative activity such as fashion that we might find activity that rivals that of what rates as "high art" on the contemporary scene—that is, not all fashion, but what Geczy and Karaminas have called "critical fashion practice."³ Not for nothing have the most successful exhibitions at major art venues such as the Metropolitan Museum of Art (measured albeit in terms of turnstile clicks) been those on fashion. Gaga aesthetics refers to not only a scrambling of sites and values that earlier tradition would find unthinkable and crazy but also the pop star Lady Gaga herself. In the early 2010s, to refer to her as an artist would have incited mockery and contempt, now far less so. In her music videos and performances, she enlists countless visual tropes and references that are from rival art and performance art. She has even teamed up with the celebrity performance artist Marina Abramović. We see her not as an exception but rather as embodying a new approach to art practice, where it features within the thick and ubiquitous texture of what Theodor W. Adorno called the "culture industry." Adorno pitted the culture industry (his specialized term for popular and mass culture) against "authentic" art. Now "authentic" art can be found embedded within the culture industry, not strictly, as he would have had it, as its "alienated" foil.

Wild art is art that has not been admitted by "the decisions made by the policing agents of the Art World."⁴ These are not just "marginal" practices but ones quite on the mainstream, such as graffiti or skateboarding. They challenge the term *kitsch* as a "nonconcept" on the grounds that it is used for what the Art World (their capitalization) disdains or does not wish to categorize, as it does not fit snugly within the narrative of art that modernism has sedulously shaped.⁵ Although Carrier and Pissarro's book focuses largely on the plastic arts, their mission spreads to all of the arts. In their conclusion, they write,

> An essay by philosopher Richard Rorty provides us with a clue as to what these new aesthetic rapports may yield. Thinking more specifically about examples from literature, Rorty refuses the use of terms such as "knowledge" or "truth" in order to apprehend the positive results from immersing oneself in a novel. He claims that our experience with literature—and it is highly tempting here to extend this claim to all the creative fields we have seen—offers a cure far less for ignorance than for egotism. As we live our experience through a novel, the illusion of self-sufficiency is broken down. Rorty goes so far as to suggest that reading a novel can best be compared with meeting new people.⁶

And it is here that we cannot fail to recognize that a growing number of people are having these imaginative, hypothetical, yet "real" experiences with characters from graphic novels. Does that make their experience counterfeit, debased? Our argument is that to think so is, to carry over the words of Carrier and Pissarro, egotism derived from ignorance.

If not egotism then jealously held standards are what have governed literary criticism until the slow, osmotic entry of more popular and vernacular forms. True, the vernacular has always been an important and creditable presence in literature: the King James Bible (1611), which was a translation from Latin into the "vulgate" of English; Mark Twain's *Huckleberry Finn* (1884); Jules Laforgue's use of common speech in his poetry, one of the influences in T. S. Eliot's *Wasteland* (1922), which, although part of the modernist canon, was a pastiche of high and low literary references; and James Joyce's endless wordplay and mimicry of everyday speech sounds in *Ulysses* (1922), culminating in *Finnegan's Wake* (1939), were all stages in the expansion of the literary genre into a more casual, freewheeling style from the Beats, such as in Jack Kerouac's *On the Road* (1957) and Allen Ginsberg's free-verse poem "Howl" (1955). Novels such as Peter Carey's *True History of the Kelly Gang* (2001), in homage to the tradition set by Twain's *Huckleberry Finn*, are written entirely in a style as if they were narrated, with phonetic spelling, thus purposely eschewing correct and proper word usage and grammar.

While commentary on literature had existed since the birth of criticism in the eighteenth century, it was conveniently thought that what constituted high literature as such was the work of the ancients. "Classical" literature for most of us today means something very different from what it meant even as late as the early twentieth century. Our habitual understanding of the "classics"—whether we mean Emily Brontë or Marcel Proust—is shaped by an inclination by a variety of thinkers and commentators in Europe and America to defend certain values that literature propounded and reflected. Such values no doubt depended on the writer, time, and culture, but they were usually based on the extent to which literature upheld systems of morality and good taste and the vividness and convincingness with which these notions were written, all of which were advanced through admirable proficiency in the language in which they were written. Stimulated by the philosophical novels *Julie, or the New Heloïse* (1761) and *Émile, or On Education* (1762) by Jean-Jacques Rousseau, it was also expected that good novels reflect sentiment and therefore a sympathetic, reflective attitude to the human condition. Good literature, as it would evolve, made us know others better in order to know ourselves better. This is why the novel would be a medium, from Goethe to Stendhal, that was arguably favorable to philosophy because it was able to intertwine the intricacies of life, where the abstractions of emotion and consciousness met the circumstances and things of the world.

In its evolution out of the eighteenth century, the novel was very much an Enlightenment enterprise. There had been annals, tales, memoirs, and accounts, and we may even cite Cervantes's *Don Quixote* (1606, 1615) as one of the principal forerunners of the novel as we know it. However, the novel flourished under conditions of independent will together with the accelerating proliferation of the written word and the popular press. The various conditions that coalesced in the increased secularization of society in Europe are not worth delving into at great length at this point except to point out that the imperatives that were entrusted to literature were in large part an antidote to a moral vacuum. Literary theory as we know it is something more encompassing than isolated judgments of critics. Rather, as Terry Eagleton is careful to point out in his influential book *Literary Theory* (1983, rev. 1996), it is a fundamentally "ideological enterprise" that was invested with weighty expectations: "As a liberal, 'humanizing' pursuit, it [literature] could provide a potent antidote to political bigotry and ideological extremism." In the manner in which literary theory was shaped in nineteenth-century Britain, the good theory of literature was one that promoted universal human values that, as Eagleton argues, were in the interests of the middle classes, curbing the lower classes from "any disruptive tendency to political action."[7] Literature was to be a more encompassing project that went beyond that of the distraction of literate men and women. This project, developed by F. D. Maurice and Charles Kingsley, who was not only a university professor at Cambridge but a clergyman, social reformer, and friend of Charles Dickens, was socially edifying. They were responsible for laying the foundation of "English" to be studied as a serious discipline. Its seriousness as a discipline was commensurate with the seriousness of the values that "literature" enshrined. In short, the transition from "literature" to "Literature" meant that the latter was inextricable from "literary theory." For it to maintain its importance, it had to be buttressed by criteria that were socially and morally defensible.

The "canon"[8] of English literature that we associate with F. R. Leavis, Q. D. Leavis, and I. A. Richards found itself inscribed with these values but reclaiming more radical views that had been shielded by the upper classes. English and its prime exponents were not only a civilizing mission; they had profound social ramifications that spanned across classes and were not limited to one or a few. To study literature was to engage in the inexorable questions of human existence and relationships with others. It was also essential to combat the rise of mass culture evidenced in colloquial free speech and glib ideas. "In literature," states Eagleton, "and perhaps in literature alone, a vital feel for the uses of language was still manifest, in contrast to the philistine devaluing of language and traditional culture apparent in 'mass society.'"[9] Under the aegis of the journal *Scrutiny*, Leavis and his followers were adamant that "evaluating literary works was deeply bound up with deeper judgments about the nature of history and society as a whole."[10] Thus, "*Scrutiny* was not only just a journal, but a focus of a moral and cultural crusade: its adherents would go out to schools and universities to do battle there, nurturing through the study of literature the kind of rich, complex, mature, discriminating, morally serious responses (all key *Scrutiny* terms) which would equip individuals to survive in a mechanized society of trashy romances, alienated labour, banal advertisements and vulgarizing mass media."[11] This is all hard for us to imagine today, not least because of the staggering pluralism of genres, material, and standards of taste. It is important to reflect, however, that this kind of literary evangelism was being carried out at about the same time as the studies of literature by Georg Lukács and the eloquent warnings against the onslaught of the "culture industry" articulated by Adorno and Max Horkheimer. Inimical as it is to these thinkers, and even if *Scrutiny* is now best remembered for the ardor of its campaign rather than its standards, what if we decided to apply such terms as *rich, complex, mature, discriminating*, and *morally serious* as a way of beginning to discriminate between good and not-so-good graphic literature? In so doing, we begin to formulate a literary theory germane to this genre.

Before we go too far into this, we must ask why, despite its avowed Anglophone bias, which is perhaps in the interests of circumscription, Eagleton's account of literary theory is exempt from the groundbreaking work in this area by Lukács, more curious still given the significant role that Marx has to play in Eagleton's thought.[12] Lukács had an inestimable role to play in the deployment of Marxist criticism on a level of seriousness and rigor that is largely lost on critics of the left today. Adorno broke with Lukács in his aesthetics over the premium given to "realism," preferring indirectness and abstraction in art, which could be sufficient for its "autonomy." It was only in art's autonomy that humans could truly grasp the alienation at the root of human existence. Lukács's *The Theory of the Novel* (1914–1915), although he would renounce many of its claims later in his career, stands as one of the first most singular efforts at investing an artistic form with revelatory philosophical power, something that Adorno himself acknowledges.[13] It is also important for its key insight that the novelistic form has shifted toward an increased sensitivity toward time, prophetic as it is useful to our present task given that the graphic novel is preeminently allied to the filmic adaptation, as numerous commentators have already shown.

The debates over the task of literature (and the other arts, but literature most predominately) that raged and coalesced before the First World War and in the wake of the next were considered more exigent as a result of these cataclysms, resulting in searching analyses of the task and the capability of literature, in its capacity for edification, empathy, and change. If we can mark out *The Theory of the Novel* as a notional starting point in the debates in continental philosophy, the other side of the critical bookend is perhaps Jean-Paul Sartre's *What Is Literature?* (1948), translated into German in 1962, prompting from Adorno another critical onslaught that resulted in one of his more famous essayistic statements, "Commitment." His reproach was similar to that of Lukács, in which he warned against literature, and art in general, being too inscribed with ideology and overly invested with social and political agency. But pace Adorno, we find ourselves aligning more closely and compellingly to Lukács and Sartre for the simple reason of the important role that mimesis takes in their literary aesthetics, for after all, the graphic novel is a fundamentally mimetic form. Although Adorno has his own version of mimesis, the kind that Lukács refers to is more immediately graspable, although his notion of realism is not a dogged matter of replication but is rooted in praxis, which is the way in which a theory is given form, realized or embodied. The following passage from his lengthy essay "Narration or Description?" goes a long way to defining the realism at the nub of Lukács's thinking. He refers to the early poetics of fairy tales, ballads, and the like: "Such poetry therefore had its significance because it is shaped by the fundamental fact of the overseeing (*Bewährung*) or the failure of human intentions into practice (*Praxis*). It thus remains alive and still interesting today because, despite its often fantastical, naïve or unacceptable premises for today's human beings, it places the eternal basic fact of human life at the centre of its design."[14] The last words are deeply resonant: "It places the eternal basic fact of human life at the centre of its design." The ancient romances, ballads, folk tales, and sagas have roles to play in the consideration of (Lukácsian) realism because of this persistence of the interminability of experience. To deny these same criteria to the graphic novel is to do so at one's critical peril.

The relevance of all of these debates, many of which have fallen from view in contemporary criticism and will be glossed in the first chapter, is the extent to which literature becomes a site of contestation, reflecting an acknowledgment of its singular position within social and political knowledge. The insights that can be gained from resuscitating some of these debates will prove especially valuable in providing evaluative criteria for graphic novels and, inversely, to demonstrate how such criteria can be productively applied in the first place.

While based on the comics that came out of the mid-twentieth century, in the last three decades, the graphic novel has witnessed a growth and a following that are hard to ignore. Its popularity is owed not only to the skills of its producers but to a new digital sensibility that is oriented to both word and image. The graphic novel and its forbears, the comic book and comic strip, have been gestating in relative autonomy for over a century, often on the very edge of graphic, narrative, and formal innovation yet marginalized as being by turns lowbrow, vulgar, confused, cheap, juvenile, geeky, and perverse. Yet it is these very qualities that are now being mined by popular culture and mass media, already a form that could adapt to the hybridization and self-reflexive metaphysics of digital culture.

The most sensible place to start in order to chart a clear position of this sometimes contested—and indecisively located—form is with a clear definition of the graphic novel: a tentative indicator of where comic theory ends and where the canon of the graphic novel begins. However, such a definition does not exist. We might begin with "a novelistic form that avails itself of both verbal and visual apparatus." Yet simple definitions should not cloud the fact that the term *graphic novel* is an already contested one. In its original designation, the graphic novel was, at its most reductive, a "long" comic book, created with a longer page count and therefore with broader narrative possibilities in mind. What has come to be lumped in with this term, however, is the so-called trade paperback (TPB), which is a publication of issues released serially, collected into a single volume so as to present a complete narrative. Being similar in length, the layman would often mistake a TPB for a graphic novel, and so the term became somewhat broadened. This has become a self-fulfilling prophesy, however. In the American market, TPBs have been growing increasingly popular, with readers waiting longer for the much cheaper alternative to buying single issues (today, the standard U.S. price for a mainstream single issue is $3.99; the standard price for a TPB, which usually collects a narrative arc of at least five issues, is $19.99). This, in parallel with a growing digital market, has had its own effect on the way people consume comics and graphic novels, with authors factoring in usually five but also six- to eight-issue narrative arcs within longer-term stories specifically designed for the TPB market. The result is that serialized stories unfold in a way much more akin to the graphic novel than the single issue, and so the inclusion of the TPB grows increasingly aligned with the graphic novel designation.

The primary argument for the separation of comics and graphic novels lies in something as simple as format: the singular comic book is much harder to reconcile as an art form because of its usually episodic nature, its relative cheapness, and its commercial subtexts (the inclusion of advertisements, for example). Even the differences between Franco-Belgian comics, which have always been presented as high-quality "albums," often adult (or "adult," if need be) in tone, and essentially the same format as the graphic novel, compared to American or British comics, which were historically extremely serialized and usually printed as cheaply as possible. Indeed, when the term *graphic novel* became popularized in the 1980s, it was often met with derision on the basis of pretentiousness. Unlike the Japanese and Europeans, comics were still considered largely for children by U.S. audiences, despite a history of evidence to the contrary. For simplicity and the purpose of this book, references to the graphic novel are inclusive of TPBs and, importantly, Japanese manga, Franco-Belgian "albums," and British and Australian "annuals"—in other words, longer-format comics that allow a greater narrative and artistic flexibility.

Is the graphic novel now a serious genre on par with literature? This book argues yes, but with its own distinctive criteria. These are not only based on the fact that word and image are closely interwoven but also due to the fact that the graphic novel has had a distinctly different genesis from literature. Like the earliest days of the novel, comics were first considered cheap, soft, and lowbrow. It is important not to forget that the novel in its earliest forms in the seventeenth century was "invented" by women such as Madame de La Fayette and was consequently considered the gossipy inferior counterfeit to serious male treatises, essays, and dialogues. Indeed, the parallel with the novels' perceivably inauspicious beginnings is something from which the graphic novel, in its own contest for status, can draw considerable sustenance. For it is now hard to contest that the graphic novel is a diverse and dynamic medium that has formed its own canon. What is this canon? What are the criteria by which to measure a good graphic novel and what it contributes to the knowledge of ourselves and our world? How is it different from literature, and what are its history and chief proponents? This book sets out these fundamentals of a now established and flourishing art form. To be sure, the theoretical setting mapped out here is not at all meant to be dogmatic, as they had been in the heated defenses of Lukács or Leavis, although their own dogmatism can help adumbrate criteria for reflection debate. Where there is serious debate, there is also serious reflection, both of which are signs that the subject is no longer a trivial detail. That is our mission with this book.

With the digital explosion of such media boundaries, image-based media are being mixed and remixed without concern for contextual segregation and is becoming a language of increasing fluidity and nuance. Perhaps the medium that has become the most widely drawn from is the graphic novel, itself already a hybrid form of word and image, imbued with its own complex and by now very well-developed structure. In addition to tracing back to the origins of the novel and its attendant perceptions (as feminine, as frivolous, etc.), an important aspect of the introduction will also be setting out the idea of a canon as a standard of value, as speculative as this will always be. Certainly, there are already examples of this intention in existence, but many spend considerable verbal mileage attempting to chart the placement of comics into a broader context. In this exactitude lies the folly: comics and graphic novels have been evolving at a rate directly linked to the advancement of the digital world, and so much has been written from a perspective of anxiety over the legitimacy of the form.

Scott McCloud's 1993 much-cited study, *Understanding Comics*, itself a graphic novel, begins with this anxiety. McCloud goes about the task of discussing the formal elements of comics in the context of a much longer pictorial history, justifying them via historical precedent, and paying particular attention to the hybridization of word and image. While McCloud genuinely succeeds in this on many fronts, being published in 1993, the text falls just short of the biggest disruption to the form since the McCarthy era, the internet, which in many ways exploded the noticeably linear thesis of *Understanding Comics*. This was remedied with McCloud's sequel of sorts, *Reinventing Comics: How Imagination and Technology Are Revolutionizing an Art Form* (2000), which addresses the digital world, winkingly drawn on a Wacom tablet. Perhaps due to the success of *Understanding Comics*, McCloud's sequel is able to use examples of the work of others to better illustrate its points, whereas before such examples were approximated by McCloud himself. This may seem like a minor detail, but *Reinventing Comics* better reflects the contemporary ease with reference-driven remix culture while offering a much clearer demonstration of the myriad approaches to the art form than could be expressed by McCloud's own hand in the earlier *Understanding Comics*. Such an observation may initially seem glib but must be acknowledged in response to McCloud's own decision to create a historical and critical analysis of comics in the form of a comic. McCloud's own graphic literacy had grown more sophisticated between 1993 and 2000, as had his reference choices, reflecting the increasing sophistication of comic scholarship and increasing breadth of accessible, mainstream comics. Read as a pair, *Understanding* and *Reinventing* form a convincing argument for the legitimacy of the form by extension of long-established principles of the visual arts.

Conversely, David Carrier's clearheaded approach to comics' hybridized place in visual culture may seem a redundancy in the postdigital world's interdisciplinary approach to visual culture. Yet prior to *The Aesthetics of Comics* (2000), relatively few analyses of comics were able to be meaningfully carried out without a number of caveats. These caveats usually pertained to the perceived high-low divide, which Carrier dismantles with minimum fuss, when considered subsequent to the angst the subject brought out in critics and thinkers such as Adorno and Clement Greenberg. Indeed, Carrier's positioning of comics appears much more aligned with that of the French—that is, that comics (like film) have been considered a legitimate art form for decades. Groensteen's succinct and penetrating text *The System of Comics* (1999) wastes little time in positioning comics via high/low debates or historically, beginning instead by acknowledging the "impossibility"[15] of defining comics before moving into the analysis of the formal visual mechanics of comics and their efficiency in this context. In terms of formal systems of reading, it is comics' hybridity that many of its critics have historically found awkward or problematic.[16] Ironically, it is that same hybridity, now suddenly of its time, that is now influencing other media.[17]

Groensteen's text is invaluable in its efficiency in deepening the established formal language of comics for a better discussion of its structure. (That comics have never been subject to a thoroughgoing semiotic analysis is worth noting and is perhaps due to the shedding of this approach in academic circles by the end of the millennium.) Comics are a surprisingly complex art form, and Groensteen lays the appropriate groundwork for an extended discussion of comics, a form that can at turns depend on word, image, and the readers themselves. Groensteen's formal observations relate less to the visual arts as a whole and more to a language that vacillates between comic and film theory. The author distinguishes himself for sharpening such a language and looking closely at what many had previously written off, laying the groundwork for subsequent analysis. The reexamination of the language and systems of comics has been made necessary by dramatic shifts in popular culture, including the mainstreaming of geek and nerd culture. In recent years, comics have become the go-to resource for the mining of ideas for film, television, and video games. Video games such as *Injustice: Gods among Us* (2013), television programming such as *Daredevil* (2015–2018) and *Gotham* (2014–2019), and a litany of films have all used mainstream comics as a source of fodder (and merchandising) for muscular financial returns, seemingly regardless of quality.

However, this renewed interest in comics has sparked little in the way of formal examination, with most criticism and academic review built around the translation of media and the mainstreaming of geek and cosplay culture. This book seeks to reassess comics in a much more rigorous fashion. Comics have a fascinating history in regard to academia; for decades, their primary mode of discussion was conducted not by cultural theorists but by fans and industry insiders. While this has changed in recent years, the established parameters are still largely the same, assessed through the lens of fandom (which often abandons formal objectivity) or industry (which focuses, in the case of retailers, almost entirely on the bottom line or, in the case of producers, on the craft of the product itself).

For many years, commentators of the medium have been arguing for its cultural elevation: the necessity of a reexamination of comics is made clear by the direction of rigorous analysis of the form itself (primarily toward canonization) and academia's long-held alignment of comic theory with film theory. This alignment has some merit and has a degree of sense (storyboarding is the key point of call), but deeper and more specific scholarship is necessary if the formal qualities and artistic possibilities of comics are to be adequately addressed. Without a serious, unifying theory of comics embraced by comic artists and writers, comics are likely to continue to be a ghettoized art form (ironic considering the huge returns that their filmic and video game approximations generate). Yet this repeated marginalization is not without its merits. After all, comics have an established and artistically rich history as a subversive form. Subversion is, in fact, an important part of its makeup just as much as its inherent formal tensions, and the best comics have sprung from harnessing these aspects of its formal duality.

On the other side of the scale, as a testament to reactive hostility to the medium of comics, is Fredric Wertham's highly influential but now widely dismissed book *The Seduction of the Innocent* (1954). It is, by all accounts, McCarthy-era panic mongering at its exploitative best. Supposedly the result of a decade of clinical research (although no statistics or evidence of actual research is included within the publication), Wertham's claims are sensationalist, alarmist, and at times outright bizarre, inciting a number of comic-burning events throughout the United States. *Seduction* almost ground the comic industry to a halt in the United States and brought about serious censorship and self-censorship in the form of the Comics Code Authority (perhaps the comics version of the Hays Code), which lasted decades, stifling many of the most artistically innovative (if subversive) creators in the business. The book's dust jacket proclaimed, among other things, that comics would lead children to illiteracy, cruelty, delinquency, and perhaps worst of all, "unwholesome fantasies" and "criminal or sexually abnormal ideas." Considered subsequently to the contemporary rise of queer theory and identity politics, Wertham's alarmist screed is ripe for a contrarian reassessment, particularly in regard to the validity of his charges against the form (assuming these are all true actually validates the form as a cultural agent of change, as radical and powerful as any media) and its apparent status as an antiliterature. Considering the contemporary context, taking Wertham's many charges for granted is an efficient way of reexamining comics as a form as equipped for subversive and critical content as any of the visual or performing arts. Bart Beaty's *Fredric Wertham and the Critique of Mass Culture* (2005) provides valuable insight into Wertham's understanding of high and low culture, a discourse that has been increasingly entangled between critical theory and passionate fandom and a division that becomes increasingly hard to define in the digital age. Wertham's claim that comic books made a "deliberate attempt to emphasize sexual characteristics" of characters could not be denied in his day, and certainly not in the decades since.[18]

Wertham's far-fetched and reproachful claims have made him perhaps the most famous and influential of the comic book critics, but it is arguable that just as damaging to the form's legitimization in the long term came from the art world. The Museum of Modern Art's *High and Low: Modern Art and Popular Culture* (1990) and *Comic Abstraction: Image Making and Image Breaking* (2007) were benchmarks for both well-meaning acknowledgment and veiled condescension. While curator Roxana Marcoci's text in the exhibition's catalog is primarily concerned with artworks that reference and borrow visual motifs from comics, its treatment of comics as a creditable resource from which to draw inspiration for "legitimate" artists is telling. Marcoci's argument ostensibly reads as legitimizing, although as an overardent apologia, it ends up as patronizing and forced. Jaundiced critical stances such as these provide excellent material for discourse for authors like Groensteen and Beaty, who examine the comic form on largely its own terms and take its legitimacy for granted as well as the cartoonists themselves, who have a long-standing and rueful mistrust of the art world.[19] Survey exhibitions such as these and their accompanying publications focusing on a multitude of facets of comics have appeared with increasing frequency, but too often such curated efforts still focus upon artists whose work can be understood through a lens of pop and artists working in its legacy (e.g., Paul McCarthy, Inka Essenhigh, Julie Mehretu, Mike Kelley) or who have been canonized as masters of the form (e.g., Robert Crumb, Jack Kirby, Art Spiegelman, Jean Giraud). Few examples exist of meaningful investigation of the comic form without silos and formal caveats.

While so much theory written about comics is specifically focused upon the form's elevation to, or legitimization as, an art form, Wertham's criticisms form, more than half a century after its publication, the most famous and vitriolic argument against such acknowledgment. It is for this reason as much as any that Wertham's puritanical stance (that comics are not only low art but active agents in the moral and intellectual destruction of a generation of youth) is deserving of reinvestigation in the context of a moralistic and pseudoscientific counterargument to the stance's theorists like McCloud and Groensteen. Indeed, there is much written on the ethics of comics, particularly the superhero; however, much of this has been dismissed for the purposes of brevity and relevance. As one might expect, such publications tend toward the safer, more acceptable platonic aspects of the superhero and steer clear of the more morally ambiguous, even disturbing registers of the genre. This continued and conscious positioning of the superhero in terms of ethics is critically tantamount to a knee-jerk response to the moralizing force of conservative American politics; the superhero has always been a fascinating sociopolitical barometer for the United States, and retrospect allows some entertaining hindsight in these terms. However, the oversimplified argument for the superhero as a moral compass for an incredibly complex country does little to parse the formal, intellectual, and artistic intricacies of the comic form. Instead, we aim to consider such concerns from alternative angles, taking into account comics' complexity as an art form and their often subversive subtext. Using Carrier and Pissarro's system of identification that is wild art and our own of Gaga aesthetics and taking into account the formal complexity and sociopolitical venom many have displayed over the last century, comics as an art form could be considered outright feral.

Film adaptations of graphic novels have become big business and have to some extent altered the way the industry is geared. While the history of such adaptations is decades old, it has been around the turn of the new millennium—and by no mere coincidence, the internet age—that the genre has become a Hollywood mainstay. The last two decades are marked by a preponderance of comic book and graphic novel adaptations of wildly varying quality but often robust financial returns. In many ways, this has drawn mainstream comics and film, which have always been related visually, closer together in both tone and theme. Writers such as Brian Azzarello and Mark Millar have taken on the pacing and dialogue of film into their lexicon to massive critical and financial success. Both writers, like Frank Miller, have worked in the film industry, a not-uncommon practice among contemporary graphic novelists and cartoonists. Comic artists have a long history of working in film and animation, particularly in storyboarding and production design, but it is in these recent decades that the visuals have become almost interchangeable, with drawings taking on the visual characteristics of film thanks to the ease of photographic reference in the digital age and the huge spectrum of colors and textures enabled by Photoshop. While many writers and artists take this narrowing gap between the two media as the basis with which to lean back into the vocabulary of comics, developed by innovators like Jack Kirby and Moebius, it cannot be denied that the feeding frenzy of Hollywood adaptations has changed the manner in which many mainstream comics and graphic novels are produced and consumed.

Like film, and unlike so many of the visual arts, comics have always been more or less exempt from redefining themselves in the face of technological advancement. This is most likely due to the alacrity with which graphic novelists are willing to embrace and monopolize such changes, seeing them as additions to their toolbox as opposed to threats to their autonomy. Another reason is due to comics and graphic novels being a hybrid of two long-practiced traditions, drawing and the written word, contributing to the even longer tradition of storytelling. Yet comics have always been *of* technology, rapidly able to incorporate the latest advancements yet seldom beholden to them. Unlike painters, who had to rethink completely their art in the face of photography in the mid-nineteenth century, or analogue photographers subsequently grappling with theirs in the face of the digital capture, cartoonists have always been a rapid study of technological advancement. In the early days of comics, printing processes dictated the limits of what could be reproduced, thereby stifling the artistic ambitions of cartoonists. The difference between the full-color, high-production-value Sunday pages of newspapers of the early 1900s and the nascent days of comics in the late 1930s is staggering (consider the draftsmanship of a 1905 Windsor McCay compared to a relatively crude early *Batman* or *Superman* comic book). Printing technology would soon improve, and along with the introduction of higher-quality papers, the scope of work that was possible to reproduce broadened.

Software like Photoshop became an industry standard almost overnight in the early 1990s, and more recently, the Wacom tablet has allowed an extraordinary expansion of drawing and coloring as well as time-saving alternatives to inking and lettering. Simply put, the graphic novel is a medium adequate for its time.

The graphic novel's historical conditions, by virtue of its relationship with film and its ghettoization as low art, have imbued the form with its own hybrid characteristics and unencumbered artistic growth outside of the bright lights of the art world. Half a century ago, the complex and geeky metaphysics of comics; their questionable pedigree of outré publishing, such as beefcake and pulp magazines; and their demand of a willingness to engage across the characteristics of different media confined them to a kind of aspirational—but rueful—wallowing as an art form. Cartoonists would simultaneously hone their craft to dizzying heights while shaking their fists at their analogues in film and the fine arts. Now with the exclusion zones between media being rapidly dismantled combined with an increasingly computerized global population at home in an advanced cognitive media consciousness, the graphic novel is not such a tough sell. Even the outlier aspects of comics' historical otherness—its queerness, its camp, its alienation, cemented by an industry of outsiders—are now celebrated in the mainstream.

With a final word with a foretaste of what is to follow, we may also reconsider the Zeitgeist of the graphic novel, and there are many reasons for its growth and appearance in the last few decades, as we have begun to mention. Yet another is that we are fast entering a new age in human evolution of bioengineering, artificial intelligence, physical alteration, and ultrasophisticated prosthetics. We are in the age of what has with some contestation been dubbed the Anthropocene, where posthumanism has overthrown humanism. What better than to have a "literary" genre that presents to us a world in which artificiality and hypothetical projection reign over naturalness (whatever that is) or where verisimilitude is enmeshed with the incontestably nonreal (it's a drawing, not a photograph!). The graphic novel is now a decisive element in our posthuman sensibility, where the artificial is the new real.

The chapters in this book compose what could be a taxonomy of sorts. It is a taxonomy that can be seen to echo, if not too earnestly and ironically in the best sense, that of Leavis's lineup of great authors, from Jane Austen to Thomas Hardy. Or it can echo, in like fashion, Lukács's own pantheon of authors (including Thomas Mann, Tolstoy, Balzac, and Dostoevsky), upheld as exemplars of the highest standards of communicating the spiritual and material conditions of the modern age. We come to this taxonomy with the same degree of ardor and enthusiasm as these great but flawed theorists but with none of their gatekeeping or ideological vigor. Rather, the lineup of authors is not an indomitable "league of legends" but rather supplies the discursive coordinates for the overarching aim of establishing a theory of the graphic novel commensurate to what literary theory did for literature, making it serve a function well beyond "mere" entertainment toward being a qualitative lens for seeing ourselves and the very troubled world we inhabit.

Part I

Theories

• •

1

Literary Theory

• •

The Relevant and the Real

The assertion that graphic novels are worthy of being taken seriously as literature and, by extension, worthy of theoretical scrutiny already carries several loaded assumptions. These are related to the assumptions implicit within literature and attendant terms of form, convention, and genre. There is also a presumption in an activity being worthy or needing a theory. The assertion is aspirational and begs justification. A countervailing position is that the graphic novel should not undergo the rigors implicit in such an assertion because it needs to be evaluated on its own terms. This is something that film studies have carved out for itself: having finally relieved itself of its need to be called an art, it now has its own history and a set of principles and schools of thought that can be marshaled for critical reflection and analysis. These are film's bulwarks that exist whether or not the evaluation of art is applied to it. Similar to many fashion photographers, many filmmakers do not care if they are called artists or not, content with recognition within the industry and history of film per se. This argument is to some extent valid, except that if used too readily can result in a radical pluralism that tends to disavow the porosity of discursive formations as they apply to aesthetics and criticism.

Moreover, if we were forced to choose, we would have to argue that graphic novels begin their journey as a form first with novels and only subsequently with film. Speciously or not, the use of the word *novel* has in some way to be taken into account. Traditionally, graphic novels and comics have also been compared to literature and, most often, negatively, with the comix reader typically stigmatized as either too inept or too lazy to handle the more serious challenges of the nonillustrated narrative. To try to locate an autonomous space for comix will quickly end in formalist casuistry, as we will demonstrate presently. We would prefer a working definition that begins with two main standards. The first is that the derogatory status of the graphic novel needs to be left to lie somewhere downriver. This is based on the second point that it is a form capable of providing searching, challenging, and compelling aesthetic sequences commensurate with literature. Like "traditional" literature, it moves us, fulfills us, and gives us a joy sustained from more than fleeting frivolity or facile pleasures. And anyone pressing against either point too hard will need to be reminded that the novel began as a debased art form and rose only gradually to the elevated status it has today.

Literature

Before it entered into the use we have of it today, *literature* was a generic term for written matter, mostly printed books, but it could be used for any printed miscellany. *Literature* as material written with the intent of some aesthetic and edifying gain is more an invention of the eighteenth century, although it had already begun to evolve since the Renaissance—that is, when contemporary literary production came to be recognized, however slowly, as on par with the writings of the ancients. The writing of Dante, Machiavelli, Vasari, and others was all modeled on ancient texts, in line with the way that visual art drew deeply and inventively from Greek and Roman art and mythology. In various ways, these writers saw themselves as inheritors of the classic tradition that they sought to emulate or surpass.

What cannot be underestimated and critical to the Marxist perspectives of literary theory is that literature is a historical phenomenon grounded in the material conditions of the day, stemming from economy and class. Around the seventeenth century, literature became unmoored from productions such as philosophy or "poesy"—imaginative composition usually following accepted formal and metrical applications—and evolved into a body of activity that required poise and learning. "In its first extended sense," explains Bernard Williams, "beyond the bare sense of 'literacy,' it was a definition of 'polite' and 'humane' learning, and thus specified a particular social distinction."[1] From this point in its evolution, literature was placed in an openly theoretical position together or against notions of nationhood and vernacular language. (Chaucer had already begun to challenge the primacy of the classical tradition in *Canterbury Tales* [1387–1400], but this was the exception to the rule.) These were exerting increasing pressure on the "classical" languages, which were considered universals until as late as the early nineteenth century, while the local vernacular languages were incidental and by implication evanescent and dispensable. Literature was a minority, elite endeavor reserved for the educated and knowledgeable. The next stage in literature's evolution was toward sensibility and taste, important concepts circulating in the eighteenth century that brought an artist's or reader's subjective experience to the fore. The understanding we have of the term *literature* is far broader, although its elitist connotations remain residual. It is no mistake that taste and sensibility arise out of the eighteenth century, as they are conterminous with the middle class. As Williams, among others, affirms, these "are characteristically bourgeois categories."[2] They gained currency together with the novel's increased popularity and its entrenchment as an accepted form in the nineteenth century.

Therefore, literature is inevitably set within theoretical contours as something that makes formal and social distinctions. Literary criticism, which requires and assumes a set of theoretical criteria, can mean criticism on the level of literature and critical evaluations as to what is or is not to be recommended as worthy of being called literature. The literary critic weighs a work of literature and cites its merits and demerits using criteria based on other works of "good" literature, hence invoking a tradition and implying a canon. Once literature is invested with the belief in its ability to communicate, reflect, and embody basic conditions of human existence to describe the subtleties of social relations and structures, it is perforce subject to debates regarding which writers and which forms are the most effective toward delivering such messages. The writers of a or *the* canon embody these criteria to which they also, reciprocally, have been responsible for shaping.

Criticism as it came to be named and practiced in literature and music evolved at much the same time and rate as connoisseurship in the visual arts in the nineteenth century. Once again, those in the know (*connaître* is French for "to know"), capable and worthy of extending criticism, were those who had had the requisite experience and ability to pass judgment and belonged to a certain class. These were the lawgivers according to taste, beauty, and morality. The birth of the art critic in the eighteenth century and the literary critic a short time after witnessed the shift of "aesthetics" away from the study of the senses and toward the consideration of art and beauty. The marriage of terms and, what Eagleton would argue, ideologies is essential for a clear picture of the coevolution of literary forms, values, and practices. To quote Williams, "What had been claimed for 'art' and the 'creative imagination' in the central Romantic arguments was now claimed for 'criticism' as the central 'humane' activity and 'discipline.'"[3]

Whether in literature, music, or art, a standard of measure that animated the critic was that of the divisions or classes of activity. To confer a judgment of "bad" art or "bad" writing required a critical taxonomy. We might say that the self-conscious widening of genres and approaches in all art forms in the eighteenth century, with the increased currency of "popular," "folk," and "light" (literature or music), required criticism to contain or at least makes sense of them. The consciousness of genre and approach and the classification of high-, middle-, or lowbrow are built into not only criticism but literature itself. The various registers in *Don Quixote*—its liberal use of deadpan and irony—can be said to be a form of criticism. We also find a strong and intuitive consciousness of kinds of writing in other early novels such as Laurence Sterne's *The Life and Opinions of Tristram Shandy, Gentleman* (1759), which is a virtuoso performance of various kinds of literary register. Sterne alerts us to this play almost at the novel's outset with his long-winded parody of legalese in a "marriage settlement" between Walter Shandy and Elizabeth Mollineux. Sterne deftly ranges across "high" writing and "low" burlesque, making the tension between high and low art part of the novel's texture. That such reflexivity occurs so early in the novel's history is evidence of the literature regularly engaging in its own internal criticism by scrutinizing its own "theoretical" status. All of this leads to the conclusion that "good" literature inscribes theory and criticism within itself.

Lukács explores the interrelation between the writer and criticism and critical writing and writing as criticism in his 1939 essay "Writer and Critic," in which he separates avant-garde strains of literature since the art-for-art's-sake movement of the late nineteenth century. His distaste for the avant-garde, which includes subsequent movements such as Impressionism, Expressionism, and Surrealism, is in their claims to being substantive. By believing to reveal a layer that is external or indeed superior to reality, these artistic strains, argues Lukács, believe themselves to be immune from the evaluations of and by the lived world. To believe in such immunity is, aesthetically and ethically speaking for Lukács, to will yourself out of business. Being lost in an abstracted world is also to deny the critical function of and in literature, and to deny this function is to settle for a degradation of art as a whole. An early example of a writer with an awareness of this essential relationship is Goethe, a paragon of the "poet-critic" (*Dichter-Kritiker*). The poet-critic is attuned to the act of critical synthesis that in literature is embroiled and aware of self and world. Thus,

> the poet-critic—regardless of how broad his social and human interests, however deep and original his theoretical thinking—will in general approach the problems of aesthetics according to concrete questions relative to his own creativity and will according to his conclusions—even when the reasoning encompasses the whole problem of time and contemporary art—return to his own work. Certainly, as we have seen, and already in a way that raises the connection between subjective difficulties and struggles to a level of historical, social and aesthetic objectivity. The point of departure for the philosophical critic—taking into account any partisanship—is his objectivity. For him, from the outset art has a systematic (in the case of the recent blossoming of thought historic-systematic) connection with all phenomena of reality. And since art is the product of human social activity, since the really important thinkers are first and foremost founders of the social, art is grasped from the start in terms of its social formation [*Entstehung*] and effectiveness.[4]

Given that art is a product of its sociohistoric moment, it is ultimately a critical reflection of that moment, and to abscond from criticism or to deny that moment is an act of self-denigration or a missed opportunity. The literary writer is critical within his or her form, while the critic, if we follow Oscar Wilde's lead, is an artist. This ontology of literature, the critical reflection on its form, history, and limits, will prove to resonate when discussing some of the graphic novels later in this book. Moreover, the status of "literature" as a social and historical category ramifies to graphic novels as well, whether it is a form to be seen alongside nongraphic novels, as film, or as a legitimate category of literature itself. Irrespective of where you wish to situate the graphic novel, the critical status of literature suggests another stage in its historical evolution.

Seen dialectically, the now inescapable presence of the graphic novel is indeed congenial to literature, literary theory, literary studies, literary criticism, and so on because it forces a new process of evaluation and definition. These processes are inherent to literature itself, historically and ontologically.

We could go so far as to extend the argument to assert that the difference between literature and comix is an ideological one—oriented around value systems such as class and taste—that is easily dismantled. After all, since its inception, the novel has had visual illustration. Any novel can be illustrated in different ways and with differing results (think about the demands of *Ulysses* in comparison to *David Copperfield*). W. G. Sebald, a celebrated author of "serious" fiction, is well known for his poetic rather than illustrative use of photography to prompt responses that enhance the narrative's uncertainty and speculative expansion.

Casuist Interlude: All Literature Is Comix

In our contemporary encounter with media, we are so regularly faced with the marriage of pictures and the written word that we are disinclined to give it a second thought. From the splash image in your iPhone to the icons on your YouTube menu, it would almost seem that not having images accompany words would be an impoverishment, confrontingly barren. However, we may confront the word-image relationship as the transition from signifier to signified, as symbiotic and complementary, or finally, as a difference that is a matter of degree as opposed to kind.

What follows is a gloss of the spirited essay "Redefining Comics" by John Holbo that delves into the formal definitions of comics only to dismantle them. Holbo begins with one of the more cited and popular definitions by cartoonist Scott McCloud from the now "classic" (and bestselling) book *Understanding Comics: The Invisible Art* (1993): "Juxtaposed and other images in deliberate sequence, intended to convey information and/or to produce an aesthetic response in the viewer."[5] Holbo rightly takes this statement to be wobbly on more than one count. McCloud's account would seem to include children's books. On the other hand, he does not admit to a one-panel gag strip.[6] To this we can add the unbearably broad "aesthetic response in the viewer." Nonetheless, Holbo agrees that McCloud's "historically revisionistic [*sic*], formalistic definitions" is necessary.[7] McCloud's historical perspective includes the Bayeux Tapestry in his genealogy, which, Holbo adds, must by extension also include Michelangelo's Sistine Chapel.[8]

The contention that single panels are not comics is also untenable because comics are filled with instances when a panel speaks for itself. Does this mean that a narrative image from the old master tradition (Holbo cites Caravaggio's *The Sacrifice of Isaac* [1603]) can join the umbrella definition of comics? Further, if a comic can be a comic without words, would then the reverse also be true—a comic without pictures? Holbo cites Frans Masereel's *Passionate Journey* and Nabokov's *King, Queen, Knave*. He is sure to take the extrapolation to its fullest effect: "Typography *is* graphic design. Novels, being typed, are *graphic* novels. . . . Letterforms *are* images. They just aren't *pictures*."[9]

Reeling back a little, Holbo examines "canonic" (we are not disposed to scare quotes, but we are aware of the terrain of contention that we are traversing) novels that have long existed together with pictures but can also exist without them, such as Lewis Carroll without the famous illustrations by John Tenniel or Jane Austen without the work of Hugh Thomson. But then, it is instructive to know about Charles Dickens, who "collaborated closely with his illustrators, even dictating placement of wood engravings in page layouts. Sometimes Dickens suited words to pictures. Dickens' novels were, famously, serialized. Monthly installments were unified by their wrappers (rich 'visual confections,' to employ Tufte's term). Each opened with two plates."[10] The extent of Dickens's receptiveness and dedication to the illustrative ballast for his work is striking. It renders his work *paracomics*, along with Hogarth, who is termed *precomics*. If these terms fail to convince, no matter: the point to be drawn is the fluency with which the works of "great," "high" art has with comics, materially, conceptually, and historically.

After then demonstrating the effects of words as image using different graphemes and font styles, Holbo concludes that "it is quite critical to see that 'comics' has expanded to the point of being a veritable synecdoche for graphic design *and* at the same time become more deeply interested in its own historic, generic roots."[11] While debates will continue to rage about comics versus written novels, as they do about the primacy or legitimacy of all art forms by fanatics, naysayers, and gatekeepers, we can at least conclude that these are subjective choices based on aesthetics and form that elide the question of function. That is, glib variances with comics seem unlikely to evaluate what they do in terms of their potential to communicate a message, condition, or sensibility. The success, immeasurable as it is, is to create a convincing narrative that has a bearing on the reader. Even when embracing the fantastic and the extreme, the narrative is relevant and thus real.

"Real" is a vexingly contested word and can end up in the same casuistry as what defines a comic due to the common difficulty of both terms straddling several categories at once. Taken on its least contentious level, realism rests on what is verisimilar, recognizable, and graspable. "Naturally," writes Lukács in a later study (*The Contemporary Meaning of Critical Realism*,

1957), "the finished work is itself an image of its actual causal process but in such a way that it does not get caught in an indiscriminate chronicling."[12] Thus the real is not a facsimile; it is a selective, invented, and judicious rapport with the living world, not a slavish itinerary. Taken further, realism pertains to what is convincing and compelling but in a sense that does not partake of propaganda or manipulation. These are still abstract terms, variable and highly subjective. We will attempt to sharpen them.

The Return of the Real

For most readers of literature, "Marxist criticism" is the name for a critical artifact, taken for something allied to a terribly failed social experiment. But this corollary, understandable as it may be to contemporary eyes unfamiliar with the details, is an unfortunate one. To begin with, what constitutes Marxist theory in literature is as unstable and as open to interpretation as "literature" itself. Aspects of Marxist literary and cultural theory are embedded in our thinking today, including the belief that a work of art is the bearer of the material and historical conditions in which it is made. Most critics and practitioners are aware of the notion of the "Zeitgeist medium," the idea that a certain medium and approach in art is more seamless in its productive and communicative values than another. This belief has its roots in Marxist aesthetics as filtered through the aesthetics of Hegel. Hegel believed in the particularity of forms and approaches to art in relation to its historical moment. Known as artistic adequation, Hegel argued that sculpture was most adequate to the life, beliefs, and needs of the Greeks, while painting and music were better suited to art from the Middle Ages until his own time.

Lukács turns realism into a universal standard when he states, "The adequate artistic representation [*Darstellung*] of all humanity is the central aesthetic question of realism."[13] Adequation in art stands for what is "truthful" and "right" (and for Lukács by extension, "real") to a given historical moment. "The Marxist theory of history," Lukács explains, "analyzes humanity in its entirety, its developmental history [*Entwicklungsgeschichte*], and the partial realization of its determination [*Vervollkommung*]." Thus, "the Greeks, Dante, Shakespeare, Goethe, Balzac, Tolstoy, Gorki together form adequate images of singular, significant stages in human development that are guideposts in the ideological struggle for the totality of humanity."[14] As Lukács notes of Tolstoy, what he shares with Shakespeare, Goethe, and Balzac "is the realism of the full roundness (*Allseitigkeit*) of life in its meaningfully illuminated dynamism."[15] He praises Maxim Gorki's "deep and genuine conception of reality: this is the common basis of artistic attainment and literary popularity."[16] Such statements are, by degrees, also intelligible when shorn of Marxist clothing: the artists are great inasmuch as the adequacy with which they speak to their time paradoxically discloses the timeless dimension of human struggle.

Whether in allegiance to Marxism or not, critics and social historians of the twentieth century were warring on the topic of what kind of art was most adequate—appropriate, productive, correct, relevant, the words have differing levels of authoritarianism and didacticism—to its time. To make matters more complicated, many of the most thoughtful and eloquent theories are identified as Marxist, although the nature of that identification was mixed and varied. "Marx" in criticism and aesthetics came to stand as a metonym for speculation about what stood to be the kinds of art—forms, conventions, and configurations—that most accurately reflected the conditions of the day. (Already we are mired in problems of definition: we can look at any one of the words just used, including "reflection," which can encompass Aristotelian mimesis as well as subjective judgment.) Fredric Jameson argues that while Marxist criticism may be used as "but one philosophical system among others,"[17] there are nonetheless components to it that make it impassable when analyzing and accounting for the cultural events of the nineteenth century onward. It does so by reminding us of the privileges inherent in cultural activity, enacting a short circuit that exposes the flaws in both cultural producer and cultural critic.[18]

One of the tenets of Marxist literary analysis is, as Lukács puts it in his essay on Friedrich Engels, the "conception of art as a special form of mirror to objective reality."[19] This is a comment that can be taken in various ways. At its most simple, it is an aesthetics that expects that art have some bearing on the immediate world to which it offers a lot more than mere escape. If it does not offer guidelines for a better life, its benefits lie in the insights it offers into its time and into both historic and paramount human experience. Lukács reminds us that literature was a preoccupation of Engels well before he began collaborating with Marx. Engels had a sizeable role to play in elevating Balzac's reputation as the quintessential novelist of social mores and economic relations, placing him at the center of discourse on class relations. Lukács quotes the comment by Engels that he learned more about economic details from reading Balzac than "all the professional historians, economists and statisticians of today put together."[20] He goes so far as to suggest that Engels's legacy is the "struggle for great realism in literature."[21] It is an extension of the task of Marxist criticism to put works of art to the test for their own critical evaluation of history and society. Lukács explains that "the really great realism, which draws its strength from the deep knowledge of the world-historical transformation of society, can only do that if it really encompasses all layers of society, if it breaks the 'official' view of history and society and brings these social classes and currents to life to accomplish a real transformation of society, the real creation of new types of people."[22] A compelling aspect of Marxist criticism is the extent to which it is seen to be participating in an authentic—mythological as that concept may be—analysis of society.

Because of or despite this, theories of modernism have found it hard to escape Marxist criticism. For instance, Peter Bürger's *Theory of the Avant-Garde* (1974) places the avant-garde within a Marxist framework, arguing that art movements of the West in the early twentieth century were guided by the effort to find a more complete link to life and society despite failing in various ways. Renato Poggioli's account of the avant-garde (1962) is less overtly Marxist than Bürger's but still acknowledges that the artist is tethered to his or her time while also maintaining the avant-garde as guided by social forces. Taken as a whole, both positions evaluate the signal art movements of modernism as campaigns for social and historical relevance and applicability. It may come as a surprise to know that Cubism, the most obscure and mysterious of styles that was a decisive watershed toward nonobjective abstraction in decades to come, was viewed by its adherents as a realism. As John Golding states in the definitive history of Cubism, "Most of the Cubists were united in declaring that theirs was an art of realism, and in so far as Cubism was concerned with reinterpreting the external world in a detached, objective way, it was also in a sense a classical art."[23] Cubism was not just a style; it was a technique of analysis and representation by which objects could be captured according to their ontic status within space and time.

The crisis of postmodernism is the shift in these relationships, the unmooring of artistic language from its context, and an uncertainty in what that context is from the start. The discussions about relevance and reality in art would ebb somewhat. The refrain of postmodernity was an echo of commentators such as Jean Baudrillard and Umberto Eco as a world swallowed by the vertiginous matrix of simulation and hyperreality. The postmodern work of art and literature must compete with or succumb to a world of plural realities that are transmitted to us with ever-increasing intensity and quantity. If we have made our peace with such circumstances or learned to live with their contradictions since the new millennium with the staggering proliferation of digital media, we would have to state that the Zeitgeist medium is film. The abstractions of the artistic and literary avant-garde are more historicized than ever. "Quality TV," as it is called, has become the inheritor of the panoramic realist novel in its settings, its range of characters, and the depth of psychological penetration. Just as there are adherents of Austen over Tolstoy, it is customary to be a follower of *The Wire* over *Westworld*. Debates over which is the superior show, *Better Call Saul* or *Breaking Bad*, take place all the time, with the originality of the plotlines and the breadth and depth of characterization being focal contentions.

Historically speaking, the global and critical "academic" rise of graphic novels has been at the same rate as that of quality TV. There can be no doubt that this growth can be attributed in no small degree to the ubiquity of film in the global culture, which has attuned audiences to be receptive to both words and images. Moreover, the staggering success of films and television series based on comics and graphic novels has expanded into its own discrete genre and industry. The collaboration, so to speak, between film and comics has meant that they are viewed as extensions of each other. This is a subject that deserves to be treated with attention and will be the subject of a later study. For now, the focus is on isolating the criteria for evaluating graphic novels in relation to their "traditional," "literary" forerunners, if we choose not to start with the Bayeux tapestry but more with the twentieth century.

One last comment about contemporary television of this kind that brings in yet another defense of invoking realism. The rise of television series that follow dramatic plotlines and allow for the characterization that shares more with lengthy realist novels than with films is attributable to a number of factors, the most salient being digital streaming. Digital streaming has facilitated greater program accessibility and resulted in extended watching patterns. While binging could be had with a box set of DVDs, it has today become something of an institution of media consumption. The form is now fairly established and includes long-form series and limited series, such as *The Undoing* (2020) and *Your Honor* (2020), which both unfold within six to eight episodes, each episode like a chapter in a book. Noticeably, none of these series follows a structure that we would associate with modernist literature—free-form, meta- or multitextual, or reflexively opaque, as in the work of Beckett or Joyce—which includes Surrealist or Expressionist literature. In both cases, form and content fold in on one another and are often in agonistic friction.

Discounting devices such as imaginary excuses or flashbacks, the "quality" television series invoke realism. *Westworld* has futuristic components but is a contemplation on humanity and mortality, while *Game of Thrones* is based on a series of novels by George R. R. Martin that, like Tolkien's *Lord of the Rings*, uses the clothing of fantasy to explore the intricacies of power, betrayal, customs, human fallibility, and so on. Similarly, when we compare this trend to graphic novels, we can also see that modernist characteristics are so few as to be the exception at best. Their recourse to fantasy makes them no less real because fantasy is used as a device for exploring human anxieties and foibles. The copresence of pictures makes fantasy an understandable value in a graphic novel in comparison to a wholly written book, which has to enframe its atmosphere and setting in a different way. for graphic novels are by nature mimetic and bear a relation to realism, even when they have recourse to the fantastic and the bizarre.

Narrative in the first decades of the new millennium is a return to realism. The most dedicated, as well as the most troubled, thinker of realism is Lukács. Our analysis will need to be selective not only for the breadth of his writing and for the sake of concision but also for the reason that many of his theoretical positions are unduly narrow or untenable. Lukács, in his Marxist thinking through his early and influential works such as *History and Class Consciousness* (1923), took a strong Hegelian leaning. Like Hegel—whether we mean Hegel and the philosophy of nature or Hegel's aesthetics—there are some embarrassing details and some overambitious claims. In between, there are many moments to be mined that continue to resonate, and many of them have unjustly fallen away, a casualty of the din of discredit.

2

Recuperating Realism

• •

Lukács

There are several reasons why Georg Lukács's work on literature and aesthetics has paled from view that are not confined by Marxism falling from contemporary fashion. These have to do with the contradictions in his thought, including contradictions and repudiations that he made himself throughout his long and colorful career. Like Schelling's philosophy, Lukács's thought slips from anything systematic for any great length of time, which means that anyone coming to him for the first time does not know from which angle or from which era to tackle him. These irregularities are possibly a factor in accounting for why only a selection of his writings are available in translation, limiting those who may wish to attempt a broad and rigorous summation of his thought. Most salient of all, however, is that his standards of what constitutes the best examples of art are widely held to be too narrow, and suffocatingly so. As would be expected, the narrowness of standards leads to the conclusion of the narrowness of vision. His antagonism to many of the tenets and achievements of modernism did not win him friends and caused him to lose many. These include Theodor Adorno and Ernst Bloch, who would offer him begrudging respect before repudiating him with exasperation bordering on spite. The intellectual contribution of his early works, *The Theory of the Novel* (1914–1915) and *History and Class Consciousness* (1923), cannot be denied, but his later work, such as his most in-depth and searching studies on realism and literature, from *Balzac and French Realism* (1945) to *The Historical Novel* (1955), to his extensive and often brilliant essays on German literature from the late eighteenth century onward and his final assertion of his position on literature over that of modernism in *The Contemporary Meaning of Critical Realism* (1957), would be discredited for the taint of Stalinism. If history has not served Lukács as well as it might, there is enough to argue against the inconsistent divisions in his thought, which we can only gloss. It is often the case that prejudices in thought are conveniently upheld to discount the need for further investigation: a thinker dispatched is a thinker resolved. Nevertheless, the generalizations, which have become rigid through time, have tended to get in the way of the details. What occupies us most forcefully in this chapter are the areas of analysis that can be brought fruitfully to bear on a literary theory of graphic novels.

One of the more convincing attempts at critical restitution is in the hands of Fredric Jameson in his 1970 essay "The Case for Georg Lukács," which many acknowledge as the text that serves as the most lucid and serviceable entrée of the thinker to the Anglophone world. Here Jameson briefly mentions a handful of disgruntled comments about Lukács, from Susan Sontag to George Steiner, quoting Adorno at his merciless best: "Lukács's personal integrity is above all suspicion. But the conceptual structure to which he has sacrificed his intellect is so restricted that it suffocates anything which might have breathed more freely."[1] Despite the chorus of disapproval, Jameson holds to the tenacity of much of Lukács's work, which continues to be referenced, while suggesting that seen as a whole, the inconsistency with which his work is branded is exaggerated and perhaps a misunderstanding. He was far from a capricious or jingoistic thinker. The division of his life into relatively discrete periods, Jameson argues, is a topos that highlights the differences rather than the continuities: "Yet what if the earlier works proved to be fully comprehensible only in light of the later ones?"[2] This is undoubtedly true, especially regarding *The Theory of the Novel*, which is too slender and, in some ways, idiosyncratic (to the point of being mystical) to be taken on its own terms while regularly being used as a touchstone when examining later works. As Jameson rightly avers, Lukács was drawn to narration as a device that draws together the superficies of life with the inner logic of life and living. As Jameson epigrammatically concludes, his ideal of the concrete finds itself in *The Theory of the Novel* and reinscribed in *History and Class Consciousness*, where he demonstrates that it "depends on the privileged historical moments in which access to society as a totality may once again somehow be reinvented. Lukács's work confirms the opinion of no less an expert than Martin Heidegger himself, who saw in Marxism not merely a political or economic theory but above all an ontology and an original mode of recovering our relationship to being itself. But of such an opening onto Being, now conceived as a social and historical substance, it is narration which is both the formal sign and the concrete expression."[3] Narration as it grew out of ancient times was for Lukács an essential key for knowledge and for situating and asserting being in the world. The great works from any time, he believed, were ones through which we can divine the interrelation of being within time, which like human existence itself was colored historically but also had inexorably similar qualities or the same.

Throughout his career, Lukács insisted that the concrete elements of life within art, particularly the novel, when elaborated in the most effective form, were able to reveal the historical moments that defined our lives and give them meaning. The problem lay in what for Lukács constituted effective form. As we will return to time and again, the error is to read his preference for realism as an ideological parti pris that was such a form; instead, it was an effective form that was realism. It is perhaps unsurprising that a muddle has resulted from the overelastic nature of the word *realism* itself, not helped by the fact that the writers that Lukács championed—preeminently Balzac, Tolstoy, and Thomas Mann—fit squarely within the tradition identified as literary realism, a tradition that he helped shape. As a lineup, they fall into further discredit because they were championed by far less subtle or courageous commentators as exemplars of "social realism" (a tendency that Lukács did not wholly repudiate but believed to be treated with caution) and, more recently, were placed into a narrow phallocentric canon. Unfortunately, this is another sweeping condemnation that discounts his sensitive treatment of Cervantes, Friedrich Hölderlin, Joseph von Eichendorff, and Heinrich von Kleist. Kleist, at least, cannot be accused of penning narratives that have the coherence of a writer like Balzac. Balzac himself had his share of superrealist dalliances. For instance, his first successful and serious novel under his own name, *Peau de chagrin* (translated as *The Wild Ass's Skin*, 1831), follows a fable-like premise, or what we might more recently call magic realism: the hero discovers a fragment of hide that grants him his every wish but at the expense of sapping his life force. The more supernatural novel *Séraphîta* (1834) tells of a hermaphroditic angel caught in a love tragedy in a castle on a Norwegian fjord. Moreover, as we shall shortly see, the conclusion that *The Theory of the Novel* draws anticipates the work of Joyce and Proust, in which time is placed at the epicenter of the narrative in a way that supersedes the stricter diegesis of the traditional realist form.

Brecht's Fortuitous Criticisms of Lukács

Bertolt Brecht was another of Lukács's contemporaries who had a constricted view of Lukács's notion of realism and mounted a most unsparing attack unambiguously titled "Against Georg Lukács." Curiously enough, however, we witness Brecht in many ways arguing the same point. Once we become unmoored from the belief that all good novelists need to be like Tolstoy, which is Lukács's reductio ad absurdum, Brecht's summation of realism chimes harmoniously with those of his rival. It is certainly beneficial to us here.

Before navigating the routine variances—that Lukács is overly rigid with his choice of form and limited by his focus on the literary genre of the novel—the most interesting for our purposes comes toward the end with the discussion of popularity and realism. Brecht begins by remarking on the slow but undeniable erosion of barriers between writer and public, to the extent that "popular" as a term has acquired a different meaning. (Brecht's essay, published in 1967, follows in a line of Marxist criticism on the encroachment of popular culture on "high" art, the watershed of which is Adorno and Horkheimer's essay "The Culture Industry," which was first circulated in 1944 and then 1947. Naturally, comics come under fire in their litany of the scourges of capitalist manipulation.) Given encroachment or normalization, Brecht admits that "the demand for a realistic style of writing can also no longer be easily dismissed today."[4] While we may today bristle at the overly general and dangerously patronizing use of the "the people" as a collective noun, Brecht concludes that the turn to the most suitable form of communication is necessary to the extent that "*popular art* and *realism* become natural allies."[5] The two terms have their relative demerits because they are deemed expedient and easy. As a result, they are "concepts that must be thoroughly cleansed before propositions are constructed in which they are employed and merged."[6] (The question that presently looms is, Have they been cleansed despite having merged?)

People and *popular*, Brecht argues, are prone to generalization because they have long been treated as monolithic. One reason for the deprivation of more nuanced definitions is that they have long been "held back from any full development by powerful institutions"[7] but are by default or design viewed as a mass as opposed to a conglomerate of individuals. "Popular means: intelligible to the broad masses, adopting and enriching their forms of expression / assuming their standpoint, confirming and correcting it."[8] As would be expected from Brecht, he argues for "an aggressive concept of what is *popular*."[9] If we have not already, we will be making a similar case, especially with an unwillingness to sanitize the residual stigmas associated with "popular" aspects synonymous with graphic novels and comics and with the intent to see the ways in which they have been deployed in unprecedented ways.

Whether Brecht's attempt to "cleanse" realism of its negative connotations is an unspoken retooling of Lukács's definition is unclear, yet his criteria are uncannily complementary. Here is not the place to quibble over the minutiae but only to acknowledge that this background, which serves this book exceedingly well, derives from a direct confrontation with Lukács. Brecht observes that "with the people struggling and changing reality before our eyes, we must not cling to 'tried' rules of narrative, venerable literary models, eternal aesthetic laws. We must not derive realism as such from particular existing works, but we shall use every means, old and new, tried and untried, derived from art and derived from other sources, to render reality to men in a form they can master." He then follows with another swipe at an overwrought circumscription derived "from a particular epoch as realistic—say that of Balzac or Tolstoy—and thereby erects merely formal, literary criteria for realism."[10] The statement demonstrates again the limited criticisms about Lukács's limitations. We only need to turn to Lukács's comment in the foreword to his book on Balzac about realism not being confined to one historical moment. It encompasses the Greeks, Dante, and beyond—all the authors who have shaped "adequate images of singular, significant stages in human development."[11]

Indeed, when Brecht embarks on his definition of *realistic*, he could well be considered a partner in arms. The passage deserves to be rendered in full: "Realistic means: discovering the causal complexes of society unmasking the prevailing view of things as the view of those who are in power / writing from the standpoint of the class which offers the broadest solutions for the pressing difficulties in which human society is caught up / emphasizing the element of development / making possible the concrete, and making possible abstraction from it."[12] While there are differences between the two authors, the overlap is visible here. What concern us are the criteria themselves that are so amenable to a burgeoning theory of the graphic novel.

In his detailed comparison of the views of the two authors, Eugene Lunn stipulates that what Lukács meant by realism was the preference for the "'visible-concrete' as against 'conceptual-abstract' means of communication—as well as Goethe's method of perceiving the general in the individually specific."[13] While it is not in the remit of this chapter to digress into the individual elements of these authors, what is worth underscoring is that not only Lukács's conception of realism but also the extent to which it embraces visibility and individuality and how these are harnessed for the expression of collective forces have been maligned as prescriptive and narrow.

A passage from a later book by Lukács from 1957, *On the Contemporary Meaning of Critical Realism*, makes this relationship unequivocal. Here he defends the emphasis on subjectivity over what he sees as the solipsistic subjectivism of the avant-garde. Subjectivity can only be thought of in the reciprocal relation to society. Citing Aristotle's notion of humans as social animals, Lukács argues that to subscribe to this is by extension to commit to realism in art (literature), given that the individual's interface is a central preoccupation. We began to circle these themes in the previous chapter, but they are worth returning to in order to affirm that Lukács describes a broad historical arc, one to which we are tentatively adding. The following passage is especially clear in linking the characters in literature that are authentic archetypes of their sociohistoric conditions: "Whether Achilles or Werther, Œdipus or Tom Jones, Antigone or Anna Karenina, Don Quixote or Vautrin: the socio-historical, with all the categories that flow from it, cannot be detached from reality, in the Hegelian sense, from its being in itself, or to use a fashionable term, from its ontological nature [a swipe at Heidegger]. The purely human, deeply individual and typical character of these figures, their artistic sensibility, is inseparably linked to their roots in the concrete historical, human, social relationships of their existence."[14] The word *typical* is worth drawing attention to here as it has a bearing on Lukács's exploration of character types: subjective distillations or concentrations that exemplify subjectivities and roles within the social fabric.

It is only a little later, however, in the same volume that we find a passage that has unforeseen pertinence to our present study. This is at the beginning of the chapter that pits Franz Kafka (the exemplar of modernist abstraction) against Thomas Mann (the exemplar of the ongoing tradition of responsible realism). The opening is worth quoting at length:

We had to describe and analyze the ideological basis and principal formal and critical tendencies of the anti-realist movement of our time [viz., modernist literature, avant-gardism, etc.] in detail because it was the only way in which a "literary" literature of the bourgeois world can develop today. It would of course be more than useful, if only in order to uncover its social basis more concretely, to extend this investigation to include unliterary literature, because certain aspects of the portrayal of life, which are determined by Being, may emerge even more concisely than that. When, for example, the cult of the abnormal, perverse is mentioned, "comics" show very clearly how the tendency toward their popularity, toward their preponderance, has penetrated literature from life and not vice-versa.[15]

This is a remarkable statement, if only for its conditional acknowledgment of comics for someone of Lukács's background, preferences, and theoretical trajectory—not to mention the status of comics at the time of writing and that he was not writing in the United States. And despite the slew of prevarications and reproaches he would make about his earliest work, especially *The Theory of the Novel*, which predates the influence of Marx, one aspect jumps out with uncanny consistency. This is the way in which the perverse agent, the hero, is an aggregate of life's processes and anxieties deployed into literature, one of the central and most valuable observations of *The Theory of the Novel*, a study that, whether Lukács would have liked it or not, is one of the most commonly cited of his works today. In broader terms, it is also a template for his many searching explorations of the role of the individual and society as it comes to us in art and literature.

The Theory of the Novel

In one of the more famous examples of backhanded praise in the annals of Marxist criticism, Adorno, before launching into a bullheaded attack on Lukács, credits *The Theory of the Novel* as among the first examples of philosophical aesthetics, which his own posthumous *Aesthetic Theory* would take up with full force. He declares that the book "had a brilliance and profundity of conception which was quite extraordinary at the time, so much so that it set the standard for philosophical aesthetics which has been retained ever since."[16] In the contemporary annals of literary theory, it is a fact that has diminished importance, perhaps because of its idiosyncrasies and occasional mysticism. It was the first work of its kind that defended the right and need of the novel for theoretical inquiry. Although he later brutally renounced its findings (a "reactionary work full of idealistic mysticism, false in all its assessments of historical development"),[17] it anticipates his sprawling and detailed writings on literature and aesthetics that culminate in the conclusion that aesthetics, the theorization of art, must be seen together with social and historical conditions and that narration is essential to our ontic nature—that is, how we configure and understand ourselves within time.

Instead of beginning, as one might expect, with the theory of the novel as it developed in the late seventeenth and early eighteenth centuries, Lukács turns nostalgically back to the Greeks and the golden age of epic narration. Although Hegel in his aesthetics had his wistful eye trained on Greek sculpture, Lukács expresses the same veneration but directed toward the unity between Greek epic narration and its seamless correspondence with the details and meanings of daily life. If this paradigm is tinged with a little generalizing nostalgia—it at least can be seen as fact or allegory—it has the function of being the corrective to the (catastrophic) rupture that is internal to the modern novel (a redundancy given that the novel is predominately a modern phenomenon). It is also a paradigm that Lukács would cling to in later writings despite having renounced his earlier aesthetic positions. The epic describes an age of balance and cohesion. While not utopia as such, its equilibrium posits it if not as a possibility then as a prevailing signifier. A passage from the essay "Narration or Description?" from 1936 captures this well: "In epic poetry, humanity wants to preserve its own broader, enhanced mirror image as a reflection of its social practice. The art of the epic consists precisely in the correct distribution of stories, in the right emphasis on what is essential. The more captivating and general this art, the more essential, the more human beings and their social practice are disinclined to appear as an elaborate artifact, as the result of virtuosity, but rather as something naturally grown, something not invented but merely discovered."[18] We do not need to extrapolate too far to argue that the graphic novel *is* an elaborate artifact, *is* the result of virtuosity *and* something unnaturally grown and purposefully invented.

This golden age of minimal contrivance passes, Lukács argues, according to the growing presence of tragedy, which suggests a metaphysical dilemma when life's abstract meaning has separated from daily existence. The tragic hero must try to hold this alienation of meaning and life in balance but must suffer its imminent collapse. Tragedy signifies a slip away from epic in another respect, as it is more conducive to theater. While Hegel saw poetry as the highest of the arts because it was the most conceptual and immaterial, it was still always a vehicle for the expression of the deeper, more exigent force of Spirit and was still only a form to be transcended, or sloughed. For Lukács, narration is central to the way in which we make sense of life and measure our reality. (This is one assertion of a more recent bestseller, *Sapiens* [2014] by Yuval Harari.)

The novel in the modern form as we know it is an effort to recapture the earlier status of the epic narrative. It is therefore both a symptom of and a solution to modern alienation: "The novel is the epic of an age in which the extensive totality of life is no longer meaningfully given, for which the meaning to life's immanence has become a problem, yet which still thinks in terms of a totality."[19] However, this totality remains both a hovering abstraction and an unstable one at that. The totality found in the epic form is a will-to-totality in the novel. As Jameson puts it, this marks the novel as an agonistic form: "It is problematical in its very structure, *a hybrid form which must be reinvented at every moment of its development*."[20] Whereas the epic hero stood for the collective, a component of an integrated world, the novelistic hero or heroine must navigate through one that is fractured and stands against the world—figure against ground, the figure-ground relation, as it is called in art history—as a sole subjectivity. "Thus the fundamental form-determining intention of the novel," Lukács remarks, "is objectivized as the psychology of novels' heroes: they are seekers."[21] The psychology of the novel's heroes can often be represented as intense and so at odds with the surrounding world that it can be perceived as madness, and the hero's actions can often be represented as misdemeanors in which the line between turpitude and heroism is slender or blurred.

These observations have a significant bearing for us when we consider the number of graphic novels oriented around destabilization and madness. Indeed, one way of interpreting the entire DC and Marvel universes is as built on the principle of the fluctuation between these two poles; in series such as *The Boys* or *Watchmen*, the interplay between heroism and madness is writ large. With this in mind, Lukács's words have renewed resonance:

> The simple fact of seeking shows that neither the goals nor the paths can be given directly, or that their psychological immediate and unshakable presence gives no evidence of true relationships or ethical necessities, but rather of a psychological fact to which there need be no correspondence in either the world of objects or norms. To put this another way, it be crime or madness: the boundaries that separate crime from acknowledged heroism, insanity from life-mastering wisdom, are but fluid, psychological boundaries, even when the established end, in all its terrible clarity and emergent obviousness, stands out from the hopeless strangeness of it all.[22]

This is brilliant if eccentric prose: the reader is pardoned from having to balk. We can apply these remarks to any variety of novelists—for example, the conflicts that occur within and between the characters of Henry James: the warring of inner contradictions and friction of different worldviews over and above any strict formula of living. There is the madness of the love that dares not say its name on which so many nineteenth-century novels are based; there is the tragic madness of the outsider, such as Thomas Hardy's Jude in *Jude the Obscure* (1895), a novel that at the time was described as obscene; and then there is the long list of Dostoevsky's heroes and antiheroes.

Extrapolating, there is also the madness of Bruce Wayne / Batman, who finds himself much closer to his nemesis, the Joker, graphic demonstrations of the shifting lines between "insanity and self-mastering wisdom." They are both prisoners of their estrangement from their broken innocence or, worse, the phantasy of an innocence that never existed. "Estrangement from nature, first nature," writes Lukács, "the sentimental modern feeling for nature, is only a projection of humanity's experience of his self-created environment into a prison instead of a parental home."[23] The end of the (graphic) novel, whether heroically triumphal or gloomily tragic, is, according to the implied laws of narrative imminence, inevitable when seen in retrospect. But the close of the narrative is only ever the close of a chapter in humanity, never a complete resolution. Yet more the case in comics, the characters are perennial: they rise to fight again, and the conflict is never-ending. In this regard, a successful telling is always infused with a metaphysical failure, as it is this failure that ensures the life of successive narratives. The successive failure, great or small, is a disequilibrium and state of being "out of joint" that can have fatal consequences, a discord that leads to perceptions of evil.

The subject in the novel is condemned to travel through his or her historic and social milieu, struggling to find meaning and hence reconciliation with the world. Whereas in the epic there is no doubt that this reconciliation will occur, the modern protagonist is broken and unsure. Hence this begins with Don Quixote, although the shape of his world still has a medieval residue, with its superstitions and religious ritual. As such, Don Quixote is defined and embroiled within formal and linguistic constraints. Although Cervantes's novel pastiches historical romances, he is still beholden to them, however much his protagonist struggles to find his own domain. In many ways, it is the failure of Don Quixote to do so that is the kernel of the novel, the root of its drollery and stylized madness. When the psychological and linguistic structures are provided by the sacred, there is greater space for nuanced disturbance. The demonic is no longer an avatar of fate but, more tragically, a symptom of the disturbances caused by a plural society and social alienation. "The psychology of the novel's hero," warns Lukács, "is a transactional space [*Wirksamsgebiet*] of the demonic. Biological and symbolic life has a profound tendency to remain within its own immanence. Men want only to live, and structures want to stay untouched, and because of this remoteness, the absence of an effective God gives the indolence and self-sufficiency of this quietly decaying life sole rulership if people did not at times fall prey to the demon's power and overreach themselves in unaccountable and unfounded ways, annulling all the psychological and social foundations of their existence."[24]

The hero, divested of God, must find some kind of logic with which to tame and make sense of the world but in so doing is imposing rules on the world, which is therefore a demonstration of his or her own willful vice. The mystic, Lukács avers, finds freedom by renouncing God. Similarly, "a hero is free when he has perfected in and of himself in Lucifer-like defiance, when—for the freedom of his soul—he has banished all the half-measures from the world ruled over because of his fall."[25] The comparison to Lucifer is taken a little further when Lukács states that the demonic character, because and in spite of his obsessiveness, maintains a "confusing and fascinating resemblance to the divine."[26] The ensuing words continue to have uncanny relevance to a large array of characters of graphic novels and, most particularly, superheroes: "The hero's soul is at rest, closed and complete in itself, like that of a work of art or a godhead; but this mode of being can only express itself in the outside world through inadequate adventures that have no counterbalance because the hero is so maniacally prisoned in himself—and this artist-like isolation not only separates the soul from any external reality, but also the areas of the soul that the demon has not infected."[27] This state is avoided by the "genial tact" of Cervantes by interweaving divinity and madness in Don Quixote's soul. Such tact is renounced in Kleist's *Michael Kohlhaas*, where, as Lukács suggests, "monomania is escalated and abstraction exaggerated—idealism is necessarily becoming thinner and thinner, more and more meaningless, increasingly an idealism of 'not all'—to such a great extent that the characters tread the edge of involuntary comedy."[28] Kleist's novella is a signal example of striated, unaccountable, subjective decision-making caused by willfulness and leading to madness.

The most sizeable counterweight to "epic immanence" comes from Balzac. In his *La Comédie humaine*, there is a litany of heroes and antiheroes embroiled in their obsessions—love, money, art, gastronomy, revenge, and more—and all doomed by some degree to fail. (*La Recherche de l'absolu* [*The Quest of the Absolute*, 1834] is a title that could not be more unequivocal about the marriage of obsession and failure.) The individual cases amass to the whole, however, aggregating to a larger if still not wholly coherent unity. With the failed quests and pyrrhic conquests of his protagonists, the demonic is everywhere, and "the inadequate relation to the outside world is increased to the utmost intensity," yet this intensity is only against a backdrop of other humans with similar tribulations and fixations. The net result is that the "demonic inadequacy" is centered on humans eternally pitted against one another in continual discord and incongruence, making humanity's conflicted interests the truth of existence. Balzac's world is a "strange, endless, confused mass of lonely souls and intertwining fates."[29]

The conclusion of Lukács's historical-theoretical itinerary is frequently highlighted by commentators, uncannily anticipating the direction of the novel in his own time by highlighting the role of time. Foregrounding time, or Time, is the logical result of extreme interiorization. As opposed to epic interiority, which "realizes itself in conscious and spatially oriented [*Abstandsvollen*] ways," when interiority "becomes an end in itself," it becomes "crass" and "corrosive in every form."[30] Lukács insists that "the inner importance of the individual has reached its historical high point," such that the value of being seems to justify the validity of only being a subjective experience.[31] This inwardness is part of the struggle against time's inexorability. The hopelessness that the protagonist undergoes at the hand of time is exemplified, states Lukács in Gustave Flaubert's *Sentimental Education*, a novel of disillusionment that is effectively a tissue of fragments signifying "the disintegration of external reality into heterogeneous, ramshackle, and fragmentary parts."[32] Similarly "the hero's inner life is as fragmentary as the outside world." The singularity of Flaubert's novel is its distillation of the problems of the novelistic form: "In the unmitigated desolation of its material, it is the only one that reaches true epic objectivity and through it, the positivity of an accomplished form."[33] This is captured through the "unrestricted, uninterrupted flow of time."[34] In the words of Paul de Man, for Lukács, "Flaubert succeeds in recapturing the irresistible feeling of flow that characterizes Bergsonian *durée*"[35]—that is, the lived perception of time as opposed to its mathematical measure. De Man follows by citing a comment made by Proust about the temporality in Flaubert's novels through the alteration of tenses and alternating scenes and sequences comparable to the episodic oneiric landscape generated by Gérard de Nerval in *Sylvie*: "The single-directed flow of mere *durée* is replaced by a complex juxtaposition of reversible movements that reveal the discontinuous and polyrhythmic nature of temporality."[36] We can fruitfully use these words, unintended as they are, again for graphic novel sequences that use flashbacks and jumps in ways that are not simply mimetic of cinematic structures but refer to examples of novels that experiment with approaches to plural time sequences. (In later writings, Flaubert would retreat from Lukács's theoretical perspectives.)

The final sections of *The Theory of the Novel* are devoted to Goethe and Tolstoy, who for Lukács, to use Jameson's words, "this metaphysical second term, the World, has imperceptibly glided into a new one, namely Society." This has the effect of shifting the tension of the protagonist from a metaphysical principle toward a more tangible and historical one. If unevenly, the hero deploys a need to change his social milieu. For Tolstoy in particular, the presentation of his world is so manifold and differentiated that it calls for a "renewed form of the epic."[37] But, Lukács warns, historical circumstances militate against this, for the moment. The novel is an imperfect form for an imperfect, if not reprobate, world: "The novel is the form for the epoch of complete sin, as Fichte has it, and remains the dominant form as long as the world is ruled by these stars."[38]

The graphic novel, it seems, is the inheritor of this state of sinfulness but where sin is brought far closer to the surface, as we shall explore again in chapter 4. While it would be tempting to delve more deeply into Lukács's extensive writings on realism ranging from Walter Scott and the historical novel to the work of Tolstoy and Thomas Mann, constraints of space force us to jump to his analysis of "type" as it features within literature.

Typicality and Types

Almost everyone who has had some small exposure to comics or just to their filmic adaptations will have been asked to name their favorite superhero. Your choice, if you are inclined to make one, is then taken to be a reflection of your inner being conjured according to the cocktail of airy subjectivism and mythic determinism, much in the manner that some choose to believe that horoscope compatibility obeys some cosmic law. The superhero is a type or indeed an archetype: the prefix *arche* deriving from *arkhe*, meaning "primitive" or "originary," and *type* from *tupos*, meaning "a model." Their origin stories, their special abilities, the other types that may associate with them, and the social circles they inhabit in their civilian aliases are all indicative of the indissolubility of subjectivity and society.

The superhero genre's reliance on type is only a conspicuous and hypertrophied case of what is a basic function of character within literature: each character is the embodiment of a set of personality traits that may be the effect of certain socioeconomic conditions, chance encounters, or generational osmosis. Among the expansive cast of characters in Balzac's *Human Comedy*, Gaudissart conjures salesmanship, Vautrin conjures villainy, and "Rastignac" has even entered into the French language as a metonym for "social climber." Graphic novels such as those of Jaime Hernandez, whom we will discuss in chapter 10, use characters that compose a social composite, much like the main characters in *Archie* comics, which are among his cited influences. The challenge of the writer is to cast his character as an embodiment of a type before they slip into two-dimensional caricature. As Lukács quotes Engels, "Each [character] is a type but at the same time a particular individual, a 'this one' . . . and it has to be that way."[39] Yet Lukács warns that "the real, structured unification of the individual and the typical, the concrete elaboration of the how of acting, thinking and feeling of individual figures is still one of the weakest points of our literature." He was writing in 1935, yet the main point is this "structured unification" (*gestaltete Vereinigung*) of individual and type and that it should be singled out as relevant at all. To be sure, it is a theme that any author and/or artist of comics and graphic novels must face, for the characters must be graspable both lexically and pictorially. Their differentiation from one another pictorially is essential to the stimulating visual dynamic and texture.

The most penetrating and lengthy meditations on type are in a later book on aesthetics, *On the Particular as an Aesthetic Category* (*Über die Besonderheit als Kategorie der Ästhetik*, 1967), in which he takes up the problem of the particular and the general beginning with the philosophy of Kant and Schelling. The category of the particular, or "specialty" (*Besonderheit, das Besondere*), as it is translated elsewhere, develops out of the eighteenth century with figures such as Diderot and Lessing, although Lukács assigns the lion's credit to Hegel, who discerns that the particular is the mediator between the universal and the individual, while Goethe believed the particular to be the abiding concern of art. In simple terms, art, as a form of representation, deals with specific things in the world, particulars that stand in for a greater whole. It is ill founded to believe that an objective and empirical representation of the world can be reached at all, and the artist (writer) must be careful not to drain his or her world of necessary points of concentration on which the central problems of life and society can turn. One way of understanding concentration is through the typical. In the words of Béla Királyfalvi, "The elevation of the individual to the level of the special [particular] means that the artistic generalization is made to reside (in a dissolved form) in every detail as well as the totality of the art-work, making it quite unlike any particular segment of objective reality, rather, a world of its own."[40] The main challenge, of which Lukács is aware, is that the artist does not fall prey to "the typical as such," which risks falling into universality and by exaggeration caricature.

This was the failure that he saw in naturalism, in which many characters go to extremes, where typicality too often tips into eccentricity. This is a criticism that on face value can be argued to apply to superheroes, except when one is willing to accept that the superhero genre is a branch of mythology and fable. Lukács mentions the way that the character type is mirrored by "typical" stages "in human life, its nature, its perspectives. This tendency is already present in the very first, spontaneous types of creation (*Typenschaffen*): in folklore, in mythology. The creation of great typical figures such as Herakles, Prometheus, Faust, etc. is coterminous with the invention of those concrete situations, actions, circumstances, friends, enemies, etc., in the context of which the figure can be elevated to a type."[41] To be "elevated" to a type is therefore to have some metonymic value according not only to interior subjectivity but to the functions that the subject performs and the milieu against which he or she is set against or embroiled in. The typicality of the type, if that is not too much riddling, is made possible through the plausibility of the circumstance and the form into which he or she is cast: "The truth of the form is based here on the fact that the unity, the uninterrupted intermingling of the type in life makes sense."[42] To use again the example of Rastignac, his status as *arriviste* is made richer and, as a character type, more rigidly lasting because his machinations are inseparable from the corruption of the era of the bourgeois king Louis-Philippe, steeped in any number of feckless wannabees and ruthless self-seekers, and the cause of its demise.

Given that most narrative forms feature more than one type and that a type can only be seen as such against the texture of other types inevitably gives way to the notion of a "hierarchy of types" (*Typenhierarchie*). The concatenation of types—seen as a conflict of forces as in the comic genre or as a deliberative to and fro of different personalities and worldviews in most graphic novels (and nongraphic novels, of course)—is at its most pungent and effective when they, through their interaction, evoke essential relations and characteristics of human interaction. The "elevation" of the type makes him or her more than a symptom within a formless whole to have a paradigmatic quality. Lukács is careful to qualify the idea of paradigm away from the ideological type of socialist reason: it must have inner contradictions and nuance.[43] It is also that the different types in a narrative can be embodiments of contradictory or complementary qualities within a subject—namely, that of the author. As we wind this chapter to a close, we quote from a long passage toward the end of the book about the reciprocal relation of type and world:

> We have already spoken of the hierarchy of types in each work, of the fact that in art there is never only one isolated typical figure, much less the sum of all typical features in a single embodiment. On the contrary, in every important work of art, the different types are the result of how their similarity, their parallelism and contrasts in character in fate etc. illuminate one another more vividly and indeed bring them, artistically, to life. The hierarchy of types as the ideal basis for composition thus transforms into a truly artistic shape: through the evocation of a special world in which, on the one hand, the individual figures, fates and situations have an independent, self-reliant sensibility, and in which, on the other hand, their concrete reality rounds off a special world in which all of these individual moments, reinforcing and complementing one another, have but the function of bringing the particularity of this new whole to life.[44]

"The evocation of a special world": it is the extent to which the reader finds recourse to a crystal of life that is external to us but to which we are wedded and embedded with avidity. This allows plenty of latitude for fancy and fantasy so long as it maintains its hold. The attributes that ensure this maintenance are what constitute the narrative's reality.

3

Classic Novels,
Classic Comics

• •

The defense of classic novels is that the written words are suitably nonfigurative to allow us to trace the images for ourselves. Arguable and unverifiable as it is, we will still assert that the ratio of complaints over filmic adaptations is far lower for graphic novels than for nongraphic ones. After the sedimentation of literary theory—literature as having philosophical import and literature as an elevated, edifying cultural enterprise—there is a certain indefinable but undeniable sanctity in the written word unencumbered by images. Never mind the—to many indelible—illustrations that have accompanied the works of Dickens, Poe, or Lewis Carroll or that these authors and the other canonic greats from Austen to Flaubert to Tolstoy have been subject to myriad adaptations in film and, more recently, in graphic versions, there remains a bias of liturgical proportions toward the original written text. Film adaptations were with us from the dawn of sound cinema, where they were viewed with apprehension because of fidelity to the original but welcomed as vehicles of popularization. Today they are a genre in their own right, their critical traction based on intertextual and comparative relations with other adaptations. And when established as a genre, they are accorded their own substantive values that render them parallel or complementary to the film as opposed to subordinate to them. Graphic novels, however, are edging in that direction but still have some way to go. Both of us recall reading graphic adaptations of literature as children while sensing the benign, patronizing air of our parents for being exposed to the accessible version (the economy of compromise to the lowbrow in the phrase "at least . . ."). The graphic component, which helps truncate and simplify the language, was not the sweetener and the lubricant, both indulgences to compensate for more arduous intellectual effort. If some of these judgments are residual in graphic novels not based on stand-alone written texts, they certainly still apply to ones that are. That graphic adaptations continue also to benefit those without the language skills to read the original novel, we contend, is not grounds to cast them as retrograde, for when we turn our attention to adaptations of novels, the critical point of evaluation is translation. There are also a couple of formal considerations, proper to any comparison between the written and the graphic novel: literalism and ellipsis.

Paradoxically, because literalism can be approached from a number of angles, it can therefore not be approached literally. Literalism is a surfeit of details up to an undefined point. It is the spelling out of excess detail to the point of exhaustion. It is the distrust of description over metaphor and figurative language. It is saying too much and ignoring what is important to omit, occluding the narrative with the elements that should otherwise be subservient to it. Literalism and overdescription have been used to critical effect by some authors, such as Alain Robbe-Grillet in *La Jalousie* (1957). The title means both "jealousy" and "blinds" or "window shades," suggesting the imperfect barrier between the said and the unsaid. That graphic novels have recourse to two formal trajectories—the visual image and the written word—can be seen as an advantage and, to the literary purist, a shortcoming. In a striking analogy with visual art, Lukács likens the propensity to excessive detail in naturalism (the main culprit being Émile Zola) with still life. He declares witheringly that "the descriptive painterly endeavors of naturalism diminish people into still-lives, and with it the painting loses its capacity for expression."[1] Further, "the descriptive method is inhuman. That, as noted earlier, is a form of expression that transforms people into still-lives, which is an artistic indication of inhumanity."[2] With expressions such as these in mind, what we need to turn our attention to are the ways in which the potential literalness of the graphic image assists in keeping reductive objectification at bay. In this respect, it must withdraw and downplay scenes and details, hence ellipsis.

Ellipsis is a selective and intuitive abstraction from the moment-by-moment flow of living. It is a process of constellating particulars—types in terms of character or situations—that amount to a narrative distilled from life and hence more concentrated and compelling. At its most simplistic, it is a necessary component of all communication in which the details that distract from the narrative or diegetic flow are instinctively edited out. On a more sophisticated level, ellipsis is a device to enlist the imaginative faculties of the reader, making him or her psychologically complicit by eliciting the need for filling in gaps and fissures in the plot. "Of course: without abstraction, no art," Lukács advises, "how else can the typical arise? But abstraction, like every motion, has direction, and this is what matters here. Every significant realist work—and through the means of abstraction—has experiential material so as to arrive at the irregularities of objective reality in order to arrive at the deeper, hidden, mediated, directly imperceptible connections within social reality."[3] It is through omission, through the process of hiding, that the hidden, in terms of possibility, causality, and inner nature, has the possibility of arising within literature. The reservations about graphic literature in this regard have been voiced too many times already and have become a glib judgment, but one we will attempt to investigate in this chapter and the case studies. Suffice to say at this stage that the process of suggestion, abstraction, and ellipsis must be done according to different means but perhaps more by degrees and not always in a consistently predictable way.

This now leads us to the third in the triad of evaluative criteria and central to the adaptation, which is translation. As stated already, films and other adaptive genres such as operas are not subject to the same negative scrutiny. Film as a medium of intertextuality, remake, and interpretation is now set within sophisticated discursive critical and academic contours yet to be had with graphic literature and comics.[4] Opera, which also does not suffer the same opprobrium as comics, is nonetheless an appropriate place to start. Some of the great operas in the repertoire include plotlines from Shakespeare (*Macbeth*, *Falstaff*) and Goethe (*Werther*, *Faust*) for which we do not decry the lapses and losses in prosody, for much of the libretto is written at the service of—and let's face it, drowned out by—the music. As a chain of cultural signifying systems, we could say that the greatness of the original play of *Macbeth* is worthy of the musical and theatrical grandeur of an operatic adaptation. Knowing the historical circumstances under which Giuseppe Verdi lived and composed is to be aware that most of his audiences would have been familiar with the play—and itself in translation (the opera premiered throughout Italy in 1847 and then in Paris in 1865). Understandably, the libretto (by Francesco Maria Piave with additions by Andrea Maffei) is a radically altered reduction of the play, which must happen in any opera to make way for the arias, chorus, and so forth. "In opera we lose Shakespeare's full language," states Carrier, "but gain the music. . . . An artist who translates is not necessarily lesser, for Verdi is as great as Shakespeare." Similarly, the graphic translations are by degrees compelled to monopolize the visual element, often proportionately minimizing the written component. The pictures take over, at best to no detriment but according to the formal demands of the medium. When we measure language-to-language translations, the tendency can be punctilious and unforgiving; in language-to-language music or language image, translation is measured as an art of transposition. What unites all the examples below is the mechanisms of visual embellishment to an extent to which the strategy can no longer be apprehended as compensation.

The Image and Memory: Translating Proust

While one might easily imagine certain novels having graphic versions, Proust's magnum opus, *À la recherche du temps perdu* (*Remembrance of Things Past*; we prefer the earlier rendition to the title), does not spring immediately to mind. To translate his enormous novel into graphic form would seem a daunting if not reckless task. Nonetheless, Stéphane Heuet's work, begun in 1988 (completed in 2013), is an extraordinary achievement on several levels, including the sensitivity with which he treats parts of the texts in which visual ambiguity is salient. Understandably, Proust's meandering, interfluent syntax has no literal visual equivalent, yet there are other relationships that sympathetically lend themselves to graphic transposition.

In spite of the immense length of *À la recherche du temps perdu*, there are factors that lend themselves to transposition, beginning with the multivalent role of translation. It is a translation of a life, but more intricately, it investigates the realm of memory, its many features and incarnations as a mode by which life is translated and given different levels of coherence. Visual comparisons and corollaries abound, most famously in the dandy Swann's compulsion to compare people around him to famous paintings. One favorite was Benozzo Gozzoli's cycle of frescoes, *Procession of the Magi* (1459–1460) in the Palazzo Medici-Riccardi in Florence, to which Swann would assign likenesses of notable Parisian doctors, politicians, lawyers, nobles, and other society grandees. His pastime becomes an obsession with his fetishized love of the courtesan Odette, in whom he sees as an atavistic reincarnation of Botticelli's Zipporah. At the end of the novel, he compares what he has written to a cathedral. And in earlier years (1903), Proust wrote a preface to the French translation of *The Amiens Bible*, then translated (with assistance) in John Ruskin's *Sesame and Lilies* (1865) two years later.

These connections are relatively well known to readers of Proust, but it may come as more of a surprise that on a more structural level, *À la recherche du temps perdu* could be considered as lending itself to graphic transposition due to its highly episodic nature. His earlier abandoned attempt at a major novel remains *Jean Santeuil* (1896–1900), which is essentially a series of short, verbal vignettes that, in sequence, amount to a narrative but when read alone seem more like mnemonic fragments. Perhaps more of a projection of his own sensibility, Proust made an observation about the way Tolstoy composed and compressed space, articulating the landscape in *Anna Karenina* according to a selective measurement of intervals, articulating select points and details, that "are like larger reserved surfaces that space out the rest, giving an impression of greater vastness" (*une impression plus vaste*).[5] Writing about his own novel, Proust is explicit about its segmentation and compartmentalizing: "My work was in my mind as if it were a vast tapestry in an apartment that could contain it as one piece that would have to be cut."[6] As memory, the revived images are selections that have been altered dramatically, like theatrical re-creations where certain things and characters are made to stand in for the unfathomable whole. A pity, then, that Lukács abjured Proust on the grounds of his hypersubjectivism, as there is plenty of evidence of typologizing in both the selective scenic nature of his fiction and his characters, many of whom are strikingly isolated encapsulations of characters and professions. (Most noticeably of all the partitioning is in the arts. Apart from historical figures, the novel features only one writer [Bergotte], composer [Vinteuil], and painter [Elstir], becoming something of an artistic trinity.)[7]

Within French literature, a key progenitor to the imagistic, episodic style of writing is in the cycle of prose poems *Gaspard de la nuit* (*Gaspard of the Night*, 1842) by Aloysius de Bertrand, bearing the subtitle *Fantasies in the Manner of Rembrandt and Callot*, making its kinship to both high art and popular imagery explicit. (Jacques Callot was a seventeenth-century artist known for his evocations of the commedia dell'arte, clowns, indigents, gypsies, soldiers, and all manner of picaresque subjects and scenes.) Closer to Proust's time was the work of Gérard de Nerval, who brought Goethe's *Faust* to a Francophone public and is best known for the collection *Les Filles du feu* (*The Daughters of Fire*), which contains what in French letters is considered among the most perfect of prose works, *Sylvie* (Proust wrote a short and beguiling essay on Nerval). *Sylvie* stands as a model of oneiric writing, its narrative hovering in midair, achieved not only due to the limpidity of the prose but again by the way that the narrative is severed into discrete units, each of which amounts to a literary *peinture*, a painting in prose.

In his graphic interpretation of *À la recherche du temps perdu*, Heuet was continuously faced with some confronting decisions that would place defining positions on a narrative that is avowedly and purposely porous, owing to it emanating from memory as opposed to the forensic pseudoscientism of naturalists such as Zola. It starts with the lead protagonist himself, who, although called Marcel, is not a slavish autobiographic corollary. Another problem is the visual depiction of the characters themselves. Commentators on Proust, including his first serious biographer, George Painter, have long delighted in speculating the various links of the fictional characters to actual people. The Comtesse de Guermantes, for instance, is generally agreed to be modeled on the Comtesse Élaine de Greffulhe, while Charles Haas is regularly cited as the source for Swann. But others are not so neat. Baron de Charlus collapses both Baron Doason and Comte Robert de Montesquiou, the former corpulent, the latter notoriously lithe and skinny. The actress Berma is a composite of Sarah Bernhardt and Réjane. Such compositing serves a number of functions: not only typing, which we have mentioned, but also the blurring, editing, and sublimating forces of memory, for when we come to the artists, the historical references are more diverse. Bergotte the author reveals signs of Anatole France, John Ruskin, Paul Bourget, Alphonse Daudet, and several more, including the philosopher Henri Bergson. Many characters, the artists preeminent among them, are shifting signifiers, ciphers of the wisdom and pitfalls of their craft. Heuet had to make some hard decisions, ultimately attempting to find some compromise between some of these historical references, which many readers are likely to have known, while also carving the figures out to have an independent shape based more firmly on how they are described than what they say. Does the reader, led along with a visual prompt, lose out? The arguments in the affirmative are quick and easy to make. To compensate, Heuet concentrates on figures against their settings and interactions. In other places, he makes the more complex figures with a more compendious provenance, such as the painter Elstir, relatively nondescript, depicting them off frame or turned and at a distance. In so doing, the mystique is retained while the reader is encouraged to fill in the gaps and account for the visual circumspection.

It is the complexity of Elstir, the cardinal role he plays in the aesthetic lessons of the novel, and the elusiveness of certain paintings that cause David

Carrier to concentrate on one scene involving all three in his prescient analysis of Heuet's adaptation[8]—in particular, the narrator's encounter with the artist in his studio in the fictive Norman seaside town of Balbec, recounted in volume 2, *À l'ombre des jeunes filles en fleurs* (*Within a Budding Grove*, the better and nonliteral translation). The painting in question is *The Port at Carquethuit*, which Proust describes in detail yet in beguilingly indefinite terms given the nature of the picture itself, its horizon, and the blur between water and sea. Innocent and unremarkable to any lover of Impressionist painting, the indistinct horizon line will grow to have emblematic importance for the narrator, who later refers to it and to the "lesson" of Elstir himself. That he refused to impose the will of what he knew and succumbed to his senses—he painted not the thing but the effect it produces to paraphrase Mallarmé's famous dictum—becomes one of the central turning points in the narrator's aesthetic and moral sense to equip him to be a capable and sensible novelist. Moreover, Elstir's painting is an imaginary picture in more ways than one, including the insight into the paradox that to be faithful to one's senses is as much the opposite of pure empiricism as it is a leap of the imagination. There are more than a few contradictions to the descriptions of it. Like Elstir himself, it is an amalgamation of numerous pictures, and if we give credence to the painting's preeminence in the novel, it can be interpreted as a critical avatar in the very process of eidetic and mnemonic amalgamation. As Gérard Genette, one of the outstanding writers on Proust, has argued, the most effective way of thinking of the formation of his scenes, images, and characters is in terms of the palimpsest.[9] With *The Port at Carquethuit*, both the narrator and the reader in different ways confront the palimpsest head-on.

This poses a problem for Heuet but also a solution, which is that he is absolved, so to speak, from representing it. Carrier observes that one scene of the graphic rendition has "Marcel looking at the back of the painting, in a scene which looks oddly like Velázquez depicting himself before his masterpiece *Las Meninas*." We are still left to ask what it looks like, but Heuet demurs. "Because the comic shows images," Carrier observes, "it focuses attention on the problem, without resolving it."[10] Carrier suggests that it is also by virtue of having images at his disposal that images can afford to be withheld. So much is forthcoming that it is advisable that so much be withheld. At the same time, there are suites of larger images in which the reader-looker is able to lavish attention on landscapes and panoramas that Proust describes. In some cases, Heuet willingly represents transversals of time, especially in those passages of memory, imagining, or some mental disorientation.

All of this is not to contend in any way that the comic version of Proust's great work is a contender for a replacement. Yet as Carrier argues, the audacity of the enterprise—that before it came along, the average Proust devotee would have found the prospect impossible; just look at the unsatisfactory filmic renditions—allows "philosophical questions about the nature of visual and verbal narratives" to be contemplated with added acuity. And like all good, challenging, or intriguing translations, it has something to teach us about the original.[11]

Graphic Violence and the Horror Genre

In keeping with the abiding theme of ellipsis and elision, the next best place to turn is the horror genre. On the face of it, it would seem that tales of horror have everything to gain from having pictures added to the written narrative. But any follower of the cinematic horror genre will be familiar with the inevitable slides between the two extremes of graphic violence: blood and gore on the one hand and psychological manipulation on the other. From a formal perspective, the horror genre in both comics and film is preoccupied with its effects, highly intertextual in its competition with its peers, and abundantly, hyperbolically visual. It presumes that the reader-viewer is passive and reactive, whereas in the psychological pole of the genre, the reader is more active and participatory because its narrative relies on supposition, presumption, and uncertainty. Evil and misdoing are not explicitly implied. In many ways, the horror genre, a move that is hyperbolic from the outset, naturally disposes itself to parody, as evidenced in the many comic adaptations of horror franchises, such as *Evil Dead*, *A Nightmare on Elm Street*, and Clive Barker's enduring *Hellraiser* (some purists will argue against its horror status, but the series always gleefully took its B-grade roots very seriously) or in films such as *Willy's Wonderland* (Kevin Lewis, 2021, starring inveterate comics lifer Nicolas Cage).

Alan Moore and Eddie Campbell's *From Hell* (1989–1998) is itself a variation of horror—the slasher—employing humor quite unlike most horror, some of which is a period-specific satire of the language, politics, and sexual mores of Victorian London and the rest firmly rooted in Moore's own (what the British would refer to as "cheeky") preoccupations. *From Hell*, a speculative fiction revolving around the exploits of real-life slasher prototype Jack the Ripper (and subject to a stylish but rather hollow Johnny Depp vehicle), coolly splits the difference between psychological- and gore-based horror. With a page count dwarfing the average novel, Moore and Campbell take their narrative time, indulging in significant character development and careful pacing, sketching as vivid a portrait of Victorian London as has been seen since Dickens. Rather than employing the comics equivalent of the cinema jump scare—a well-placed page turn revealing a shock, often embellished with gore (see the work of Robert Kirkman's *The Walking Dead* and *Invincible* and Erik Larsen's *Savage Dragon* graphic novels for bravura examples)—*From Hell* inverts the slasher staple with remarkable effectiveness. Eschewing the visually dynamic splash page one may expect, the pages never stray outside configurations based on the nine-panel grid. This deliberate device grounds the substantial narrative in a metronomic, almost real-time pace, which is not particularly noticeable during normal character interactions. However, in depicting the Ripper's murders (and occasional postmortem desecrations), it is a highly effective technique, akin to an overlong camera shot, moving beyond the shock of a stabbing and well into its immediate physical and psychological consequences.

The preeminent story in this vein that has become something of a standard for later writers, filmmakers, and graphic novelists is Henry James's novella *The Turn of the Screw* (1898). While it has been regularly adapted for television and film under its own and altered titles (*The Others*, 2001), it has as not yet received much attention from comix artists, with only one rather mundane and generic version from 1984 by Academic Industries and an unnamed author.[12] The source of the fear and disturbance is according to the perceptions of the protagonists, principally the governess and the two small children under her care. It is left unresolved whether the events are caused by supernatural phenomena or are part of a mass of delusions and fears, thus bringing the tale closer to the ambit of our own realm of possible experience. A graphic transposition must perforce avail itself of the devices discussed above, for to render events too explicit is to betray the essence of the story.

The literary horror genre's reliance on visual evocation makes it a natural choice for artists seeking sympathetically adaptable sources. *Dracula*, *The Island of Dr. Moreau*, and *Dr. Jekyll and Mr. Hyde* have all become staples of the comic repertoire. Two that stand out for notice are Junji Ito's rendition of Mary Shelley's *Frankenstein* (1994–1998) and Richard Corben's adaptation of Edgar Allan Poe's "Fall of the House of Usher" (which Corben has adapted twice: in 1989 for Pacific and in 2013 for Dark Horse). It is also relevant to mention that it is routine practice to refer to such books, especially when they have a respectable following, with the name of the original author omitted, an indication of the extent to which the translation from words to

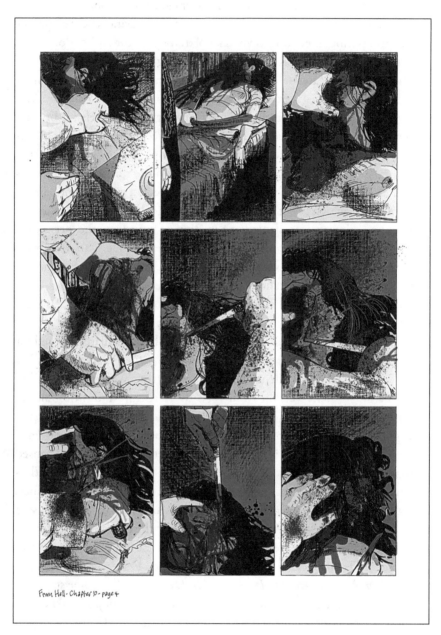

From Hell - Chapter 10 - page 4

FIGURE 3.1 Alan Moore and Eddie Campbell, *From Hell* 10 (2020): 4.
Courtesy of the artist.

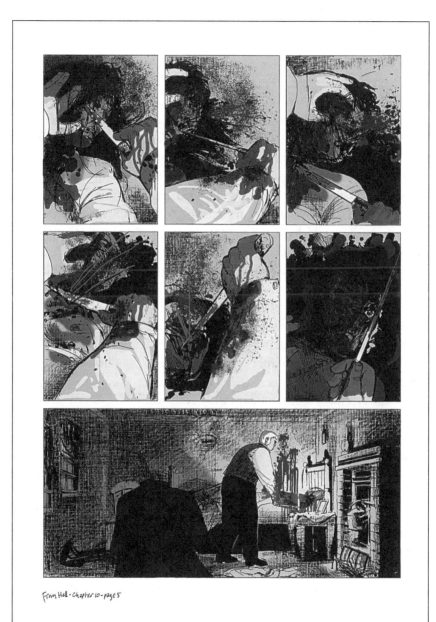

From Hell - Chapter 10 - page 5

FIGURE 3.2 Moore and Campbell, *From Hell*, 5.
Courtesy of the artist.

images is dramatic enough to warrant acknowledgment of a new literary life (hence "Ito's *Frankenstein*"). These and many reputable others have ensured that these key progenitors of horror maintain widespread currency. After all, to any contemporary ten-year-old, Shelley's eighteenth-century prose is impenetrable, and Poe's byzantine style, so incongruous to a verbal blog world that vaunts the virtues of writing the way you talk, presents quite a barrier, perhaps being a disincentive to picking up the original books again at a later stage. In their originals, these two works provoke visual realization yet at the same time rely on psychological spaces of uncertainty, aphasia, psychic overstimulation, disavowal, and disorientation—all-natural human responses to being exposed to unfamiliar, extreme, and threatening stimuli. Both Ito's and Corben's versions are sensitive to honoring these states of disruption, with one device being to place the onus of affect on the protagonist: we are not always offered a scene in question but instead the reaction to it, thereby sliding readers into his (Viktor Frankenstein, Poe's nameless protagonist) realm of experience.

Junji Ito is a much-celebrated manga artist known also for his highly inventive approach to body horror, frequently using the genre as a subversive rupture from contemporary society. Ito's detailed, black-and-white graphics are put to wonderful use in his monster, a long-limbed, shambling horror much more akin to Shelley's original than many subsequent versions: the creature's stitches are the only Hollywood innovation to remain. However, unlike many of his colleagues in the horror genre (whether film or graphic novel), Ito's grasp on pacing is first rate, building considerable suspense. When the creature is finally exposed to readers in full, he is genuinely unnerving and horrific, in part due to Ito's pungent visualization and his development of Viktor Frankenstein himself, a character with his own impulses and values and a sense of horror upon the realization of his creation, as outlined in Shelley's novel. In terms of adaptation, Ito is faithful but not slavish, making judicious excisions in order to keep the pacing at an enjoyable clip yet taking the time where necessary to develop and grow the principal cast of characters, unchanged from Shelley's text, itself a rarity when it comes to adaptations of *Frankenstein*.

Pynchon Postscript

Readers who come to the works of Thomas Pynchon for the first time and who are not so versed in the techniques of postmodern fiction, with its

FIGURE 3.3 Richard Corben, *The Fall of the House of Usher* 2 (2013): 3.
Courtesy of Dona Corben.

FIGURE 3.4 Corben, *Fall of the House of Usher*, 21.
Courtesy of Dona Corben.

multiple registers, reflexivity, digression, and wordplay, will balk and perhaps put the book down before the end, intimidated, irritated, disheartened, and bewildered. Authors such Sterne, Joyce, and Rabelais are frequently cited as predecessors. Joyce turns up frequently in Lukács's writings as the great exemplar of dissociative subjective abstraction and the descent into self-referential formalism, a tendency that brutally eschews, in his view, the writer's duty to find concordance with his or her historical social conditions. Given the primacy on language over lot, attempting a graphic translation of *Finnegan's Wake*, a kind of horizon of literature in its own right, is arguably impossible, whereas *Ulysses* and *Tristram Shandy*, themselves linguistic tours de force, are nonetheless a composition of episodes, many of them disconnected from or with tenuous relation to the plotline, such as it is. Sterne's novel has an adaptation by Martin Rowson. Rowson availed himself of a commensurate intertextual arsenal, pastiching, quoting, alluding, and parodying other sources, including Albrecht Dürer, Aubrey Beardsley, and Georg Grosz, as well as drawing from queer theory and film noir. Rowson explains, "If *Tristram* is a novel about the impossibility of writing a novel, which it is, then my version is a comic book about the impossibility of adapting into a comic book a novel about the impossibility of writing a novel."[13]

Much of the same could be said of Pynchon, although the intertextual and intermedia characteristics are free-form and are part of his works' substance. Pynchon blends "high fiction" with journalism, dialogue, and internal monologue, constantly weaving in references to high and low with the intentional view of their friction and collision. Further, the structure of his narrative is highly episodic to the extent that it continually obscures the narrative thread so that the reader must retain faith in the reading while surrendering the need to know exactly what is going on. It is perhaps because of this that his work lends itself to graphic adaptation—not least of which is its mine of popular culture and the glee in casual diction—but one in which the written component is all but subsumed by the original. This is precisely the technique employed by Zak Smith in his interpretation of Pynchon's acclaimed opus, *Gravity's Rainbow* (1973), set around the Nazis' design and production of V-2 rockets during World War II.

Conquering the dazzling verbal vicissitudes of Pynchon's brilliant but controversial novel, Smith makes a painstaking approach of a page-by-page comic transposition in his 786-page *Pictures Showing What Happens on Each Page of Thomas Pynchon's Novel "Gravity's Rainbow"* (2006, and itself a rather Pynchonesque title). Rather than attempting a typical adaptation, a task that would be close to impossible, Smith instead approaches each page as more evocation than illustration. This gels with the spirit of Pynchon's baroque narrative, which is in itself composed of elaborate detours and at times confounding attention to detail. As such, Smith's undertaking is faithful, as opposed to literally slavish, to the spirit of the original. The project has been presented as both an exhibition and a graphic novel, and while the exhibition was by all accounts visually compelling, it was its graphic novel form that represents Pynchon's work with appropriate fidelity. While recognizable scenes do "appear" periodically, other pages are harder to decipher in their minutiae, not unlike the original novel. Smith's drawings are largely devoid of text, which casts the work as more of a formal translation than adaptation in the first instance, offering a compelling variation to Chekhov's gnomic imperative of *show don't tell*.

It may be argued that the work is not a graphic novel, particularly considering Smith's own history as an exhibiting artist and the fact that the work has been exhibited in full several times. However, even in its gallery presentations, *Pictures Showing What Happens* is still defined by sequence, with each drawing corresponding directly to a page of Pynchon's text and is hung as such. This kind of debate has become prevalent in recent years, which have seen cartoonists presented in the gallery context, and thus out of context, not in terms of drawing or painting but in terms of its experiential components. An original comic page will be lost on a gallery wall, just as a painting will lose detail in a reproduction, and so a friction of intent and experience is created between the book and the wall. However, by any measure, *Pictures Showing What Happens* is actually more faithful to the original designation of the graphic novel—that is, a longer comic created with this format in mind—than what the form has evolved into, which includes collections of single issues that form longer narratives. In this way, Smith's work is a satisfying resolution of this rupture, the cartoonist having created a graphic novel that is easily transposed to the context of the gallery wall and an inventive exploration into the borderland of the graphic novel, the gallery, and word and image.

4

Was Wertham Right?

• •

Comics as Antisocial
and Subversive

If comic culture could say that it has a bête noire, it would be the psychologist
Fredric Wertham. He looms over it like no other. One of the first major critics, or indeed commentators,[1] of the increasingly popular art form, Wertham's
often reactionary message caught the attention of the mainstream and helped
bring about a strict industry-wide censorship code. Wertham attacked the
genre with a singular vehemence that bordered on the pathological. Perhaps
it is telling that a psychologist tapped into a broader and increasing anxiety
over the effects of popular culture as it had begun to take hold after World
War II. What cannot be denied is that it was by dint of the effort to discredit
them that comics received their most sustained analysis to date: after several
articles on the matter, Wertham's book *Seduction of the Innocent: The Influence
of Comic Books on Today's Youth* (1954) was, for all its flaws, one of the first
substantial publications focusing primarily on comics, if not strictly a work
of comic theory. Many of Wertham's critics denounced his views as alarmist, a knee-jerk dismissal that was almost as reactionary in itself, in turn denying serious critical discourse of a form historically known for its self-denial

of subversive content.[2] This denial, however, usually came from publishers, eager to keep their business economically viable (by 1945, comic books were selling in volumes at around the twenty-five-million mark every month,[3] to say nothing of the medium's half-life through swapping and junk stores) in the precarious cultural landscape of McCarthy-era United States.

Wertham's stance represented an anxiety in U.S. society over different forms of popular media and communication, for which comics were singled out for special mention because they were seen as having a deleterious influence on the minds of the young. Wertham's criticisms are predictably that of any contemporary alarmed over the erosion of "high" culture, uncomfortable to the point of paranoia over the skill of popular media to infect all areas of life so insidiously and effectively.[4] Wertham's book appeared in the same year (1954) as congressional hearings in the United States linking comics with juvenile delinquency, which led to the establishment of the Comics Code Authority. A year later, the news show *Confidential File* assembled child actors for a segment against the negative influence of comics. "What *Confidential File* put on film," observes Christopher Pizzino, "already existed in the writings of midcentury comics crusaders, and thanks to the extensive strictures of the new Comics Code, the fate of comics books in the United States had already been sealed."[5] Pizzino suggests that the fear that comics instilled in so many at the time was not confined to literal content but had as much to do with the haptic content, the heterogeneous visceral ways that comic strips and their devices address themselves to readers. These devices had, and have, an immediacy that is not always easily accounted for or properly described.[6]

Wertham's objections, some reasonable and some hysterical, were a symptom of a contemporary Zeitgeist of postwar United States that, in wake of the might of the Nazi propaganda machine, was hypersensitive to any medium that exerted ordinate power and garnered widespread interest, especially new media not sanctioned with the abstract notions of high culture. Wertham can therefore be used here as a particular instance but also metonymically for the kinds of reactions to communication in the contemporary vulgate that favored the volatile and the colloquial over the serene and the moral.

Comics, which could no longer be counted as a peripheral medium, were accused by Wertham of eroding literacy, propagating wild fancies, feeding baser appetites, and so on. In hindsight, we may respond to such accusations in a number of ways, should we want to respond at all. But the collapse of high and low culture, the very pervasiveness of popular culture, and the myriad and fundamental alterations that this ubiquity of popular culture has precipitated tempt us to ask the question of whether many of Wertham's concerns over comics were in fact right, particularly in reference to their engaging and subversive potential. This is more than a dialectical provocation on our part; it has more to do with the rise of new genres and the repositioning of others, which, after all, is one of the key justifications for this book. Maybe his worries are not worries anymore but symptomatic of epistemic changes.

The Other History of the Novel

Before we dive into the case of Wertham, it should first be noted that the origins of the modern novel from the late seventeenth century were equally inauspicious and prone to the same kinds of reservations and criticism. To the freshman student of Literature 101, it may come as a surprise that the novel has quite seamy origins: lowbrow, derivative, mass-produced, cheap, and consumed in haste or by those who knew little better by those unversed in philosophical nuance or in the classical languages. In other words, the shady origins of the novel are not dissimilar to that of comics.

When researching the origins of the novel, casual searches will cite, as we did in the introduction, Cervantes's *Don Quixote*, or they may gesture further back to Murasaki Shikibu's *The Tale of Genji* (1010), *The Life of Aesop* (620–562 BCE), Petronius's *The Satyricon* (ca. 50 CE), or Lucian's *A True Story* (125–180 CE). There are others we can add to the list, but they are not extensive. In many ways, the classifications we make for novels are retrospective, based on the form that grew gradually out of the eighteenth century, stirred by precedents such as Madame de La Fayette's *Princesse de Clèves* (1678). The isolated works of antiquity and the Middle Ages are classified within the novel family by virtue of being prose narratives, placing them apart from the epic verse tales of Virgil and Homer. *Princesse de Clèves* is an important marker in the historical itinerary, as it tends to emphasize that at the time when prose narratives gained in popularity and circulation, novels were mostly women's affairs, inferior versions of the loftier scholarly texts.

The examples cited above are of prose known and available to a minority. La Fayette was no hack, but she was a woman, and her book is about a woman and concerns affairs of the heart. While it may be deemed as marking the beginning of the modern novel and indeed the psychological novel, at the time, for anyone weaned on a literary diet of Tacitus or indeed the dry, sententious, but verbally meticulous sermons of François Fénélon or Jules-Bénigne Bossuet, it would have been received as little more than a penny dreadful. Novels were not an isolated case; the eighteenth century was also the time that witnessed more pornography on an inventiveness and scale than ever before. Pamphleteering, from the latest fashions and art criticism to rousing and seditious polemics, was popular currency. Novels were racy affairs with as much sex and violence as could be suffered by the censors, smuggled through with innuendo and metaphor.

Although numbered among the writers who elevated the novel to the status of "serious" literature, Honoré de Balzac spent his earliest years as a writer tossing out narratives that had been cannibalized, recalibrated, and riffed from other popular accounts and according to tested formulas, not unlike early comic journeymen such as Jack Kirby, Joe Kubert, or Russ Heath. In his early years as a writer, Balzac was faced with the novel following strict templates of plot that staggered from one cliché to the next. As one of his biographers, Graham Robb, explains, "In the 1820s, it was not the sort of writing that normally brought distinction. In France at least, what we think of as the nineteenth-century novel did not exist. The Empire variety, as one of Balzac's characters puts it, was a crude combination of plot summary and speech for the prosecution."[7] Under the guise of a variety of noms de plume—most memorably, Lord R'Hoone—Balzac began his career as an imitator and ventriloquizer of popular trash, ensuring that he had enough to pay his rent and his meals. His output is mostly self-consciously veiled parody, regularly using names that were anagrammatic or personal jokes, such as invoking the imbecilities of his father. He worked for a time in the early 1820s for a roué and editorial hack, Auguste Lepoitevin, to which he first sent his raw material to be tidied up then graduated to substantive screeds. Robb describes Lepoitevin as presiding over "the slime pit of satirical journalism,"[8] who would later claim to have created Balzac.[9] Even if not the case, there is plenty of evidence, passed over by some biographers, of the seedy origins of one of the fathers of the modern novel, a production that did not scruple to put mercantile interests over any consideration of quality or pretension to the truth. As Robb concludes, Balzac's apprenticeship in turning tricks for money surely had something to do with the role that money has to play in his greater oeuvre: "There is even a pleasing irony in the fact that market forces helped produce a series of novels which Marx and Engels, after Victor Hugo, hailed as a brilliant, unintentional diatribe against capitalism."[10] At the time, these works did not conform to the etiquette of "higher" literature, part of which was due to the way that dealt with the minutiae of life.

This brokering for discursive ground and the debate over what is seemly subject matter are a central part of literature's growth and formation. Debates over what constitutes fair and plausible treatment are still alive today, especially with regard to racial and gender sensitivities. In Balzac's time, there were plenty of intertextual and veiled strategies within his work and that of others—very much in tune with what occurs in comics as well. For instance, his novel *Le Lys dans la vallée* (*The Lily of the Valley*, 1835) was inspired at least in part as a gibing riposte to the rather prim morals of the novel of the preceding year, *Volupté* (1834, roughly translated as "Fertility" but published as *Voluptuousness*) by Charles Augustin Sainte-Beuve, now best known to us as the most influential literary critics of the period. Balzac had been motivated to do this by a caustic article of Sainte-Beuve's, "On Industrial Literature," in which he reproached Balzac for his mercenary attitude to literature, evidently in both figurative and literal senses.[11] And in a review six months later, Sainte-Beuve reprised these criticisms.

The fecund ground of Balzac's early literary activity was indeed shady and disreputable: pastiche plagiarizing, cynically rehashing and permutating plots, finding ploys like side stories to string out the publication run (as most materials of this kind at this time came out first in installments, another parallel with early comics), all for meretricious effect and with scant regard to anything we would now call the dignity of great literature, the standard that Balzac is repeatedly said to uphold. His literary production was spawned from the gutter. If the reader does not want to see parallels with the early life of comics, then at least this historical detail can serve as a corrective to the censorious trumpeting of moral values in literature, which Wertham took pride in espousing.

Balzac's is not an isolated case, just one that is eminently citable because of its strong contours. In Britain in the late eighteenth century, books were one of the most growing commodities, but in the early years of the following century, their still high prices were being addressed through lending libraries and other such consortiums. The increase in both the consumption and production of literature meant a widening of subject matter, which is to say not quite of the highest quality. One of the more entrepreneurial figures to see the benefit of a swelling market was William Lane, who founded Minerva Press and Library, which, in the words of Kathryn Sutherland, "specialized in the most sensational Gothic romances and sentimental novels, and offered from the 1790s to the 1820s complete circulating libraries, ranging from a hundred to ten thousand volumes, for sale to grocers, tobacconists and haberdashers eager to extend the trade into the profitable area of book-lending."[12] (One can hardly help but think of the comic book available in the local corner store.) So successful was Lane's enterprise that it fueled fears of what so many works were doing to the moral fiber of their readership: "Elsewhere Lane's successful marketing of lurid Minerva titles like Regina Maria Roche's *Children of the Abbey* (1796), Mary Charlton *The Philosophic Kidnapper, a Novel, altered from the French* (1803), and Agnes Maria Bennett's *Vicissitudes Abroad, or the Ghost of my Father* (1806) raised fears for the welfare of his large, semi-literate reading audience and saw the beginnings of moral and literary dismissal of the popular novel by the established guardians of taste which has dogged much fiction, and certainly best-selling fiction, ever since."[13] Sutherland goes on to cite Samuel Taylor Coleridge, who complained in his *Biographia Literaria* (1817) about the way that reading books such as these had quickly evolved to be distraction and entertainment: "Call it beggarly daydreaming, during which the mind of the dreamer furnishes for itself nothing but laziness and a little mawkish sensibility; while the whole *material* and imagery of the doze is supplied *ab extra* by a sort of mental *camera obscura*."[14] While there are uncanny resonances with the tenor of disapproval, it is also notable how the acts of visualization are considered lapses of mental effort.

Wertham: Beginning with the End

Considering comics in the context of contemporary identity politics, particularly queer theory, Wertham's *Seduction of the Innocent* becomes a kind of Rosetta Stone for a reconsideration of comics as not only antiart but also antiliterature. The hybridity of comics thus becomes problematic rather than unifying. This reading, while tongue in cheek and, to some extent, farcical, is nevertheless intended to expose the more difficult aspects of the medium and its history that don't sit flush with literature, film, and the visual arts and to celebrate this distinction.

Wertham's charges against the medium were varied, but in his mind, the effects of reading comics were quite specific:

1) The comic-book format is an invitation to illiteracy.
2) Crime comic books create an atmosphere of cruelty and deceit.
3) They create readiness for temptation.
4) They stimulate unwholesome fantasies.
5) They suggest criminal or sexually abnormal ideas.

6) They furnish the rationalization for them, which may be ethically even more harmful than the impulse.

7) They suggest the forms a delinquent impulse may take and supply details of technique.

8) They may tip the scales towards maladjustment or delinquency.[15]

It is important to note here that while many of Wertham's targets were not without justification (his observations on the racist depiction of non-Western cultures in comics were particularly damning and cannot be disputed, and, indeed, the psychologist was willing to testify to that effect in an era where others wouldn't dare[16]), it is his method of using histrionic rhetoric, choosing to mention rather than produce or cite data to make his cases, that ultimately undermines his own views. In many cases, Wertham's charges of comic books being "sexually aggressive in an abnormal way" or making "violence alluring and cruelty heroic"[17] have often been at least partially accurate. However, to present Wertham's "findings" of comics-as-mental-retardant under the guise of science rather than op-ed or sociology seems increasingly problematic with each subsequent generation of educated, successful, and/or high-functioning, self-avowed comic fans. A recent example: during the pro-Trump storming of the White House, CNN interviewed renowned ethics lawyer Norm Eisen in front of a much-envied cultural artifact: the original Kirby/Sinnott drawing for the cover of *Fantastic Four* #100 (1970). Eisen is far from the kind of reprobate Wertham so avidly condemns for their predisposition toward comics. Wertham's reading of the medium as entirely capable of subversive and powerfully compelling content is difficult to dispute by virtue of the medium's predisposition toward graphically compelling visuals and certainly through the wide-ranging obsessions and fetishes of their creators. However, the ill effects of comics upon the malleable minds of children are easily debated.[18]

Wertham's diatribe must be considered from a historical perspective and cannot be cited in isolation. It is first a reflection of the conservatism and paranoia that McCarthyism embodied, a defense against perceived Cold War threats to the hard-fought liberties and opportunities of postwar prosperity. But before McCarthyism took hold, there were other regulations in place in the United States to protect against the transgressions of decency and public morals. Preeminent among these for the arts was the Motion Picture Production Code, commonly known as the Hays Code after its promulgator, William Hays. The Hays Code was a set of moral guidelines for the film industry active between 1934 and 1968 that prohibited content perceived as socially untoward. Looking further back, Wertham was of a generation that was influenced by Oswald Spengler's influential work, *Decline of the West* (1918), and perhaps also the more obscure and eccentric *Degeneration* (1892) by the Hungarian physician Max Nordau, who railed against the decadents, symbolists, and aesthetes of the fin de siècle, diagnosing their work as neurotic and a sure sign of the ruination of culture. For him, Wilde was an immoralist, and Huysmans (the author of the bible of the decadents, *À rebours* [*Against the Grain*]) was an enemy of a fair and just society. Wertham forms something of a lineage of the guardians of culture and, in doing so, defines the enemy much better than what they are the enemy of, albeit in pejorative terms. Once the moral anxieties have been relaxed or reoriented, these reservations can be revisited with a less jaundiced eye.

What is also true is that Wertham's diatribes did not entirely hit their intended mark, for over the intervening years, rather than cementing his reputation in the field of psychology or behavioral science or as a guardian of children's rights, Wertham has been largely cast as a villain by the comic industry and fans of the art form, with little objective analysis subsequently conducted outside the psychiatric mainstream of his day.[19] This is in part due to two main factors. The first is the ease with which the research presented in *Seduction of the Innocent* can be debunked. While his writing is emotive—one gets a palpable sense of slavering outrage coming through Wertham's hand-wringing—there is no clear clinical evidence put forward to support his theories. Wertham's research is heavily represented by unattributed quotes from children he has supposedly treated, quotes that are often challenging to accept as the children's words verbatim. Wertham's text has the feel of too-convenient quotes being written or adjusted to support its arguments. "I am a mainliner. . . . I want to get rid of the habit. I have been popping myself. I have been hitting the main line," reports one unnamed fourteen-year-old heroin user, supposedly a comic enthusiast that Wertham treated.[20] Many of these quotes are highly emphatic, repeating the particular focus of Wertham's point, bordering on mania: "Sometimes I read comic books ten times a day. I look at the pictures a long time. I just imagine as if they are real. They go around stabbing people. They have eight knives, and they rob a liquor store. They stab a woman with a knife. They stab two women with a knife. One man starts killing people: five cops, six women and eighteen others. If anybody crossed him, he didn't give them no chance."[21] "Quotes" such as these are littered throughout the text, themselves strangely reminiscent of frenzied, all-caps, hyperbolic comic book dialogue of the crime and horror comics Wertham condemns.

The second factor is the collective desire of many comic fans and professionals to see the medium receive respect as an art form and thus an eagerness to deflect or dispense with criticism altogether. Ironically, the stifling or outright of Wertham's critical voice had an adverse effect on comic culture, stunting the growth of serious debate around the validity of comics as an art form in the United States, perhaps the greater of sins in retrospect than arguing the finer points of Wonder Woman's lesbianism and Superman's fascism. Cultural criticism and theory have taken much longer to develop in response to comics than in their sibling forms, film and animation. Comic theory really did not emerge as a fully-fledged field of research or study (outside some isolated occurrences) until the 1970s and 1980s. Yet despite his designation as the whipping boy of comic culture, Wertham's claims, though rarely justified, were somewhat prophetic, even if it was the fans and professionals that were ultimately responsible for making it so.

More recently, parallel to the rise in geek culture and comic scholarship, Wertham's claims have been reevaluated. This reevaluation is in part due to Wertham's enduring reputation as a hack, a tyrannical critic, and an industry bogeyman and the rise of neoliberal regulation and censorship, the homogenization of the arts, and the comic industry's (or at least comic studies') continued anxiety over the definition of the form. Comic theorist Bart Beaty's *Fredric Wertham and the Critique of Mass Culture* (2005) remains a remarkable exception in that it does allow for a deeper examination of Wertham's effect on television in particular, which is often overlooked in favor of the more sensational (and juicy) criticisms of *Seduction*, and builds context around Wertham-as-cultural-critic rather than Wertham-as-industry-killing-zealot. Rather than dismissing Wertham out of hand as so many have done, Beaty unpacks the psychologist's work in the broader context of the perceived effects of mass culture (including, notably, television), a still-new anxiety in postwar United States. While Beaty gives Wertham some credence with respect to his so-called clinical research, focusing instead upon his career more holistically, he does consider this research in the context of what was assumed to be anecdotal by virtue of the author being bound to patient confidentiality.[22] However, Carol L. Tilley's article "Seducing the Innocent: Fredric Wertham and the Falsifications That Helped Condemn Comics" (2012) is a damning account of Wertham's work in terms of the validity of Wertham's findings.[23] Subsequent to Beaty's erudite analysis, Tilley gained access to Wertham's remaining papers and systematically revisited Wertham's cited casework and, where possible, carried out comparative analyses against the psychologist's notes and annotations.

This comprehensive study reveals Wertham's willingness to conflate, confabulate, manipulate, and embellish his own research to the benefit of his claims, in effect compromising his own research.[24] This is ironic considering that it is not the claims of homosexuality and the disregard for authority that so enraged comic culture but rather the manipulated notes presented as research that ultimately undermine Wertham's arguments. Had Wertham made some judicious edits, including the overzealous framing of the book as the result of sustained clinical research, *Seduction* would be much more apt (and harder to dispute) as an editorialist polemic and would have potentially maintained its own legitimacy. Indeed, even in his own time, others from Wertham's own field had their own issues with the presentation of his research, even if they agreed in spirit with his claims.[25]

With Wertham's dogged argument of comics' insidious and pervasive influence on youth, combined with the findings of his (at best, questionable) research, it would seem a miracle that the United States survived the postwar era, were his claims about the subversive power of the medium taken to heart, for while comics are now a well-established and (mostly) accepted mainstay of popular media, culture, arts, and studies, they do not sell anywhere near the level they did in the World War II and postwar eras, and especially not among children. There are still some niche titles created for and marketed to children, yet the bulk of the industry is now primarily geared toward adults with disposable incomes. The multiplicity of media available in the twenty-first century cannot be underestimated, and a popular character like, say, Superman, whose exploits were being published through comics and radio as well as various merchandising licenses, is now a genuinely multimedia entity. The comic industry has invariably changed, as have the technologies that produce them, engendering creative innovations. But what of the social context? The 2020s are not unlike postwar years in terms of a highly unstable global economy and a general sense of social unrest grounded in recent collective trauma. As Wertham describes them, comics must surely be the most corrupting influence on children ever created, outstripping television, rock 'n' roll, and video games by a considerable margin, turning children into criminals, drug users, homosexuals, communists, and sexual predators.

While Wertham's outlandish claims can be (and have been) debunked, what if they are taken at face value through a contrarian deconstruction? Overlooking Wertham's clinical research (or, more accurately, its barely referenced interpretation) and assuming that his claims are sound and uncontested validate comics as a deeply effective media. Such a consideration would recast comics in a subversive, critical, and ultimately compelling light, particularly in the conservative, neoliberal political climate we are now experiencing and the increasing cross-media influence of comics via film and video game adaptations. An important distinction to make, however, is that between film, video games, and so forth and their source media. For example, in recent years, through which the rinse-and-repeat formula of Marvel films has achieved a staggering cultural primacy through fairly standardized narratives (good versus evil), representation (largely male and White), and politics (a rather disturbing deference to the military-industrial complex), comics have diversified. Where many comic books now model themselves around their filmic adaptations (real or hoped for) with a vague visual realism rooted in quasi-realistic anatomy and the armor favored by Hollywood rather than comics' old go-to spandex, others have leaned harder back into the specificity of the medium, maintaining the subversive edge that drew Wertham's scorn in the first place. Comics are now a sanctum for diversity previously unheard of, with increasing—and increasingly celebrated—representation of minorities, notably the many stands of "deviant" that had Wertham so vexed.

Sex, Violence, Nudity, Horror, and Emphasizing the Sanctity of Marriage

While Wertham's analysis of comics rarely strays outside a literal worldview in regard to the representation of women and cultural minorities in comics, he does betray a certain Bavarian tone deafness when it comes to the idiosyncrasies of humor and satire. Many of Wertham's prime targets were produced by EC Comics, a relatively aberrant publisher in terms of its incredibly high artistic standards counterbalanced by an enthusiastic and subversive vein of black comedy. Helmed by publisher Bill Gaines and cartoonist, writer, and sometime editor Harvey Kurtzman, the "EC New Trend," born out of the need to boost sales, made stories more shocking while at the same time exposing modern America in ways hitherto impossible in other media.[26] To put EC Comics in an appropriate historical perspective, the publisher had launched *Mad* in 1952 (its longest-running title by a significant margin), but its bread and butter was genre fare, contemporary and innovative takes on horror, war, science fiction, crime, and occasionally romance. With their comics' twist endings and their investment in artists (who were themselves prone to particularly inventive and fanciful approaches to violence and horror, surpassing at that time the abilities of most film studios, often single-handedly), EC Comics became a recurring point of reference for Wertham's wrath, both in and out of print. In retrospect, this is somewhat ironic, as the political viewpoints of Wertham, Gaines, and Kurtzman were not necessarily incompatible: all three parties leaned to the left and often demonstrated progressive or libertarian viewpoints, particularly when it came to war and civil rights. However, the way these beliefs manifested themselves could not have been more different. During an infamous Senate inquiry, many cartoonists and publishers wisely steered clear or kept their statements brief, though not Gaines, who was skewered, in some ways the true ideological polar opposite to Wertham in terms of the debate around comics.

Cast as Wertham's opposite number, Gaines—puckish, audacious, satirical, intelligent—makes a foil for Wertham equal to Lex Luthor, a perfect adversary but undercut by his own preoccupations: in Gaines's case, a vivid and provocative sense of violence. EC Comics was decades ahead of other publishers in this sense, and it was not until France's *Metal Hurlant*, Britain's *2000 AD*, and the "grim and gritty" United States of the mid-1980s ushered by Miller and Janson's *Dark Knight Returns* and Moore and Gibbons's *Watchmen* (themselves ex-*2000 AD* contributors) that such lurid, compelling, and subversive ultraviolence be found in mainstream comics. In terms of violence, Hollywood still trailed behind EC Comics. Sam Peckinpah's *Straw Dogs* (1971) was a shock to the Hollywood establishment (itself referenced in the *2000 AD*'s *ABC Warriors* strip and memorably satirized in an episode of *Monty Python's Flying Circus*), but it wasn't until the obsession with genre fare such as the horror (the *Halloween*, *Friday the 13th*, and *Hellraiser* series, to name but a few) and beefcake action movie vehicles (*Commando*, *Cobra*, etc.) in the 1980s when ultraviolence would become imbricated within the Hollywood mainstream. As in Gaines's EC Comics, audiences were, through subversive narrative, satire, and ultraviolence, given permission through ironic detachment and humor to enjoy such a campy spectacle—to be taken with a grain of salt, tongue firmly planted in cheek, and definitely not for children. McCarthy-era United States was no more ready for EC Comics than it would have been for a Pinhead film.

Gaines's disastrous appearance in front of the 1954 Senate Subcommittee on Juvenile Delinquency (and Wertham) is well documented; suffice to say, EC Comics, like many publishers, collapsed under the new government-mandated guidelines, formalized in what became known as the Comics Code Authority. The Code is composed of forty specific stipulations, prohibiting everything from the obvious and expected ("All scenes of horror, excessive bloodshed, gory or gruesome crimes, depravity, lust, sadism, masochism shall not be permitted. . . . Profanity, obscenity, smut, vulgarity, or words or symbols which have acquired undesirable meanings are forbidden. . . . Nudity in any form is prohibited, as is indecent or undue exposure"[27]) to the moralistic or prudish ("Females shall be drawn realistically without exaggeration of any physical qualities. . . . Divorce shall not be treated humorously nor represented as desirable. . . . The treatment of love-romance stories shall emphasize the value of the home and the sanctity of marriage"[28]) and the outright bizarre ("No unique or unusual methods of concealing weapons shall be shown. . . . No comic magazine shall use the word horror or terror in its title"[29]). EC Comics, who perhaps more than any other publisher was hampered by the specificity of the Code and the brilliance of its artists, was obliged to cancel its comics. Only *Mad* survived, repackaged in magazine form. This marked the end of the golden age of comics. The EC New Trend was a brief but highly influential period in comic history, predating similarly subversive and artistically innovative comics as France's *Metal Hurlant* (1974–1987) and England's *2000 AD* (1977–), both of which are steeped in horror, fantasy, and particularly science fiction genre fare. Post–Comics Code war, romance, and science fiction titles became a shadow of their former selves, and crime and horror comics became close to impossible to publish. Perhaps EC Comics had the last laugh, with a 1957 *Mad* magazine lampoon of Wertham (dubbed Frederick Werthless, MD), the mock article furnished with drawings by Wally Wood, one of EC Comics' most talented (and lustily red-blooded) cartoonists. However, in perhaps the only public evidence of owning either a piece of mass culture or a sense of humor, Wertham had the piece framed for display in his office.[30]

Filthy Degenerate

Certainly, superhero comics, a continually published source of imagistic pseudomythology since the mid-1930s, have incorporated violent and erotic imagery since the form's inception. Wertham singles out the superhero genre, categorizing it as an offshoot of the crime genre.[31] It is important to note that the crime genre more or less begins with Edgar Allan Poe's tale "The Murders in the Rue Morgue" and that it is incorporated with a considerable degree of perversity. From the beginning, many of the superheroes' identities and their relationships were unconventional. This stands to reason that since by definition the superhero defies human conventions, it therefore follows that their exceptionalism will affect other aspects of their behavior, including their relationships with others. We might start with the love triangle of Superman, Lois Lane, and Clark Kent, but then there are the overt and recurring bondage themes of Wonder Woman, Batman as a product of obsession inherited from a traumatized childhood, and, perhaps most notorious, Batman and Robin's inappropriate domestic situation. After *Seduction*, which was particularly wary of the way the Dynamic Duo's relationship could be construed by young, impressionable readers, the Batman and Robin "situation" proved to be problematic. Publishers quickly introduced regular girlfriends for Batman and Robin in order to throw critics off this worrisome homoerotic scent. But countervailing efforts such as these cannot gloss over what are now precedents burned into the fabric of popular memory. The now celebrated campiness of the 1966 television series *Batman* starring Adam West and Burt Ward embraced the weirdness of the crimefighters and their rogues' gallery with hip dialogue, a swingin' soundtrack, and lush Technicolor. West-era Batman found spiritual successors in *Batman Forever* (1995) and *Batman and Robin* (1997), directed by the late, openly gay Hollywood mainstay Joel Schumacher, reigniting speculation about the sugardaddy, rough-trade Batman and Robin relationship. Even Batman himself (George Clooney) proclaimed that he played the role as if he were gay.[32]

It is a common misinterpretation that Wertham criticized Batman and his sidekick Robin for their homosexuality.[33] Homosexuality, of course, was firmly denied by the character's owners, who went into damage control by quickly incorporating (female) love interests for Batman and Robin and even replacing their patrician butler Alfred Pennyworth with a female counterpart for a time. Perhaps the most revealing response to Wertham's claim came from readers, who categorically and emphatically rejected the notion, despite the argument's evidence.[34]

Notably, as Glen Weldon points out in *The Caped Crusade: Batman and the Rise of Nerd Culture* (2016), Wertham's attacks were aimed not at Batman's homosexuality per se but rather at the potential confusion or anxiety that the presentation of Batman and Robin's civilian domestic situation could cause in a juvenile with latent homosexuality.[35] Of course, context is everything. Much of the discourse around this particular aspect of *Seduction* has swirled around the vehement denial of Batman and Robin's perceived gay or pederast relationship or resulted in the dismissal of Wertham himself as an overzealous crackpot. One such denier is Mark Cotta Vaz, writer of *Tales of the Dark Knight: Batman's First Fifty Years: 1939–1989*, who strenuously denies any such "incredible" homosexual readings.[36] Vaz also rejects assertions that the character has unresolved hostility toward women, which he accredits to his witnessing of his mother's death, perceived by the infant mind as abandonment, casually responding that "the Caped Crusader's only negative attitude toward women has been an old-fashioned chivalrous manner around the ladies,"[37] before listing Batman's various (female) love interests.

Whether Vaz is correct, however, is irrelevant. To deny Batman's gayness is to deny a crucial, recognizable, and deeply subversive aspect of the character that has been resurfacing in comics and other media for decades. Weldon, a self-professed fan of the campy shenanigans of the Adam West *Batman* television series, spends considerable time establishing the importance of Batman's gayness and the multivalence of the character. Grant Morrison, perhaps the most notable (and studied) Batman writer of the last two decades, also subscribes to this view.[38] This is an interesting tidbit when considering a scene in the bleak, Dave McKean–illustrated graphic novel *Arkham Asylum* (1989), Morrison's first work with the character, in which the Joker grabs Batman's (bat) buttocks, with a provocative "Lighten up, tight-ass," to which the Batman snaps, saliva flecks spraying from his mouth: "Take your filthy hands off me!" The Joker then insinuates, "What's the matter? Have I touched a nerve? How is the boy wonder? Started shaving yet?" to which Batman froths, "Filthy degenerate!"[39] Perhaps Batman doth protest too much? This brief exchange but purported telling has been debated thoroughly by those who read Batman's response as homophobic, those who categorize the three panels as a metacriticism of the "grim and gritty" 1980s incarnation of the character, and those who believe this reading is a retroactive cop-out.[40] While homosexuality had certainly been toyed with in relation to the Joker previously (one cannot overlook Frank Miller's unforgettable white-suited Joker-by-way-of-Noël-Coward take on the character in *The Dark Knight Returns* [1986]), this must surely be the first example of a mainstream comic character displaying gay panic.

The debate over Batman's queerness is only one discourse that the superhero, a somewhat complex cultural avatar, is subject to. Mainstream comic books have incorporated sex and violence into their form in a variety of subtle (and not-so-subtle) ways. Cartoonists employed to create comics do and do not necessarily share the same view as their publishers and have in some instances incorporated what was once fringe material into the narrative fabric of comics themselves. As Wertham would note, "The supermen are either half-undressed or dressed in fancy raiment that is a mixture of the costumes of SS men, divers, and robots. . . . Blood flows freely, bosoms are half bared, girls' buttocks are drawn with careful attention."[41] This is as true in 2021 as it was in 1953.

Consider Wertham in a nonbinary or queer reading. If taken at face value, Wertham's reading of comics could be extrapolated, particularly in relief to David Halperin's overview in regard to the "queering" of workplaces and vocations that are typically associated with masculinity (the priest, the sailor, the lumberjack, etc.).[42] No doubt superheroes can be applied to this overview. What we end up with is a clearly queer or nonbinary reading of a medium that is formally and inherently hybridized. Just as bisexuality would open an individual to a broader spectrum of sexual experiences than cisgender, so too does the combination of word, image, and the complexities of the grid open the cartoonist up to a broader spectrum of narrative possibilities.

Kindergarten *Übermensch*

At the time *Seduction* was published, Superman was the most popular and influential comic book character in existence and was subject to Wertham's critique on various fronts, notably for being, in his own words, "an offshoot of Nietzsche's superman" before going on to quote the philosopher without context ("When you go to women, don't forget the whip") and asking how Nietzsche has infiltrated the nursery.[43] Erroneous and hyperbolic recontextualization aside, this is a fascinating leap of logic and postwar alarmism. Granted, some readers of the day may have been familiar with the Nazi embrace and inflated recontextualization of Nietzsche's *Übermensch* (literally "overman") allegory, but the idea of such an esoteric philosophical footnote radicalizing or disturbing children in daycare, even if it was intentional, is laughable. Wertham was clearly engaging with shock tactics, relying on the conjured association of the Nazis rather than facts to make his point. "With the big S on his uniform—we should, I suppose, be thankful that it is not an SS," the author quips.[44] Clearly, Superman is bad news.

Created by writer Jerry Siegel and artist Joe Shuster, the character's earliest exploits were rather socially conscious. Before any recurring supervillains were ever introduced, Superman was battling domestic abusers, union busters, and greedy industrialists. Surprisingly, it was not so much these often Marxist ideologies that attracted Wertham's criticism of the character but Superman's apparent psychological undermining of authority figures in the eyes of youths.[45] This may seem an exaggeration, but Wertham was not the only one who has interpreted this differently. Gershon Legman's *Love and Death: A*

Study in Censorship (1949), while not focused solely on comics, remonstrates many of the same perceived moral issues that Wertham would emphasize in *Seduction* seven years later, particularly in the context of crime and super-hero comics. In fact, Legman and Wertham have a mutual professional respect, and Wertham borrowed liberally from Legman's work.[46] It has even been suggested that Legman may have ghostwritten *Seduction*.[47]

Wertham's views on ostensibly wholesome (if Marxist) do-gooders like Superman are not unlike Legman's and extrapolate the basic tenets of the character to some rather hyperbolic lengths. Legman proclaims that "the Superman virus was sown not, of course, by the two nice Jewish boys who take the credit, Messrs. Shuster and Siegel, but by Hitler. With only this difference that, in the ten-year effort to keep supplying sinister victims for the supermen to destroy, comic-books have succeeded in giving every American child a complete course in paranoid megalomania such as no German child ever had, a total conviction of the morality of force such as no Nazi could ever aspire to."[48] On a side note, perhaps not of interest to (or in the interest of) Wertham, Superman, like all other comics from the United States, was actually banned in Nazi Germany for its close association with, and innovation by, the Jewish race. Wertham, himself a Jew, was somewhat coy about the matter, but certainly his denunciation of Superman as a fascist in the wake of World War II, a war in which many cartoonists personally fought and sometimes perished, guaranteed a particular brand of scorn that continues to this day.[49]

By the time *Seduction* was published, Shuster's failing eyesight was preventing him from taking tight deadlines and a heavy workload of comic book work. Instead, Shuster had taken to the less demanding (and perhaps more enjoyable) work of illustrating BDSM stories for underground publications such as *Nights of Horror*, which was almost completely invisible to criticism, despite incorporating far more subversive content into its stories than the pages of *Action Comics* or even many EC Comics titles. *Nights of Horror* routinely featured nudity, spanking, flagellation, bondage, torture devices, voyeurism, lesbianism, and other activities considered risqué at the time.[50] In an artistic sense, freed from the confines of the tight panels and grids of *Superman* and *Action Comics*, this was some of Shuster's best work, even if the characters within did (compellingly and tellingly) resemble in turns Superman, Lois Lane, and Jimmy Olsen.[51] Whether Wertham ever discovered Shuster's uncredited connection to the publication remains sadly undocumented. (Legman, though equally excitable, seems to display a greater understanding of the nuances of style and genre and may have had a better chance at making this connection—Wertham's scorn for cartoonists appears consistent and impartial, despising each with equal fervor.) However, Wertham was certainly well aware of *Nights of Horror*, being asked in 1954 to testify as an expert in the trial of the neo-Nazi youth gang the Brooklyn Thrill Killers, where he used the publication to emphasize the potential vulgarities of the comic book.[52]

If we survey contemporary television shows such as *Watchmen* and *The Boys* (both based on comics written by *2000 AD* alumnus whose worldviews are distinctly subversive and deeply steeped in the metahistories of comics as a medium), it would be hard not to refute Wertham's accusation of the delinquency of the characters in them. Superheroes are larger than life, so their flaws and foibles are commensurately magnified. As inordinate beings, they defy the ordinary in human interaction, which naturally leads to many inferences about their aberrant nature. Heightened powers lead to heightened misunderstanding. In some more recent television series, the idea of a Galahad-like goodness is jettisoned in favor of characters that are willful, manipulative, insecure, and prone to self-interest and self-aggrandizement. That they are inordinate beings also allies them to queerness in every sense of the word. Perversity, oddity, corruption, and extreme appetite are all notions that abound in the superhero genre and in the comic genre more generally. On a simple formal level, it might be asserted that it is precisely the graphic component that lends itself to the temptation to supersede the natural and the prosaic. But that they move toward our desires and fears makes them more real as a result. Wertham's reactionary intuitions may have had something to recommend themselves after all.

5

The Balzac of Comics

• •

Jack Kirby, World Building,
and the Kirbyesque

For there to be a scholarly, analytical value for comics or any other endeavor, there needs to be a set of values. These are examples and abstractions that act as gravitational principles for what standards or benchmarks are the most conducive to advancing and developing the most fruitful modes of analysis. A canon, a pantheon of names, a set of eminences—whatever label one chooses to give them—are a natural by-product of this process. Lukács's literary aesthetics is formulated according to the premise that humans make sense of the world through stories, and therefore it is to the benefit of us as individuals and as a collective to formulate the best stories and to find the best criteria for judging them. By now all too familiar to us, the names that Lukács continually refers to are Balzac and Tolstoy, to whom he devoted detailed, albeit criticized, studies. To throw up an author as the gold standard for a genre, a generation, or an entire aesthetic system is immediately to leave innumerable spaces of critical vulnerability. Balzac is taken to task for his erratic prose, flights of brilliance that suddenly lapse into garishness, repetitiousness, and careless characterization or plot development. These are there for those who wish to look closely and ponderously at his huge edifice. And to be sure, he is not the exalting stylist of Flaubert, nor does he match the ironic concentration of Austen, but then there is no such thing as a perfect work of art (the impossibility of which Balzac wrote in the *Unknown Masterpiece*, 1831). Balzac was known for his frenetic working methods and his vertiginous energy (fueled by inordinate coffee consumption), which led to his extraordinary output and his premature death. As a social panorama, a template of his times, putting aside our ideological bias for a moment, it is hard not to side with Engels's view that his example is unrivaled in providing a sociohistorical portrait as well as characters and stories that transcend them. To be clear, we are not interested in an argument about the greatest novelist, only one who has become a critical benchmark for successive novelists and theorists based in large part on the scope of his work. The analogous figure in comics, we would like to suggest, is Jack Kirby.

Like Balzac, the scope of his ambition and the extent of his output were prodigious. Like Balzac, he was an artist full of easily citable flaws and inconsistencies. Yet just as Balzac, more than any one writer—albeit not alone— transformed the novel from a marginal to a substantive art form, Kirby was a prolific innovator of comics. Although he did not have the same ambition to devise a work as multitudinous and embracing as Balzac's *La Comédie humaine* (*The Human Comedy*), an ambition that is perhaps more rooted in the totalizing structures that many romantics were inclined to try to build, Kirby was the creator of multiple imaginative universes that have stayed with us in countless forms to the present day (not least in Disney's Marvel Cinematic Universe). Like Balzac, his world is filled with a panoply of types that became sedimented into contemporary discourse and mythology. His influence is inestimable in bringing comics from a marginal practice and as a cultural irritant to the high-minded, to something that within (popular) culture could be neither ignored nor denied. Until now, a large emphasis has been on the writerly component or, more broadly, the comic and graphic novel as multivalent text offering several formal registers. As the next segue into our argument, the emphasis here is more on the image-based component.

Recognition for Jack Kirby (née Jacob Kurtzberg, 1917–1994) within comic scholarship is a relatively recent phenomenon. Although the cartoonist reached a certain level of recognition in the eyes of comic fans and professionals relatively early on in his career, it has been through the increasing academic study of comic books that Kirby has been retroactively canonized as one of the geniuses of the field.[1] Mainstream comics, being a predominantly collaborative form, can be complicated by such an assignment of genius or auteur status. For Kirby to be thought of as an auteur, others' contributions, particularly inkers, might be minimized in the same way that artists' assistants have been obscured throughout art history. Consider Kirby's posthumous inclusion in the Hammer Museum's *Masters of American Comics* exhibition as an example: The artists who collaborated with Kirby on the pages featured in the exhibition and the accompanying publication were omitted from the credits.[2] This contentious accreditation is the result of the Fordist method of comic book production and publication—it was also a cause of endless troubles for Kirby himself. Kirby cocreated many popular characters under work-for-hire agreements, receiving little credit and few royalties for their use for decades.[3] The return of original pages had to be fought for, staggering considering that the original pages were the legal property of the artists under U.S. law and the sheer number that Kirby produced.[4] This again reflects the slow fight for legitimacy that the artists of comic books faced. (We might recall some of the details of the previous chapter regarding the derogatory status that novels, still a relatively nascent form, were accorded into the early nineteenth century.) The benefits in finances and reputation associated with the medium grew with the reputation of the medium as a legitimate art form. Kirby is therefore not only an artistic influence on several generations of artists and cartoonists but a martyr for intellectual property, corporate ownership, and cartoonists' struggle for agency. While on an artistic level Kirby is highly influential, upon closer inspection, his artistry is in no small part a response to the pressures—and in the early days of comics, the technological limitations—of the comic industry.

Scholarly research on Kirby is now commonplace, driven in part by his enduring popularity and influence upon the visual conventions of comics themselves. A less frequently examined phenomenon of the "King of Comics" himself is a direct result of Kirby's influential stature: what we call, for the purposes of this chapter, the Kirbyesque. While, as this chapter will establish, there is a tradition of reference, homage, swipes, and satire in comics, the subtle to outright overt mimicry of Kirby's style by many artists has become a convention unto itself, arguably unrivaled by any other in the comic field. While many artists reference and imitate the work of a select few master cartoonists without fear of reprisal (some to be mentioned later), it is rare that a fellow cartoonist would make a career of it. There could be many reasons for this, but there are two primary ones. First, Kirby's style is fast in terms of execution and effective in its allusion (the parallels with Balzac are again rather strong). So specific and developed—and in many ways unusual—a cartoonist needs only reference a particular kind of facial construction, figure, costume, or even visual effect to begin to pastiche the King of Comics. And second, Kirby enjoyed a sustained career, making significant contributions to the conventions of the narrative form of comics itself. This was notable in the very visual lexicon that one of the cornerstones of the industry, the superhero, was built upon, including an astonishing number of comics for the United States' two largest comic publishers. Hence the Kirbyesque and the countless ways this unusual convention has situated itself beyond simple visual stylings.

Defining the Kirbyesque

The Kirbyesque is a convention that takes place, often uncredited, in a context that insists upon credit—such is the extent of the recognition of Kirby's contributions to the visual language of comics, now osmotically absorbed into the conventions of the medium. Perhaps in response to early comics' shabby treatment of cartoonists' intellectual and artistic rights, an unspoken yet rigid approach to quotation has emerged from the comic industry, itself quite different from other visual arts, even its filmic cousin forms, in that homage is to be credited, indicated either beside the cartoonist's signature ("Dave Johnson after Jim Steranko," for instance, as emblazoned on a *100 Bullets* cover) or just as frequently with an intertextual visual wink (Gotham City, for instance, must have three dozen parks, suburbs, rivers, avenues, and train stations named after Bill Finger and/or Jerry Robinson, two cartoonists responsible—and until recently, largely uncredited—for shaping key parts of Batman's narrative mythology). While Kirby has been acknowledged in this way many times, there is an additional—and close to unique—register to homage when it comes to Kirby. It is embodied by cartoonists who quote the aesthetics or conventions of Kirby's style so slavishly as to transcend mere imitation, becoming a language unto itself. Thus, cartoonists operating in this vein can be said to be using a Kirbyesque language, which can be named a subgroup of the comic form itself.

No other cartoonists have been so widely emulated as Kirby, although there are some international analogues: Japan's Osamu Tezuka, Belgium's Hergé, and France's Jean Giraud (otherwise known as Moebius or Gir). However, upon closer examination, these examples have a distinct disadvantage in the context of emulation in that they are all cartoonists who employ a highly technical and considered drawing style, whereas Kirby's work relies far more on a kind of primitivist momentum. To ape Kirby's style can itself be a signifier of the past, of the so-called golden age of comics (approximately from Superman's first appearance in 1930 through until the postwar genre explosion) or, more frequently, the silver age of comics (usually charted from DC's sleek, science fiction–infused mid-1950s superhero revival through to Marvel's own "superheroes with problems" revival of the 1960s, usually ending in 1970), with which he is so heavily associated. Kirby's style used thus becomes shorthand for signaling the inbuilt history of the comic narrative as well as a broader metanarrative that often spans the entire "universe" in question. (Prime examples of this are built into the very fabric of Kirby's runs on the *Fantastic Four* [1961–1970] and *The Mighty Thor* [1964–1970] and his Fourth World Saga [1970–1973], which are widely considered his crowning artistic achievements.)[5] Kirby drew a broad variety of genre fare in the postwar years, particularly western and romance comics, but no cowboy or lover ever developed such an elaborate and imbricated accretion of narrative density as the superhero. Case in point: the Phantom, perhaps the oldest superhero in continuous publication, has been running in dozens of countries and languages since 1936, with a status quo that has been edging forward the entire time.

Even what this chapter seeks to explore, the Kirbyesque, has been somewhat underwritten in the very history of comics, a parallel of the industry itself to the extraordinary array of characters created by the cartoonist. Hopping, as he did, from title to title, often while keeping personal projects afloat for extended periods, many comics contain the distinctive Kirbyesque basis in design. This is evident in a character's either costume (consider Mister Miracle, Galactus, or Big Barda, all Kirby creations who, when drawn by other cartoonists, sometimes appear as overwrought sartorial nightmares) or locale (Thor's glittering home, Asgard, and the burning hellscape of Apocalypse from the Fourth World Saga spring immediately to mind). Beyond the narrative blueprints laid out through Kirby's propulsive world building. Just as Balzac shaped his voluminous and panoramic *Human Comedy* (and to a lesser extent, in its wake, Zola's *The Rougon-Macquart* cycle), Kirby's preeminence is as one of the great world builders, whether the unit of measurement was page count, creations, or pound-for-pound protean comic book protein.

The very inclination to build fictional worlds is itself as historic as the novel itself and runs in tandem with its evolution. It is no surprise that it should have added impetus in the comic realm that too often, in the effort to keep comics trivial, has not been viewed as part of a much deeper human inclination. True enough worlds are constituted through myth and religion, but these are intended as more than fictional and are generally more than the work of a single author. The modernist (and postmodernist) penchant for building worlds is a reflection of the capacity for a worldview that is a result of the growth of a global economy beginning with the imperial rush from the sixteenth century onward. From a philosophical standpoint, it is an urge that arises from the encyclopedic and lexigraphic impulse that gained momentum in the eighteenth century from Denis Diderot, Jean-Baptiste le Rond d'Alembert, and Samuel Johnson, among others. At the end of his essay on Balzac's *Peasants* (*Les Paysans*, 1844, 1855), Lukács makes one of his more rounded statements about the fictional creation of a detailed and multifaceted world as a vehicle for social understanding: "The concrete formation of socially cohesive relationships is only possible if they are raised to such a point of abstraction that from a level higher than abstraction than abstraction the concrete is sought and found as the 'unity of the manifold' (Marx)."[6] He explains that to concretize the details is to lose sight of the understanding of social relationships that the role of abstraction can afford. In other words, the world maker must seize relationships and transactional elements and see the characters as abstract elements within a greater form. Just as with Balzac, Kirby achieves, or is the closest to achieving, this "unity of the manifold" in which the characters only take shape by virtue of their relations to others and their circumstances and hence are always components within the complex of social relations. No matter the outlandishness of the details, it is in fact by dint of the supernatural elements that the integrity of such relations can be asserted and maintained.

Visually, Kirbyesques are easy to identify. Kirby's tendency toward dynamic, perspective-defying poses; his affinity for simple panel configurations and anguished expressions; and his own distinctive visual shorthand for comic book necessities such as explosions, rubble, and raw energy (known as Kirby Krackle) all developed to cut through the reproductive limitations of 1940s print technology. These styles, techniques, and devices remain salient and, if anything, have only increased in their effectiveness in growing relief to the digital slickness of many contemporary mainstream comics. There is also the gradual absorption and metabolization of Kirby's approaches by the rest of the industry, particularly between the 1960s and 1970s, during his stints at Marvel and DC. Next-generation cartoonists such as Herb Trimpe, Jon Buscema, and Don Heck, while developing their own distinctive visual approaches to comics, absorbed, whether by proximity, reverence, or editorial direction, the visual tics and linguistic conventions of the comic medium that were—if not created or adapted by Kirby in the first instance—a result of his innovations.

While, for the purposes of this chapter, cartoonists such as Trimpe, Buscema, and others are not Kirbyesques themselves—insofar as there is no reflexive emulation of Kirby's style for any reason other than an approximate adherence to what was then considered the Marvel house style (which was largely based on Kirby's dynamic graphics)—these were just around the corner. Those who deliberately incorporated elements of Kirby's visual lexicon into their own work, not by editorial fiat or gushing fandom but as commentary on the narrative continuity of comics, were a result of paying homage to or continuing the process of metaphysical world building. Jim Steranko is an early proponent of the Kirbyesque. His influential run on *Nick Fury, Agent of S.H.I.E.L.D.* (1966–1969) fused Kirby's boldness and physicality with Steranko's slick, commercial approach, honed during his years in advertising. Nick Fury, cocreated by Kirby in 1963, was a World War II–themed comic, a kind of throwback to Kirby's past work during comics' postwar genre explosion, peppered liberally with his knack for rollicking, momentous action set pieces and cigar-chomping, blue-collar protagonists. Further, Fury, like several other Kirby creations, carries a strong fan association as being a kind of cipher, if not quite a doppelgänger, of the artist himself. Steranko, one of a new generation of cartoonists coming to prominence in the 1960s, updated the character, retroactively incorporating him into the Marvel canon and ditching World War II for a James Bond / *The Man from U.N.C.L.E.*–influenced spycraft theme (a genre enjoying considerable literary, film, and television success in the Cold War era).

Such strategies may not appear particularly groundbreaking in a medium often concerned with maintaining currency and therefore keeping a watchful eye on its media siblings, particularly film, but this does reflect the growing influence of Kirby, who by this point had been working in comics for almost three decades and had influenced three generations of cartoonists. It also highlights comics' increasingly valuable cultural cachet and a growing self-reflexivity in terms of narrative density and global fandom. Select characters, such as Batman and Superman, were by then entering their fourth decade of continuous publication, an unprecedented amount of narrative content to uncoil. This was a rich, increasingly elegiac, and interlinked history to draw on and for fans to pore over, debate, and analyze. It was in these years that fanzines began to proliferate, and with them, the narrative metaphysics of the medium.

In this way, Kirby was well placed to influence subsequent generations—hence, the Kirbyesque. His fingerprints were all over the comic medium, particularly its visual language and genre conventions, extending within and without the architectural blueprint for the superhero. But the question remains, How did Kirby go from being merely influential to becoming an indexical narrative shorthand representative of an entire (postwar) epoch of American comics? Few if any cartoonists had the extent of his influence. While the comic industry was already around when Kirby began working professionally, it was still forming, still finding its own visual lexicon, when contemporaries began to notice the boldness and innovation of Kirby's work. It would not be an exaggeration to say that Kirby would continue to test the strengths and limitations of the comic medium until well into the 1970s, with several grand experiments, most notably the Fourth World Saga, a sprawling superhero space opera that bled across four monthly titles, all astonishingly written, penciled, and edited by Kirby himself (between forty-eight and ninety-six pages per month, a velocity of production hard to match, then or since).

The following sections are an attempt to delineate the different forms the Kirbyesque can take, but it is important to note that these forms exist on a spectrum. Comics are a notoriously self-reflexive medium, and to adopt a Kirbyesque storytelling style can signal different things at once, dovetailed as appropriate.

Homage or Swipe: Contextualizing the Kirbyesque within the Intertextuality of Comics

If we begin with the premise that Homo sapiens are mimetic animals, we can accept that all endeavor is built on precedents, something that the modernist myth of artistic originality still likes to keep at bay, as it is a reticence that is good for profits and notoriety. Given that it is a myth, copying is the subject of repeated scrutiny in art, not least because of the industry of fakes, but it is a practice that requires more attention with comics. Until recently, it has remained an insider concern because comics have long been seen somewhere in the realms of tomorrow's fish-and-chip wrapper, as they used to say about newsprint. Just as in the Renaissance artist workshop system, where apprentices copied from the masters in order to learn the fundamentals of their craft through a combination of muscle memory, osmosis, and the conscious practice of observation, comics have always incorporated imitation into their heuristic structure. In fact, the comic industry is one of the closest contemporary equivalents for the apprentice system, with many cartoonists honing their "chops" under the tutelage of the established veteran. There is, however, a fundamental difference between these two contexts that linger even today, which has developed from necessity, instigated by a concept not yet dreamed up during the Renaissance, which is that of secular narrative properties. While the Renaissance master may have surreptitiously embedded personal interests and narratives into his work, these narratives were surreptitious or subsidiary to Christian dogma and Greek mythology. The complexities of intellectual property were still centuries away, ushered in with the advent of copyright law in the early 1700s, when publishing had entered into a new phase of proliferation.

Kirby's work is representative of the contested territory that comic books and other hybrid art forms sometimes occupy: the distinction between what constitutes comic books and art grows increasingly obscured. The relationship between artists and cartoonists is problematic at best, with cartoonists often vexed by the frequent use of their beloved medium as fodder for appropriation or inspiration.[7] This appropriation itself can reinforce the idea of comics as a disposable medium and therefore denies, or at least hampers, comics' acceptance as an art form.[8] The defense of comics' claims to validity as an art form has been reinvigorated by a spate of comic book exhibitions at major art museums as well as the crossover of comic artists such as Kirby (2015), George Herriman (2017), and Robert Crumb (2012) into the museum context.[9] (In tandem with this encroachment into the museum sphere, it is tempting to digress into the way that fashion has done so with equal vigor and audience approval.) Indeed, as Beaty points out, even scholars whose work predates the recent crossover of comics to the museum context had difficulty finding consensus in defining the form itself.[10]

The contemporary cartoonist has learned from those who have come before, particularly the legally overlooked and the financially ignored creators of multimillion-dollar properties, of whom Kirby is perhaps the greatest example, given the sheer volume of his creations. The tragedian roots of the superhero would seem to be directly informed by the experiences of their creators. Among the more citable examples in comics' history are Jerry Siegel and Joe Schuster, having created Superman under a $130 work-for-hire contract in 1938. Siegel and Schuster did not receive royalties of any kind until 1974. Bill Finger is another example. Finger went uncredited as Batman's cocreator until 2015, thirty-nine years after his death. Indeed, in the early days of comic books, many cartoonists went uncredited entirely, unlike comic strip artists who enjoyed far more prestige and celebrity. Such is comics' history of exploitation and cultural ghettoization.[11] For every credited homage, there are innumerable cases of the obverse, the uncredited "swipe."

To use industry jargon, the swipe is a complicated and, at least until postmodernism, pejorative term for an image, panel, or layout that was closely based on another cartoonist's work but uncredited. To the uninitiated or to the eyes used to the intertextual freedoms offered by the search engine, remix culture, Pinterest, YouTube, memes, and supercuts, it may seem difficult to see any harm in this practice. However, it is grim news, especially to artists of Kirby's generation, who were, by contemporary standards, underpaid and undervalued. DC and Marvel cartoonists today receive not only named credit but also a share of reprint royalties, comps (complimentary copies) of their published work, and returned original art boards for lucrative resale. None of this was available to the first several generations of cartoonists and only slowly began to change in the 1970s after considerable legal action and advocacy work by cartoonists such as Jerry Robinson and Neal Adams, particularly around the case of Siegel and Schuster and Superman.[12] Kirby himself was an active proponent for the return of original art boards, and with good reason: he was probably owed more than anybody, being such a workhorse. In 1987, after years of legal wrangling, the cartoonist was returned some 2,100 pages of original art by Marvel, a significant victory in principle but only a fraction of the pages he had created for the company.[13] So while the swipe became common practice among cartoonists, particularly those on a tight deadline, it courted reproach for many years. This also frames, from the perspective of the cartoonist, the historical context surrounding the proto-postmodern forays of pop art into the aesthetic world of comics and the anger of those referenced.[14] (After all, "everybody" knows Roy Lichtenstein, not the artists he copied.) The attitude toward the swipe, or perhaps the politics of appropriation surrounding it, would change dramatically with the more nuanced and elastic understanding of authorship that became more mainstream with postmodernism.

Popular culture's embrace of postmodernism was fast and, in many ways, inevitable, as it seemed to signal that art theory had caught up and was now finally in on the joke. While there were still some issues, particularly between divisions of high and low, these would become increasingly esoteric and destabilized as the years wore on. The Greenbergian holdouts still existed but had to find their own access points (à la Jeff Koons or Laurie Anderson), lest they be rendered passé. Quentin Tarantino, the poster child of postmodern cinema, included dialogue about the Fantastic Four in *Reservoir Dogs*. Jerry and George would discuss the minutiae of Superman on *Seinfeld*. *The Simpsons* referenced . . . everything, including Kirby, which we will return to shortly. Where the swipe was, for many years, considered a shameful practice, by the time of Kirby's death, this attitude was beginning to soften if not begrudgingly accepted as common practice.[15] Subsequently, the complexities associated with the swipe would seem to be transferred, at least in terms of source material, into the digital realm, with cartoonists such as Greg Land obtaining imagery using search engines and making slight alterations to their vectorized forms through programs such as Photoshop.[16] While it is likely that much of the controversy surrounding Land is due to the fact that many of his source images have been found in pornography (this is fairly new to comics only insofar as it was done with digital tools, for comics have a rich and often fascinating history with pornography since the medium's earliest days), it is noteworthy in that it is a contemporary example of comics' complicated attitude toward appropriation. Continuing debates such as this also underscore the remarkable nature of the Kirbyesque. There are a great many cartoonists who regularly incorporate "Kirbyisms" into their visual lexicon and even those who have built careers entirely around pastiching (right down to mimicry) his highly distinctive visual and sometimes narrative style. Kirby's innovations have become so wholly integrated into his art form that the two have become somewhat indivisible. Kirby is the comic book, and the comic book is Kirby.

A Roll Call of His Creative Epigones

José Ladrönn is a popular and recognizable Kirbyesque stylist who has worked within both the American and European traditions of comics and is notable in that he also often incorporates distinct elements of Giraud, creating a surprisingly cohesive fusion between the two influential cartoonists, often vacillating between them according to the project (compare Ladrönn's work on his *Cable* run [1997–1999] to *Final Incal* [2014]). This is perhaps attributable to the common ground of a prevailing visual touchstone in the technological sublime and adds another register to the changes in understanding around appropriation and homage.

Mainstream cartoonists such as Walter Simonson and Jon Bogdanove, both already indebted to the King of Comics in terms of their anatomical dynamism and crisp, graphic sensibilities, turn the (Kirby) dial up to eleven whenever dealing with aspects of, in particular, the vast Fourth World mythos, resulting in an exuberance rarely found in the po-faced self-seriousness of the late twentieth-century superhero.

Alternative cartoonist Lale Westvind, perhaps more than any other cartoonist, takes Kirby's pronounced and recognizable stylings as a starting point and pushes comics far beyond standard narrative fare, embracing a highly experimental and esoteric aesthetic. Taking queues in terms of color and the abstraction of figurative and expressive forms (such as Kirby's shorthand for comic book go-tos), Westvind also experiments with printing techniques such as the risograph to further expand comics' narrative language.

Like Westvind, Gary Panter is another whose work extends far outside of the ordinary narrative boundaries of the comic form, well into the contested territory of the fine arts. *Dal Tokyo* is easily one of Panter's most overtly Kirbyesque works, evolving in parallel with Panter's artistic inclinations while subverting the strip's own momentum.[17] As in Kirby's finest work, *Dal Tokyo* is a self-enclosed world, akin to Bosch's feverish dreamscapes or the compressed crowds of artists such as Benozzo Gozzoli or Vittore Carpaccio. Denying a formal narrative, this complex world is populated by hundreds of characters, each with their own traits, each playing a small part in a fragmented and nervous drama. Panter actively subverts the formal mechanics of the comic book, as outlined in Groensteen's *The System of Comics*, particularly in the mechanics of the page and panel layouts, many conventions of which Kirby had a hand in developing. Groensteen breaks down the physical complexity of comic books by assigning units of reference to both pages and panels that create a narrative whole.[18] In this way, Panter brings the visual language of Kirby, and by extension comics, full circle, a postmodern Ouroboros built around the subversion of an established formal narrative logic in homage to one of that form's innovators.

Kirby as Index

Kirby's industrious work ethic allowed the cartoonist to build the visual groundwork for the new wave of superhero comics (re)popularized by Marvel Comics in the 1960s. Many of these titles were credited to being written by Stan Lee, but there is significant and undeniable evidence suggesting that the division of labor was not so clean cut in terms of Kirby's narrative contributions. The so-called Marvel method of comic production grew from necessity, with Lee writing several comics per month, and involved a loose conversation around plot, which is then drawn by the penciller and scripted after this step, often in direct response to the imagery. The Marvel method differs greatly from former comic-scripting practices, which closely

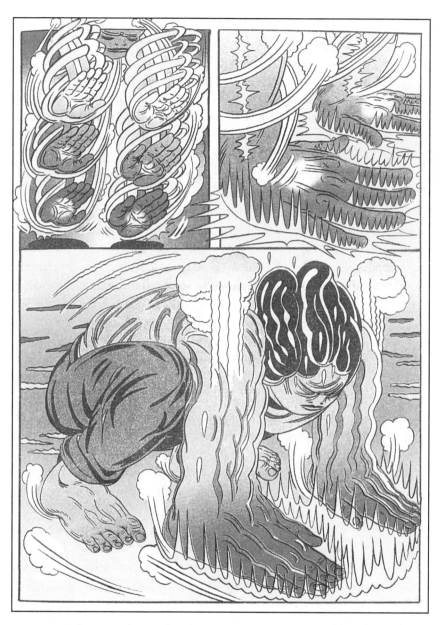

FIGURE 5.1 Lale Westvind, *Grip* 2 (2019): 13.
Courtesy of the artist.

resembled a film script. Much scholarship has been dedicated to this rather complicated creative partnership and will not be investigated in detail here; suffice to say, Lee had an uncanny nose for public relations and hyperbole and was always happy to take credit for the work of others, particularly Kirby. It was typical in these years for Kirby to be assigned to the first several issues of a new title to lay the narrative groundwork and build popularity (*The Avengers*, *Uncanny X-Men*, and *The Incredible Hulk*, to name but a few) in tandem with his long runs on his personal passion projects (in particular, *The Mighty Thor* and the *Fantastic Four*).

As touched upon with the example of Steranko's visual treatment of the Nick Fury character, most Kirbyesques approach from a place of reverence. But there is usually more to it, especially in contemporary comics. While mainstream comics have largely moved away from the bold graphics that made Kirby's work so appealing and eminently reproducible with better printing capabilities, digital tools, and so forth, the respect for Kirby in terms of sheer visual dynamism has only grown in stark relief to the contemporary version of "realism" (i.e., photographic realism) found in mainstream comics. Today, a cartoonist's decision to reference Kirby's distinctive style is not necessarily in direct relation to the characters he created. As often as not, such references work as an indexical shorthand to signal a particular era, most often the World War II era, the 1960s, or even a particular fictitious era invented by the cartoonist him- or herself.

Evidence of Kirby-as-index, so to speak, can be found with increasing frequency, perhaps in tandem with an increasing sympathy for Kirby's own complicated auteurism and an understanding of the creative difficulties faced, uncovered by increasing interest in, and sophistication of, comic theory. In recent years, several series have made use of a nuanced understanding of Kirby in historical, sociopolitical, and metaphysical contexts and deployed visual and narrative references to Kirby as shorthand accordingly. A small sample of these includes Paul Jenkins and Jae Lee's *The Sentry* (2000), Darwyn Cooke's *DC: The New Frontier* (2004), Jeff Lemire and Dean Ormston's *Black Hammer* (2016), and Lee and Michael Allred's *Bug! The Adventures of Forager* (2017).

One of the most effective uses of Kirby-as-index is represented by the second issue of *Radioactive Man*, a spin-off of the seemingly perennial animated series *The Simpsons*. Written and penciled by Steve Vance and inked by Bill Morrison, the 1994 issue (cover-dated 1962 and marked issue 88) emulated a typical 1960s Marvel Lee/Kirby joint through the filter of *The Simpsons'* bug-eyed, three-fingered, canary-yellow-skinned aesthetic. The brilliant conceit of the initial six-issue series was to move through the history of superhero comics, altering the visual and narrative elements of each issue accordingly, complete with satirical, period-specific advertisements. Ironically, it was this issue that was the most naturalistically "comic book" (and therefore effective) read for the uninitiated; such is the extent of Kirby's absorption into the superhero paradigm. Here, Kirby was indexically deployed to demarcate specific metanarrative and historical moments, effective as both satire and homage.

British cartoonist Shaky Kane's oeuvre is similarly indexical. Veering toward the bold graphic geometry of Kirby's linework, Kane is an emphatic Kirbyesque, in some senses more Kirby than Kirby, pushing certain Kirby-isms (Kirbydoms?) to a point that is at once a reverent homage and loving (if ironic) satire. Kane is also an early example of a cartoonist building a career entirely in the Kirbyesque mode, perhaps initially made possible with the cultural detachment of his UK upbringing, not unlike the embrace of American popular culture by the British originators of pop art. In *Soul Gun Warrior* (1993–1994, presented in British anthology comic *2000 AD* and written by Alan McKenzie), Kane's Kirbyesque graphics are a highly effective signifier for Kennedy-era United States. *Soul Gun Warrior* explores the space race through a nutty and inspired plot involving the astral projection of a deliberately suicided astronaut, culminating (of course) in a showdown with a USSR cosmonaut. *Bulletproof Coffin* (2012 and 2017, cocreated with writer David Hine) also playfully explored tropes of 1960s United States but this time filtered through a much darker stew of referents, including William Burroughs, CIA incursions, frontier-style vigilante justice, and the Vietnam War. Once again, the Kirbyesque signals far more than just the cartoonist himself.

Kirby as Process

It is important to note that the Kirbyesque is not solely a matter of aesthetic homage or a postmodern deployment of metanarrative references but often extends well into the process of cartooning also. This stems largely from Kirby's fast working method and prolific output and the way his writing (or his well-documented but largely uncredited narrative contributions, in the case of his 1960s Marvel output) incorporated the drawing rather than the scripting process. This method was developed in response to the fast-moving assembly line of mainstream comics and was adapted by Stan Lee and his many

FIGURE 5.2 Shaky Kane, *The Bulletproof Coffin: Disinterred* (2012): 18.
Courtesy of the artist.

FIGURE 5.3 Shaky Kane, *Good News Bible: The Complete Deadline Strips of Shaky Kane* (Seattle: Fantagraphics, 2017), 31.
Courtesy of the artist.

artistic collaborators in the 1960s with the Marvel method, which formalized the delegation of the finer points of comic storytelling—interactions, action sequences, story beats—to the pencillers from the merest plot outlines. For cartoonists such as Kirby, this was a double-edged sword: while the Marvel method allowed greater artistic and narrative freedom, it also created long-term issues around authorship, especially in the mercenary, work-for-hire days before concepts such as creator-owned characters and royalty checks were commonplace. Kirby's rising dissatisfaction with Marvel, particularly in light of Lee's self-mythologizing as the public face of the company[19] and his creative decisions around Kirby's most beloved creations (such as his thwarted desire to reboot *The Mighty Thor*), led him to their biggest competitor, DC Comics. There he applied himself with an added—indeed, vengeful—energy, committing himself to a narrative more ambitious in scope than he had hitherto attempted, exploding the Marvel method while he was at it. This time, he would have the writer's credit and would create a mythology to rival those of Norse, Greek, and Judeo-Christian, and he would do it in his own inimitable fashion.[20]

In his excellent and committed analysis of Kirby, *Hand of Fire: The Comics Art of Jack Kirby* (2012), Charles Hatfield probes the claim of the Fourth World Saga as the cartoonist's masterwork.[21] Hatfield's definition of *masterwork* is understandably comics centric, hinging on a sense of self-completeness and balance and cohesion in the overall narrative, something occasionally lacking in Kirby's work. That this would seemingly discount virtually the cartoonist's entire body of work is not the point, and Hatfield instead focuses on specific issues of the sometimes confusing, sometimes overwrought narrative arcs to hold up as examples of masterworks.[22] In other words, it is actually this very quality of Kirby's vast oeuvre, a kind of propulsive cosmic melodrama that never settles long enough for a breath, that has become as emulated as his energetic, roughhewn figures and dynamic linework. The sense—from the cartoonist's 1960s and 1970s output, in particular—of a sort of freewheeling narrative abandon, or "breathless conceptual overflow," can be directly attributed to Kirby's studio practices.[23]

Where other cartoonists often plan each panel—and its place in the larger design of the page—meticulously with thumbnails and rough sketches before ever touching pencil to Bristol board, Kirby instead pushed forward with gusto, penciling each panel left to right, top to bottom, without an overall plan for the page itself, let alone the rest of the comic.[24] Kirby's narratives were, as Hatfield so accurately puts it, created through "an improvisatory graphism: the propulsiveness of the sketch," emerging, panel by panel, on the page itself.[25] Yet such narrative momentum could be as much a weakness as a strength. Stories would crackle with an exciting unpredictability (often tempered by more sober-minded collaborators like Lee, Joe Simon, or oft-derided inker Vince Colletta); however, characters would be forgotten and subplots left dangling for the throbbing gristle and flying debris of battles or the close-up and dramatic lighting of existentialist melodrama.[26] At the time, this was thought of as an unusual but negligible quirk associated with the cartoonist. The day of the cartoonist-as-artist/auteur had not yet dawned, nor were extended artistic runs on titles commonplace (now we have examples like 400 issues of Dave Sim's *Cerebus* and 254 issues [and counting] of Erik Larsen's *Savage Dragon* at the time of writing), to say nothing of television. (*The West Wing* and *Game of Thrones* both spring to mind in terms of increasingly inverted narrative ratios of nuance and melodrama as the shows progress and a habit of forgotten characters and plot threads.) Thus, Kirby's propulsion becomes a method for simulating his narrative tempo, informing work on a deeper level, particularly if the cartoonist is aiming to visually emulate the King of Comics.

Tom Scioli is, like Kane and Ladrönn, one of the more aesthetically faithful of the Kirbyesques, having completed significant runs on several titles (notably *Godland*, a thirty-six-issue tribute to Kirby and other cosmically inclined cartoonists' epics of the 1970s), illustrated with bombastic Kirbyesque flair. But Scioli's work reflects influence well beyond visual elements. Unlike *Godland*, written by Joe Casey, which moves along at a decidedly non-Kirbyesque pace, Scioli's contributions extend into writing in the breakneck Kirby way, as evidenced in the madcap, maximalist *Transformers vs. G.I. Joe* (2014–2016, cowritten with John Barber), *Fantastic Four: Grand Design* (2019), and *Jack Kirby: The Epic Life of the King of Comics* (2020). While *Grand Design* can be dismissed somewhat as a curio, truncating and paraphrasing Lee and Kirby's memorable 102-issue run on *Fantastic Four* into—that's right—four issues, this is in itself an overstuffed narrative folly of Kirbyesque dimensions. As such it could be considered a homage par excellence, were it not immediately followed up, and overshadowed, by Scioli's biography of the cartoonist. *The Epic Life*, unlike *Grand Design*, has no affiliation with Marvel, DC, or any major publisher, allowing Kirby's life to be explored in his own (sometimes contradictory) words, untrammeled by editorial intervention. Crafted and adapted from multiple sources, *The Epic Life* is, ironically, perhaps the least Kirbyesque work of Scioli's oeuvre due to its biographical trappings. Beyond the choice to draw Kirby as a kind of cartoon antic with massive eyes, the graphic novel is largely grounded in a carefully researched, period-specific reality, an engaging narrative choice given the subject matter. While Scioli and Barber's *Transformers vs. G.I. Joe* deserves further attention in terms of its toy-box backstory and metaphysics and sheer narrative density, it must be noted here as a propulsive read, executed in a feverish fashion along the lines of "What if Jack Kirby had access to these properties in the 1980s?"[27]

Perhaps the most successful use of this is exemplified in the pages of *Savage Dragon*, written and drawn (ostensibly) monthly by cartoonist Erik Larsen since 1992. In *Savage Dragon* #76, Larsen moved his creator-owned series into a narrative arc that served as an overt homage to some of Kirby's most outré (and visually daring) material from his DC period in the 1970s, particularly *Kamandi: The Last Boy on Earth* and *OMAC: One Man Army Corps*. Entitled "This Savage World," the story is in essence an alternate-reality narrative and freed Larsen from what was by that time an increasingly byzantine continuity and provided him with an opportunity to play in Kirby's wheelhouse, with robots, gods, and giant monsters on a vast and elaborate postapocalyptic stage. Larsen even introduced hyperbolic, pulp-style text panels to better emulate Kirby's writing, a breathless commentary of the rapidly unfolding plot twists and action set pieces. One could almost hear Kirby's gruff, Lower East Side cadence narrating the steroidal melodrama.

If there can be said to be a spiritual successor to Kirby, it is Larsen, most notably for embodying the creative freedoms for which Kirby strove. For those who have not been paying attention to American comics for the last two decades, Larsen is one of the founding cartoonists who launched Image Comics, a creator-owned company built in response to poor treatment at Marvel. While Image was not the first publisher to experiment with creator-owned properties (Kirby himself had two creator-owned comics published in the early 1980s by the short-lived Pacific[28]), it was highly successful and irrevocably changed the nature of the relationship between creators and publishers in the United States.[29] In fact, Larsen and one of his fellow Image cofounders, Todd McFarlane, both cited Kirby's exit from Marvel to pursue his own projects as a key inspiration for Image.[30] In a fitting coda to a career spanning five decades, it was Image that published Kirby's last comic, *Phantom Force* (1993), a year before his death.

FIGURE 5.4 Erik Larsen, *Savage Dragon* 57 (2000): 1.
Courtesy of the artist.

6

Figurative Pseudonyms

• •

Biography and Confession

It is commonplace to say that art is born from experience, the extent of which is mostly immeasurable. In narrational art—which in addition to literature can include paintings, tapestries, and drawings as well as the musical-tone poem genre (the work of Mahler springs to mind, such as his song cycles and his first five symphonies)—the role of biography and autobiography is inevitable and inexorable but also contentious, as the rendering of experience exposes the infidelity of memory itself. Graphic novels and comics are a rich reservoir of memoir, testimonial, and autobiography but in a manner that requires special attention. While a written testimonial is still credited with some credence to truth, as it may relate to a legal document, once a story is told about oneself using pictures, the distortions that may be mythically or ideological downplayed in a conventional written text are immediately brought to notice. The figure in the comic, as a reduction, embellishment, caricature, or invention, is from the start an avatar of the cartoonist, a figurative pseudonym. This is different from actors who look different from the people that they play who nonetheless wish audiences to have faith that they channel the spirit beyond that of the superficial image (Jonathan Rhys Meyers as Henry VIII, for instance). Instead, the comic character is at once a reductio ad absurdum and an idealized figure. One prominent example is that of Robert Crumb, who uses his comic alias as a confessional and therapeutic device, a navigation tool to describe his failures, embarrassments, and disappointments. In contrast to the pseudopornographic discomfort we may feel to be privy to a private act (surveillance, eavesdropping) or the warnings that come with explicit sequences in film, the rendering of odd or unforeseen events into comics has a disarming effect in which the obscene or taboo is mitigated by a visual language that is a signifying system implicitly related to humor and not so distantly to childhood innocence—or just unserious lowbrow fare. Both factors have the capacity to make the pathos of autobiographical comics more profound, bringing the tenuous line between comedy and tragedy to the fore, where the good humor is the ostensibly benign vehicle for underlying misery—a textual wolf in sheep's clothing.

The Problems of Biography and Autobiography

The moment that a story claims to be biography, it places its stakes in the factuality of day-to-day life, which also means an etiology different from that of an invented story line. The problem is that biography must collude with invention for the sake of a captivating narrative and in so doing foregoes its relationship to truth. Autobiography is yet more fraught, as it is vitiated from the start by self-interest. It is an art of self-exculpation or self-exculpation through self-excoriation, which is what we find, for example, in Rousseau's *Confessions*. The alternative to self-dramatization is to recount the unremarkable, which, as the word suggests, is hardly worth remarking upon. As Lukács writes in the chapter on Conrad Meyer in his book on the historical novel (1937), "The everyday of everyday people comes to us as vapid, degraded prose and nothing beyond that. These lives are not bound up with any historical upheaval. A hero is, as Burkhardt says, 'what we are not.'"[1] Bluntly stated, this distinction makes autobiography structurally tenuous, since it is an effort to make a hero of one who is not, or if one were a hero, then the question that immediately goes begging is the motivation for the autobiography in the first place. What we will shortly come to see is that when autobiography has the advantage of both pictures and words, it becomes fertile ground for the lurid, the abject, the bathetic, and the self-emasculating. It is the platform for the performance of negativity and (self-) betrayal that, by dint of being directed inward, is saved to some extent by the reproach of cruelty.

Given that the novel flourishes at the time of the modern, self-determining subject, biography is a determinate factor, whether in the foreground or background. For a character to relate convincingly within a narrative, it must bear some authentic relation to its sociohistorical moment. Lukács's contemporary and friend Arnold Hauser articulates well the close interlacing of autobiography in modern fiction and how it relates to an ever-hungry and increasingly independent reading public that blossomed in the late eighteenth century:

> The autobiographical form of the modern novel, whether a story told in the first person or in letter or diary form, merely serves to intensify its expressionism and is only a means of stressing the shift of attention from outside to inside. From now onwards the diminution of the distance between the subject and the object becomes the principal aim of the literary effort. With the striving for this psychological directness, all the relations between the author, the hero and the reader are changed: not only the author's relation to his public and the characters of his work, but also the reader's attitude to these characters. The author treats the reader as an intimate friend and addresses himself to him in a direct, so to say, vocative style.[2]

These words could not be more relevant to the autobiographic genre in graphic fiction, in which there is an assumed intimacy from the outset. It is confessional and, as with the staging of confession dating back to Rousseau, often luridly so—the presumption being that the authenticity of the confession hinges upon the unwelcome details. The vocative style is prevalent: the author speaks to you as a friend with at times intoxicated intimacy.

Such intoxication has its benefits and paradoxical outcomes, as it has the potential to distance as much as to render close. We choose to suspend the fact that the intimacy is false or an ingredient in the communicative mode, since the protagonist is always the hero, and more people share in his or her plight than in yours. When faced with heroism (or madness), the task is to balance the ordinary with the extraordinary without, as Lukács would have it, descending into Expressionistic hysteria, which can be an inhibitor of pathos. For Lukács, the exemplary figure for one who manages the raw ingredients of biographical data is Goethe. He begins with his early and sensational novel *Werther* (full title *The Sorrows of Young Werther*, 1774), which for us is also a good place to start, as it is feasibly a point of lineage to the histrionics in which graphic novels play a large part. What Goethe drew from was a "seed" of the resultant story.[3] Goethe demonstrates that an author must build something wholly new from the minutiae of life. It is only by not copying reality to the letter that the artist can begin to compete with reality's richness: "Since reality as a whole is always richer and more varied than even the richest work of art, reality traced exactly, that is, in biographically accurate detail, a real episode, etc., as it actually is, can never touch reality. In order to attain an impression that amounts to reality's richness, *the whole context of life has to be rebuilt, the composition must be given an entirely new structure*."[4] When the artist is fortunate enough to have an event that can be inserted effectively within a narrative, the notion of insertion is operable: the "context" of before and after have to be curated for the sake of the narrative and the faithfulness to the actual events overturned for the sake of a different set of coordinates that are constitutively aesthetic, in which the sensuous aspects of life are rebuilt.

If we are to accept this line of argument, how then, asks Lukács, can we hope to make the lives of "great people" valid, aesthetically tenable, and "artistically possible"?[5] Goethe's *Wilhelm Meisters Lehrjahre* (1795–1796) is another serviceable example. It is one of the first examples of the bildungsroman, or a book of maturation and learning, as indicated in its title (*Lehrjahre* is translated as "apprenticeship" but literally means "years of learning"). In Lukács's words, *Wilhelm Meisters Lehrjahre* is "a *novel of learning* [*Erziehung*, which can also mean 'training' and 'nurture']: its content is the education (*Erziehung*) of humanity toward a practical understanding of truth."[6]

Many of the redrawn events in this novel reappear in his later autobiography, *From My Life: Poetry and Truth* (1811–1833). However, transposition is not only of degree but of kind: "Goethe also makes a decisive correction to his hero's makeup: he removes him of Goethian genius [*Genialität*]. And similarly, Gottfried Keller in his even stronger autobiographical novel, *Green Henry* [*Grüne Heinrich*, 1855]. Why? Because both great novelists—Goethe and Keller—saw clearly that the biographical structuration [*Gestaltung*] of genius [*Genialität*], the unfolding of a person of genius and related achievements as portrayed in a biography is at odds with epic art's means of expression."[7] *Genialität* is used here operably instead of *Genie* (genius). Whereas both mean "genius," *Genialität* also denotes "ingenuity" and "resourcefulness" with subtending ideas of "brilliance" and "refinement." Goethe and Keller drain their characters of the genius of ingenuity and refinement in order to set them within the world as opposed against it—hence Lukács's reference to the integration of protagonist and circumstance that characterizes the epic genre. He may be suggesting not that such tales attain the status of ancient epic but rather that they have more of the qualities of the epic than had they followed the line where the genius is painted in constant contrast to his or her surroundings. The "task" of the novelist, as Lukács would have it, is "to lay out the development of genius, that is, to create *organically* [*genetisch*] the ingenious character of a great person and the individually ingenious achievements through life facts and episodes that are directly presented, narrated and described."[8] Further, we must be judicious with "those life episodes with which the artistic biographer or autobiographer as a *designer* of life [*Menschengestalter*] has, above all, to work. These connections can only be brought to light on the basis of a broad, deep, very generalized *analysis* of the epoch."[9]

To return to *Genialität*: a noticeably regular device in the graphic novel is to present something of the obverse in the dissolute and objectionable. It is neither genius nor genial but far more an orgy of self-flaying and censure. This reversal is by all accounts the flipside of the hero as perverse antihero or madman and yet another instance of Marx's dictum that history occurs "first as tragedy, then as farce." The farce in many graphic novels is also scrubbed of its power to elicit sympathy, if farce ever did have that power (perhaps sometimes in the commedia dell'arte). Several (auto- or semiautobiographical) instances come immediately to mind. Robert Crumb, Chris Ware, Noah Van Sciver, Alison Bechdel, Simon Hanselmann, Yoshiro Tatsumi, Nina Bunjevac, Josh Bayer, Gabrielle Belle, Marjane Satrapi, and Keiji Nakazawa have all made significant works as graphic novels that are situated at various points along the *Genialität* continuum, all demonstrating various degrees of tragedy and farce. Yet there is a clear demarcation between those whose autobiographical avatars, analogues, and ciphers are worthy of sympathy and those who are worthy of outright scorn.

What is the net effect of this parade of pathos by so many cartoonists? It is interesting to note that the vast majority of autobiographical comics are created by cartoonists who handle both writing and drawing duties. Exceptions exist, such as Harvey Pekar, who worked with many different cartoonists to handle the visual aspects of his comics, but this is surely a matter of clarity of storytelling. After all, who better to tell the cartoonist's story (or a version of it) than the cartoonist him- or herself?

FIGURE 6.1 Josh Bayer, *Theth: Retrofit Giant-Size Annual* (2014): 27.
Courtesy of the artist.

Robert Crumb: King of Fools, Triumphant

Crumb is easily one of the best-known cartoonists to explore autobiography, yet at the same time, he embodies many of the complexities of the tradition. One key mitigating factor is the cartoonist's well-known public persona, posited as an extension of the private: horny, socially awkward, and neurotic, the traits, incidentally, that all too many stand-up comedians assign to themselves. Crumb's public prominence is due to not only his activity as a cartoonist but also him being something of a representative celebrity in this domain. In many ways, Crumb is the quintessential confessional figure of comix, the man who laid his heart bare—*mon cœur mis à nu*, as Baudelaire famously put it. He is the subject of two documentaries, several major retrospective exhibitions, and countless books and articles, to say nothing of being a character in the 2003 film adaptation of sometime collaborator Pekar's comic series, *American Splendor* (Crumb illustrated several stories between 1976 and 1987).

Crumb-as-character is at the crux of this issue, as the cartoonist's penchant for catharsis and self-examination (for good or ill) is not always bound by autobiography proper. In Lukács's terms, he embodies the alienated condition of the striving and discordant self, navigating uncomfortably amid an unsympathetic society, regularly disaffected and afoul of the situations he is forced to stumble over with more or less success. The plights of the graphic Crumb and the human Crumb have tended to fold into one, making it next to impossible to separate between Crumb's actual life with what he sometimes self-consciously refers to as his shtick. Consider, in the first instance, Crumb's costume, which is largely unchanged since the 1970s: horn-rimmed, coke-bottle spectacles; buttoned shirt; bow tie; brown suit; and straw boater. Whether a 1971 or 2021 depiction of Crumb, he is highly identifiable to the point of iconicity. (What other cartoonists are so recognizable? Only the massive, bearded, glowering visage of Alan Moore and the toupee-and-shades, 1970s Hollywood swag of Stan Lee spring to mind.) Reading Crumb, one must consider whether Crumb, qua character, is being presented as an autobiographical representation or a self-parodic avatar. Moreover, there are many characters that can be considered analogues for Crumb's own interests, kinks, and fetishes, ciphers upon which he can project himself, such as Fritz the Cat, Doggo, or Flakey Foont. It is within the variety of Crumb's self-representations (clear or obfuscated) that complicate a clear reading of Crumb as autobiographer, perhaps deliberately so, but his work can almost universally be considered confessional. This aligns closely with the way the cartoonist views his own work, a kind of uncontrollable, cathartic outpouring.

Crumb has created works of autobiography that align with the broader literary tradition in the clearest terms as well as several that contain only a passing resemblance, despite casting himself as the central protagonist or, in his own eyes, victim. In many ways, his works build on the literary genre of the bildungsroman. Notwithstanding, where Crumb departs from the traditional novel of this kind, drawn from personal experience, is that instead of a rousing ending, his works are usually essays in bathos, a device also used by his contemporaries in stand-up comedy, where autobiographic license is laced with self-deprecation. While there are examples of the author driving his literary self into a hole of turpitude—Malcolm Lowry's great *Under the Volcano* (1947) springs to mind—such a position, or path, is arguably more effective either in the performative mode (stand-up) or with the support of images, where the tragedy of human life is offset by figural representation that has the effect of bringing the pathos out of the metaphysical and into the realm of the real and the visible and thus what we all share. It would have been very interesting to have seen Samuel Beckett teaming with a comix artist, if his own stylistic scruples would have allowed. In many ways, the spirit of Molloy haunts the Crumb alias. But Crumb is, in the first instance, less interminable, although the interminability sneaks up on us as an aftershock. As with Beckett, humor provides a kind of cushioning for a much harder fall.

Several works created for *Weirdo* in the 1980s (such as "I Remember the Sixties" and "Footsy") are straightforward recollections of his youth, experiences at school, and early professional life. These stories are embellished with Crumb's own thoughts, split between the narrator's panels, which are looking back to the moment in question, and the character's thought balloons, which are of the moment, yet they are framed within a timeline of events in the cartoonist's life and therefore maintain a sense of narrative momentum and authorial accuracy. Whether or not we are willing to accept these events as unembellished—it is a given that any representation, especially literary, derives from a process of culling and selection—these comics can be accepted, easily, as autobiography. Again, we are willing to assert that abjection and bad circumstances are more conducive to visual rendition, and so (as ever in the work of Crumb) the most labored-over drawings are most often panels depicting the objects of Crumb's desire (almost universally women with shapely legs wearing Mary Janes or spool-style high heels) or indeed a kind of self-portraiture at the moment of realization of desire (usually a variation of the artist grimacing, with either befogged spectacles, a knitted brow beaded with sweat, or emotive linework radiating toward the cartoonist's head in a kind of reverse-halo).

However, just as there are instances where a narrative about the anthropomorphic character Fritz the Cat could be interpreted as autobiographical, there are instances of Crumb-as-character appearing, as it were, as a kind of guest star. (A parallel might be Proust's narrator, Marcel, who by the middle of the novel is as much a fly on the wall or eavesdropper as an introspective subject.) This version of Crumb might break the fourth wall, appear in a mock advertisement, or participate in the visual tropes of comics we associate with humor comics: pratfalls, spit takes, fainting at the punch line, or shoes flying off in exasperation. This is undoubtedly Crumb, but it is a version of Crumb who is not tethered to an autobiographical context such as time or place. This is Crumb as a character study. Such complications, however, rarely appear deliberate. Though depicting himself as neurotic and chronically self-aware, Crumb evinces little interest in the metaphysics of autobiography, usually favoring a more straightforward (if improvised) narrative. Beyond his densely cross-hatched drawings, Crumb's most influential legacy could certainly be considered the confessional comic. As Kirby looms large over the superhero and Tezuka over manga, Crumb is indivisible from the confessional—the act of confession, most notably in relation to highly specific sexual fantasies, and occasionally the self-conscious anxiety and criticality associated with self-expression, tropes that have made confessional comics a genre unto itself.

Crumb's imitators are legion, but there are few who have managed to avoid aping his distinctive aesthetic. Chris Ware, a noted Crumb devotee, has managed to harvest Crumb's sense of pathos, particularly in regard to the cartoonist's highly self-critical relationship with his chosen art form, and even managed to notch up the anxiety and social alienation by several degrees, despite appearing far more well adjusted. While Crumb's work is often denigrated as either racist or misogynist, Ware's own hatred is usually turned inward, a much safer proposition, and in some ways buried within the cartoonist's elaborate, highly constructed worlds. Ware largely replicates Crumb's self-reproach, yet the end result is quite different. While, as Beaty argues, Crumb's confessions may equate to political martyrdom,[10] Ware's own are far more calculated in terms of *Genialität*. In the final chapter of *Comics versus Art* (2013), Beaty unpacks Ware's complicated relationship with both comics and the visual arts at length, pointing to Ware's strange casting as poster boy for, and commentator of, the "alienated, overlooked genius."[11] Thus, "Ware himself has contributed to the image of his own genius through his interviews, writings on comics, and the publication of two volumes of his sketchbooks, all of which are presented as an outpouring of his direct and unmediated creative process . . . and suggest a harsh worldview evinced in his fiction is not simply a carefully tended persona or authorial mask. Much of the work in Ware's published sketchbooks depicts him as a misanthrope, perpetually unhappy with his life and his work and disappointed with his talent."[12] Beaty neatly summarizes the complex issue of authenticity in autobiographical comics: "From this standpoint, his comics are not read as products of a particular time and place, but are seen as stemming inexorably from the initial experience of the artist's personal psychic and emotional history. . . . His work is seen as inextricably linked with his own personal subjectivity as a result of the ideology of personal genius, Ware's issues become those of comics as well."[13] This is *Genialität* in its purest form, a case of directorial self-casting in the vehicle for one's own benefit. However, it must not be overlooked that such arguments for genius, no matter how unfashionable, must be considered on some level, as Ware's contributions to the medium are far from slight. Putting aside considerations of skill, which are historically imbricated with those of the master and the genius, Ware's narrative and formal contributions themselves have been hugely influential and innovative, perhaps more so than his mentor prototype, Crumb. To expound upon Ware's innovations of the comic form is less hyperbolic than observational by virtue of their striking complexity, power, and depth.

Beaty has written about both Crumb and Ware extensively in the context of their complicated relationship as cartoonists who have penetrated the fine arts and used this as the principal ingredient for auto- or semiautobiographical musings. Furthermore, his essay "Autobiography as Authenticity" provides a framework for understanding autobiographical comics' ascendency to primacy in alternative comic circles and the problems therein. Beaty articulates the unavoidable inconsistencies that arise between a lived experience, or truth, and its narrative representation, positioning autobiographical comics as referential rather than factual.[14] This is an important caveat, particularly in consideration of cartoonists such as Crumb and Ware, whose use of autobiography so often vacillates between series of recollections, avatars for the cartoonist, and cartoonist-as-character. Unlike cartoonists such as Satrapi, Bechdel, and Nakazawa (discussed in the next section), who appear to keep some sense of chronological structure through the provision of narrative detail, Crumb's and particularly Ware's approaches are far less concerned with presenting themselves as autobiography, instead allowing for broader narrative sweeps not necessarily constricted by actual events. For example, while Ware's oeuvre is frequented by characters that can easily be read as avatars for the cartoonist, Ware has also puckishly disrupted such autobiographical readings with the addition of the cartoonish version of himself in *Rusty Brown* (2001–2019), the somewhat pitiable art teacher at Rusty's school. This version of himself is a direct contradiction of the characters (theoretically) more closely aligned with autobiography as well as a perverse commentary on his own success and perceived rejection by the visual arts world, as established by Beaty. Even when Ware has reached a level of success shared by perhaps five other living cartoonists, he can still only cast himself as an outsider.

Cartoonists as Outsiders: Confessions of the Marginalized

While cartoonists such as Ware and Crumb consciously play with the boundaries of the self as a vehicle for autobiography, the self as a character, and ciphers for the outward projection of autobiography, it is Crumb that has been a mainstay of comics almost since the beginning. Superman, or more specifically his civilian identity Clark Kent, serves as a synecdoche for the American immigrant experience: the outsider blending in, excelling at a chosen profession, and longing for acceptance. Superman, in turn, is a cipher for the unencumbered id, the outsider's wet dream of power and confidence. Both, of course, pine for the same object of desire, fellow reporter Lois Lane, a love triangle wrung by Superman's cocreators, Siegel and Shuster, both children of Jewish immigrants, for all the pathos they could. This compelling dichotomy became a primary template for the superhero for decades to come, from Spider-Man right down to Invincible.

It is important to note that while in broader cultural terms the cartoonist is synonymous with the outsider, particularly in its ghettoized situation to film and the visual arts, comics have historically either mirrored or subverted the status quo. While the creations of Ware could hardly be considered overtly masculine in a narrative sense (indeed, Ware's own depiction of himself as more or less of an effete, pretentious wimp with a deeply internalized sense of desire precludes this), his elaborate compositions coupled with his recurring narratives of the misunderstood genius (established by Beaty) could be read as overtly masculine in an artistic sense. As Jacob Brogan notes in reference to Ware's most well-known avatar, "We can read Jimmy [Corrigan]'s alienation from his sexuality, and perhaps his alienation in general, as an allegory of the status of comics."[15] Alison Bechdel, Gabrielle Belle, and Marjane Satrapi are three cartoonists who have created compelling and fully realized works of autobiography unmoored from the conventions of Crumb and his many imitators. In this way it is an effrontery to frame these cartoonists' work in terms of White, male, heterosexual cartoonists such as Crumb and Ware; however, it is a useful comparison to underline the differences in approach that are possible not only in relation to Crumb but in relation to each other. Unlike Crumb, Ware, and others whose autobiographical and/or confessional works often obscure as often as reveal, Belle, Satrapi, and particularly Bechdel have a much less anxious relationship with autobiography. This relative comfort within the conventions of autobiographical comics allows for a less complicated depiction of the self (no avatars necessary) that, free from the limited attention span of Crumb and the elaborate metaphysics of Ware, are successful in presenting engaging works of autobiography and confession.

All three cartoonists use the drama and inherent peculiar dynamics of family to tell their own stories. All three situate their narratives in relief to significant life events, thereby lending each narrative a sense of urgency as well as a useful framing device to build upon the specifics of each autobiography. Bell's *Everything Is Flammable* (2017) is perhaps the most comfortable in mining the family unit for pathos. Considered a memoir, Belle's narrative centers on her return to her hometown after her mother's house burns down. Significant pages are devoted to building the complex relationship between the cartoonist and her mother, complemented with asides that take the readers down all manner of rabbit holes, narrative ellipses that serve to develop backstory. A particularly hilarious (if slightly disturbing) example is a passage in which Bell recounts and catalogs each instance she has experienced or been somehow responsible for that has led to the death of a cat.

Satrapi's *Persepolis* (2003) largely takes the form of a coming-of-age story, set against the Iranian revolution. Drawn in bold black and white, Satrapi's familial drama appears light-years outside the mainstream, equally indebted to political posters and social realist printmaking. Satrapi's story revolves around her progressive Iranian family, who find themselves on the wrong side of the political upheaval, thereby finding themselves designated and subsequently persecuted as upper-middle class and therefore decadent. Satrapi's simple, stylized aesthetic neatly belies a complex sociopolitical narrative, as growing up, she began to understand that the overthrow of the Shah and the 1979 creation of an Islamic republic would have continuing and increasingly violent repercussions on her family, her class, and her sex, eventually causing the renunciation of her faith and expatriation from her country, both compounding the character's outsider status. Bechdel's *Fun Home: A Family Tragicomic* (2006) begins with the death—and possible suicide—of her father. Jumping around in time, the cartoonist weaves different strands of her life, providing evidence for her theory that her father's death was deliberate. This also provides a pretext for the author's discussion of her self-discovery of her gender and sexuality, realizing at a certain point her attraction to women, precipitated through literature and the discovery of her father's own homosexuality. The literature in her formation is a neat catalyst and guiding line within the narrative. Bechdel appears to have inherited her parents' voracious appetite for reading, and book recommendations form an important form of communication, particularly with her emotionally distant father.

While autobiographical comics have flourished in recent years, they are by no means a new phenomenon. Unlike the analogues and ciphers so often used in the superhero genre, which tend to be more implicative or evocative than confessional, the autobiography can be highly specific and conditional to time and place. Keiji Nakazawa's seminal manga *Barefoot Gen* (1973–1987), a ten-volume epic set against the lead-up and aftermath of the bombing of Hiroshima, is a harrowing account based on Nakazawa's own experiences. As in *Persepolis*, the family members of Gen Nakaoka (Nakazawa's titular avatar) do not prescribe to the reigning status quo and are considered troublemakers by the nationalist government. Of course, this status is soon upended by the bombing of the city, turning *Barefoot Gen* from a narrative of defiance to a narrative of survival. *Barefoot Gen* is a confessional of an entirely different stripe to those of Crumb, Bell, or Bechdel. The harrowing events of the narrative align closely with a sense of catharsis, an attempt to process the horrors of war, at the epicenter of one of the defining moments in human history. Nakazawa's drawings are highly stylized, perhaps the only way forward for such an intensely bleak narrative: were the story rendered in a more photorealistic style, it would perhaps become unreadable. Conversely, being of the *shonen* style,[16] Nakazawa's work verges on cute and so is a highly effective vehicle for delivering a narrative of such thematic weight. Images of victims of the bomb blast or those suffering from radiation sickness, for example, are paradoxically softened and intensified by their rendering in the *shonen* style.

In a particularly bleak passage, Gen has passed out after hours of combing the ruins of Hiroshima for fellow survivors and is found and placed on a pyre by soldiers with the heaped bodies of the dead. Alight, the boy wakes

FIGURE 6.2 Gabrielle Bell, *Everything Is Flammable* (Minneapolis: Uncivilized Books, 2017), 44. Courtesy of the artist.

up and is saved by the soldiers, who extinguish the fire on him. He ends up becoming attached to one of them and follows him around the ruins. They chance upon cisterns filled with the bodies of those who sought escape from the intense heat from the blast to no avail. The soldier, who came to Hiroshima as a part of the rescue efforts, quickly succumbs to radiation sickness in a rather gruesome fashion.

It is worth recalling Lukács's assertion, which was by no means unique to him, that the modern novel is oriented toward the limited freedom of the protagonist based on the forces of alienation. There is very little in literature that is not in some form autobiographical, yet when it moves into the fantastic and arcane, which was his criticism of Franz Kafka, literature loosens its links to reality and its purchase upon it. The graphic dimension in the autobiographic genre of comics—which we can now claim as a substantive genre to the form—serves two ostensibly contradictory functions. First, it brings the circumstances of life and confession into sharper—graphic—relief in a way that Lukács would have decried in his criticism of naturalism, with its overabundance of distracting detail. Yet second, the inclusion of the visual in the written narrative affords a number of measures that mitigates what is potentially the affective burden of such a genre. Earlier, we used the term *cushion* when we referred to the humor of Crumb and Beckett. Before we are thrust too deeply into life's inexorability, its cruelty, and its loss, we are at first distracted by the ridiculousness of it, which is too often found in the grisly, random details. In graphic novels, tragedy is trapped within life, with life being the gory details of humble, banal reality. We become idolaters of the visual contours and details before which we find ourselves to have penetrated deeper than we thought we might have. Readers, when using the two guns of words and images, beware . . . the cartoonist has twice as many tools for their confessions as well as their obfuscations.

Part II

Case Studies

● ●

7

Josh Bayer

●●●●●●●●●●●●●●●●●●●●●●

According to Gérard Genette, a powerful and compelling way of thinking of literature is as a palimpsest, writing on erasure. Naturally an analogue relation, palimpsests occurred in administrative, legal, and even philosophical documents when policies, laws, or beliefs became altered through revelation or coercion. For Genette, the palimpsest is a more sympathetic metaphor than, say, intertextuality for the way it has a distinctly material, visual connotation, where the traces of the past glimmer forth in unforeseen ways that subtly affect what has supplanted it. In some writers, this process is more conscious and present than in others. Proust is one of Genette's prime examples, as his work is the result of countless revisions, while the content is itself a dense and layered reworking of memory, which itself is always colored and defined by the present. Looking from a very different angle—and making a comparison that could be heretical to the purists, and for that, all the better—a similar argument can be made of Josh Bayer, whose work is the result of constant revisions, building up and cutting back and collaging into existing drawings, which end up resembling skeins of paint rather than the typically flat surface of drawing. Even considering comics' historical (pre-digital) engagement with erasure and collage, Bayer's work takes the page to the nth degree, an imbrication of old and new marks that resembles that of a Cy Twombly as much as a Frank King. Bayer's work is a complex concoction of autobiography, tempered with a deep knowledge of comic history while deploying references and homage with sincerity. Bayer's practice is fascinating in its complex, frequent vacillation between the lore of comics and his own personal narrative, both of which are interwoven to an extent in which it becomes increasingly difficult to divine his own story from that of the metaphysical histories of his chosen referents. This intricate layering results in a dense and febrile aesthetic, often verging on horror vacui. His narratives become as imbricated with references (to both the personal and the meta-narratives of comics) as his drawings.

In the many delineating conscious and unconscious fluctuations of the palimpsestic relation in literature, Genette coins the term "self-pastiche," which can in turn be intimately related to Bayer. Pastiche was a literary form popular in the nineteenth century that was used as either homage or parody by writing in the style and voice of another. Like all forms of mimicry, it was hard to do well. Pastiche would subsequently be used as a definitional word for postmodernism in art, sitting alongside parody as a deconstructive device. According to Genette, authors are to engage in self-pastiche involuntarily, but when it is done voluntarily, "it requires a writer gifted with both a high degree of stylistic individuality and a great aptitude for imitation."[1] Mentioning Joyce and Nabokov in passing, Genette again turns to Proust as an exemplar of such a practice. It is an approach that is not without its difficulties, since it is "to write in the style of oneself,"[2] but what makes it notable is its self-observed intentionality that "fatefully tends toward caricature."[3] Although Genette does not pursue this any further, the caricature that he means is not to lapse into a grotesque copy but rather to move into self-irony that reflects a stress on the self-reflection and self-limitation of the author. Self-pastiche can therefore also be self-parody, and its limitations are that it is a process that is always definite, the definitions being when the style oversteps that of those that are inherited. It is an act of self-referentiality that only serves to highlight the lack of autonomy and the myriad web of references that make up the tissue of one's personal style.

Noted comic theorist M. Thomas Inge approaches self-reflexivity in comics through the lens of literature. Such comics—or metacomics, as he refers to them—share an intentionality in commenting on the author's (or cartoonist's) experience by commenting on the creative process of the form itself.[4] Couching the self-reflexive aspect of comics in postmodernism is an interesting proposition, for the art form predates the idiom by some decades, being, as Inge notes, a decidedly twentieth-century art form in terms of philosophic uncertainty and self-questioning.[5] While Inge establishes that

FIGURE 7.1 Josh Bayer, *Theth: Retrofit Giant-Size Annual* (2014): 43.
Courtesy of the artist.

comics have incorporated self-reflexivity since their earliest years (this is widely accepted), he arrives at the conclusion that, rather than offering a different *kind* of self-reflexivity to, say, film or literature, comics have engaged in the practice in ways "rather more than we were allowed possible."[6] This statement would seem to take into account the relatively delayed development of comic theory compared to film and particularly literature and flags the need for sustained analysis of metacomics.

Yet there are earlier attempts at such analysis that struggle to identify exactly what it is trying to describe evident in some early critical responses to comics, such as Wertham (as discussed earlier) and Marshal McLuhan. McLuhan's 1964 attempt to analyze the narrative metaphysics of *Mad* magazine (which was, in the 1960s, still a highly innovative and trailblazing site for subversive humor and satire) revealed some remarkable gaps in comic-specific terminology, which theorists like Inge, Groensteen, and Carrier would eventually fill. While the essay is primarily concerned with comics, the still-new phenomenon of television, and their impacts upon youth (shades of a more reasonable and evenhanded Wertham), McLuhan grasps for his argument, revealing in his recognition of alternative modes of thought, consumption, and calling for a media-specific terminology to better understand them. As Marshall McLuhan writes, "Teachers today frequently find that students who can't read a page of history are becoming experts in code and linguistic analysis. . . . Above all, it is a print [media] form of expression and experience whose sudden appeal is a sure index of deep changes in our culture. Our need now is to understand the formal character of print, comic and cartoon, both as challenging and changing the consumer-culture of film, photo and press."[7] Consumer culture and media have only proliferated in the intervening decades, particularly in the post–digital world, as well as the language and terminologies to discuss them, but McLuhan had identified the necessity of building an appropriate language to adequately discuss their particularities.

Bayer's work exemplifies many of the self-reflexive tendencies that Inge points toward as well as, intermittently, Genette's notion of self-pastiche. Drawn in a visually busy, roughhewn fashion, Bayer creates dense, semiautobiographical narratives that incorporate as many fictional plot twists and characters from comics and popular culture as they do from real life. *Theth: Tomorrow Forever* (2019), a typical example, follows the story of the titular and semiautobiographical character and incorporates fictional characters from the real world (ROM), fictional characters from the fictional world (Black Star), and real characters from the real world (punk singer Wendy O.

Williams). Drawn with dark skeins of linework, Bayer's is a singular yet amorphous aesthetic, comics by way of Kirby, Crumb, Panter, and Herriman. Overly encrusted or incomprehensible panels and speech bubbles are often cut into with paint or correction fluid or simply collaged over in order to make improvements, itself a conversation with, and extension to, the traditions of the media. While these techniques are not uncommon in cartooning practices, much of the need for such revisions is rendered unnecessary through the planning process. Not so with Bayer: this technique affords the work a lively, visceral nature that diverges heavily from the slick aesthetic of mainstream comics. Any preparatory process typical of cartoonists is subsumed into Bayer's finished work, which develops a tactile crust, a level of comic expressionism almost entirely lacking in contemporary comics. Indeed, beyond a certain point, the most efficient way of producing comics for many cartoonists has become digital, tablet drawings and Photoshop coloring speeding up the process considerably, eliminating the necessity of at least one step of the traditional comic book production line (usually writer, penciller, inker, letterer, colorist, all overseen by an editor). Of course, there are many holdouts, cartoonists too steeped in their craft to change, or younger cartoonists uninterested in working digitally, preferring instead to opt for tradition. Bayer could easily be considered a holdout were it not for his recent embrace of computer color as a means of speeding up production on longer projects, like *RM* (2018) and *Black Star* (2019), which employ a highly idiosyncratic coloring style that, while digital, sits far outside the slick, cinema-influenced digital color of contemporary mainstream comics. Bayer's approach is far more expressionistic and textured and once more suggests parallels with painting and collage as much as comics.

Metacomics and Self-Reflexivity

Put simply, metacomics are comics that have, to a greater or lesser degree, self-reflexivity. This can mean a self-consciousness of itself as a comic, as a narrative, as written and drawn, as a narrative set within visual-narrative dimensions, and usually as a combination of these. Its basis is in metaphysics, which is the study in philosophy of mechanisms and relationships that exist outside of the physical—*meta* coming from the Greek meaning "outside." Without digressing too far, suffice to say, metaphysics, while an established philosophic category, has no consensus as to its definition. In the same vein, we can assert that there is no quintessential metacomic, which can be best

FIGURE 7.2 Josh Bayer, *Theth: Tomorrow Forever* (Denver: Tinto, 2019), 11.
Courtesy of the artist.

defined as a comic that has regular indicators of uncertainty as to what it is, therefore requiring signs and strategies for addressing this anxiety with the ever-deferred possibility of a comforting answer.

From the form's nascent years, comics have operated at a particular register when it comes to self-reflexivity, embodying a readiness, even eagerness, to subvert narrative convention, breaking the fourth wall at will, commenting on the hybrid nature of the form and its construction. This is most likely a result of the form's interchangeability of word and image as well as its formal multiplicity of word and image, which constitutes the mechanics of the form's reading. Moreover, with its early reputation as a low art form, cartoonists were able to experiment and play, largely free from critical discussion so long as readers were kept happy. Lighthearted commentary on comics' particular representation of (or deviation from) reality became common practice from the very beginning, most notably with the Yellow Kid character.[8] Appearing in Richard F. Outcault's *Hogan's Alley* (1895–1898) strip, the Yellow Kid wore an oversized shirt that was emblazoned with witticisms, taglines, and satirical statements that would change from panel to panel, thereby addressing the reader who is immediately made aware of a set of intentions that exist outside (hence *meta*) of the diegetic flow. Windsor McCay's titular character from *Little Nemo in Slumberland* (1911–1927) would often address the reader upon waking (as he did in the last panel of each elaborate Sunday page), a bemused cross between narrative expediency and wonder. Thus, a language, even an expectation of some level of reflexivity, has become ingrained in the conventions of the form, which has continued even into the Hollywood comic book adaptation in films such as *Tank Girl* (1995) and *Deadpool* (2016), both of which gleefully engage in the skewering of its own respective fiction. Although such examples are far from a ringing endorsement of the translation of comics' self-reflexivity (this has been achieved far more effectively elsewhere in films unhampered by the cumbersome formulas required by the superhero film craze, such as *American Splendor* [2003], to say nothing of nontranslations [from comics] such as *The Royal Tenenbaums* [2001] and *Synecdoche, New York* [2008]), they do speak to the indivisibility of comics and their particular brand of visual multivalence.

Roy T. Cook's analysis of the self-reflexive media specificity of comics is made based on differentiating the interpretation and mechanics of comics and film. While Cook acknowledges that there are, no doubt, formal parallels between the two forms, he insists upon a forthright consideration of the differences in presentation and consumption (projection or screening versus turning pages) as a significant rupture between the two forms.[9] The most robust argument for a distinctive consideration of the medium, Cook argues, lies in metacomics, which contain properties unreproducible in film by virtue of the formal differences of each medium.[10] Cook's definition of metacomics aligns with and acknowledges Inge's, and both extend upon Patricia Waugh's earlier meditations on the topic of metafiction in literature. Cook's loose taxonomy of the varieties of metacomics is worth reproducing in full for its succinct summation of some of the medium's most anarchic and definition-resistant narrative conceits:

- A *narrative metacomic* is a comic whose plot involves the production, consumption, or collection of comics (or any other aspect of the comics subculture and its trappings).
- A *cameo metacomic* is a comic whose plot involves interaction with characters, locales, or other elements that are not in the same continuity, or whose plot involves parodying or spoofing other comics.
- A *self-aware metacomic* is a comic whose protagonist (or perhaps some other character) is aware he or she is in a comic.
- An *intertextual metacomic* is a comic whose content interacts, in some manner, with the content of some other text or artwork.
- An *authorial metacomic* is a comic whose plot involves the appearance of the writer, artist or other creator as a character in the comic.
- A *formal metacomic* is a comic whose plot involves formal manipulation of the conventions of the comic medium.[11]

It must be noted at this juncture that Bayer's work usually embodies several—and occasionally all six—approaches at one time. Bayer is among several contemporary cartoonists whose work moves easily between modes of pastiche, satire, and quotation, building a personalized and specific narrative style out of a patchwork of references, wholly original yet constituent of its many parts. Waugh's 1984 examination of metafiction, though primarily concerned with literature proper and, periodically, popular culture in its broadest possible terms, is applicable to Bayer's work and metacomics in general. Building a clear line of literary criticism back to Leavis, Waugh creates a clear progression of literary steps toward metafiction, which reaches back to Cervantes's *Don Quixote*.

It is worth pausing on *Don Quixote* for a moment, given that it is one of the most striking early examples of a metatext for the way it uses comedic elements to toy with voice and genre as well as the way it addresses aspects of the social upheaval of its time. As Lukács observes,

The resolutely comical conception of Don Quixote, the basis of which is Cervantes' resolute position in the struggle between dying feudalism and the emerging bourgeois world, not only allows the comic nature of the portrayal to be uninhibited toward a resolute human dissolution of what is outdated [*bis zur menschlichen Vernichtung der Veralteten*], but at the same time leads to the fact that Don Quixote's subjective human integrity—in contrast in many cases to the moral inferiority of that real world, replaced in his dream world with historical necessity and dissolved in laughter—so that his purity, bravery, and decency clearly emerge to be the limit of the tragic.[12]

This passage can easily apply to Bayer's work not only in the use of laughter as a vehicle for social and personal critique but also in the way that a self-conscious, layered approach is used to grapple with a multivalent and troubled world. Further, the power of the built literary world, Waugh asserts, is its "provi[sion of] collective pleasure and release of tension through the comforting total affirmation of accepted stereotypes."[13] In other words, genre and formula provide a familiar and fertile context for more daring literary conceits. This is doubtlessly applicable to comics.

Perhaps above all, Bayer is an avowed artistic disciple of Kirby not only for his crackling visual energy; massive, heaving figures; and tireless work ethic but as a symbol of the pitfalls of cartooning, particularly related to ownership of intellectual property. Kirby has largely been cast (by himself as well as others) in this role after several notable battles with Marvel and Stan Lee (longtime Marvel editor, publisher, and figurehead) for the return of original artwork and commensurate recognition for his many contributions to the industry. Such legal battles litter the history of comics, but Kirby and Siegel and Shuster (creators of Superman) have become icons of cartoonist rights, less for their actual progress (it was the next generation who began to make real headway in their name) and more for taking up the fight in the first place and for the crushingly incommensurate rewards for creating some of the industry's most profitable cornerstones, still wildly profitable today. Kirby's stoic, working-class attitudes gel with the do-it-yourself mentality of punk culture and the visual discomfiture of Raymond Pettibon (a sometime collaborator) in Bayer's work, which vacillates between self-expression and the schizoid politics of contemporary United States.

Greater Good (2013, cocreated with Pat Aulisio) is a metacomic about Steve Ditko (cocreator of Spider-Man) and his battles with Stan Lee over creative control of the character and is filled with minutiae only a diehard comic fan could penetrate. The Stan Lee of *Greater Good* is a winged, multiple-teated,

FIGURE 7.3 Bayer, *Theth: Tomorrow Forever*, 55.
Courtesy of the artist.

manticore-like creature with the toupee, sunglasses, and mustache of the "new and improved" 1970s iteration of Stan Lee and is an exploitative capitalist. Ditko is a cartoonish, angry caricature, punching through original drawings in rages and spouting the objectivist, Randian philosophies the cartoonist became associated with. In a particularly memorable sequence, a hulking, grotesque Mickey Mouse character bursts through a wall, the characters exclaiming, "Marvel and Disney . . . are the government!!" referencing the 2009 US$4 billion acquisition of Marvel by Disney. Mickey Mouse then proceeds to dangle a living, bare-assed Spider-Man puppet in front of our heroes; rips off the head off Bayer and Aulisio's Krazy Kat–like avatar; and explains the vagaries of copyright law with manticore Stan Lee. The comic ends with a sequence featuring, among other things, Jack Kirby and Steve Gerber making comics in the afterlife; Destroyer Duck[14] dancing and singing "Old Black Joe," which is itself laden with references to cotton slavery; and the manticore Stan Lee uttering his huckster epithet, "Make mine Marvel." It is a bizarre and memorable satire of both the comic industry and those who work in it.

Birth of Horror (2013) is a similar examination of comic lore and intellectual property, this time involving another tragic figure, Bill Everett (creator of the Namor the Sub-Mariner, and cocreator of Daredevil and one of the most accomplished first-generation cartoonists, who died at fifty-five of heart failure after years of alcohol abuse) as well as Gary Friedrich (creator of Ghost Rider and Son of Satan) and once again featuring Bayer's manticore version of Stan Lee. This time, the act of creation is parodied as an occult incantation, referencing Everett and Friedrich's 1970s work for Marvel, which featured an overabundance of shlock supernatural themes. Everett is depicted in star-spangled wizard robes, and together with pseudo-manticore Stan Lee, Larry Lieberman (Lee's real-life brother and cartoonist), and Friedrich, they raise the character Simon the Zombie from a grave (filled with liquid mercury, black ink, and atomized pig retina) with a spell. It is a deeply silly plot that reveals an intimate knowledge of the minutiae of 1970s comics (Simon the Zombie, like Son of Satan and Man-Thing, both of whom also appears briefly in the story, is a character highly specific to this period and has not enjoyed the continued popularity of Ghost Rider, another such relic of 1970s Marvel), including Stan Lee's carnival huckster dialogue, which littered comics from the 1960s right through to the end of the century. Bayer's wiry, nervous drawings do not attempt to replicate the Marvel house style, instead rendering characters as manipulable wax models, bending and expanding far outside the prescribed proportions of post-Kirby mainstream comics. It is at once deeply personal and highly fanciful, an incisive look into the creative process, a pastiche of a highly specific period of comics, and a satire of the industry as a whole.

Greater Good and *Birth of Horror* are striking examples of a subset of Bayer's work that examines the politics of ownership in comics, remixing and appropriating freely, in turns sincere and satirical. While these comics tend more

FIGURE 7.4 Josh Bayer, *Birth of Horror* (2013): 1.
Courtesy of the artist.

FIGURE 7.5 Bayer, *Birth of Horror*, 3.
Courtesy of the artist.

FIGURE 7.6 Bayer, *Birth of Horror*, 16.
Courtesy of the artist.

toward humor, there does remain a through line to Bayer's more personal work in that the division between corporate intellectual property and vehicle for self-expression is understood and subverted in the context of this understanding. *The Great Society* (ca. 2012), *Transformer* (2012), *Bloggers* (2014), *2010* (2015), and *Suspect Device* (2010–2014) all freely play with popular characters, engaging in shenanigans often far outside the remit of the owners and publishers of the actual characters. This kind of pastiche often centers on a central conceit, best exemplified by *Suspect Device*, which uses a panel of a cartoon collaged onto the page at the beginning and end of the page or pages. Thus, the cartoonist must fill in the action and dialogue between, whether by way of faithful homage or, more frequently, taking the opportunity to riff on the tropes of the characters, usually well-established (though somewhat out of vogue) properties such as the Phantom, Little Orphan Annie, Popeye, and Garfield and usually with lashings of subversive content. The project, which Bayer instigated and edited over its four oversized issues, invites an assortment of alternative cartoonists to explore this format, with the starting and finishing panels selected by Bayer. While this strand of the cartoonist's practice does not offer the depth of pathos of *Birth of Horror* and *Greater Good*, it is a useful insight into Bayer's attitude toward storytelling and his understanding of the multivalence of comics. The process also proves to be a useful teaching device and a favorite icebreaker among Bayer's students.

Aspects of these comics also appear in Bayer's coproduced series, *All Time Comics* (2016–2020), a loving pastiche of 1970s comics, which incorporates aspects of the era into its four marquee characters, Atlas (an avatar for Superman with the addition of the "troubled superhero" trope pioneered in the 1970s by Dennis O'Neil and Neal Adams, among others), Crime Destroyer (a kind of blaxploitation version of Batman), Bullwhip (a sexploitation and militant feminist version of Wonder Woman), and Justice (an avatar for the bizarre, freakish, and supernatural fringe characters of the era, as mentioned earlier). The stories, which replicate the hyperbolic, overwrought dialogue and captions; sociopolitical themes; back matter; and even deliberately misregistered color of the era, are a gleeful riff on a somewhat forgotten corner of comics and even incorporated some cartoonists of the era, such as Al Milgrom and Herb Trimpe, into its roster of contemporary practitioners. Once again, Bayer demonstrates the flexibility of pastiche, incorporating registers of satire and sincerity into the very structure of the series.

FIGURE 7.7 Josh Bayer and Pat Aulisio, *Greater Good* (2013): 8.
Courtesy of the artist.

Bayer and (Semi)Autobiography

An interesting aspect of many of Bayer's more personal projects is their own
relationship to corporate properties. One of his recurring personal avatars,
Theth, a young comic fan whose parents disapprove of his chosen reading,
is himself closely woven into the Marvel comic *ROM: Space Knight*, itself

based on a Parker Brothers toy license. The axis of ROM, Theth, and Bayer is complex and amorphous, with Bayer creating a bootleg comic, *ROM Prison Riot* (2013), "covering" issues 31 and 32 of *ROM: Space Knight*. The cover comic is itself a relatively recent phenomenon and reflects changing attitudes toward satire and quotation, though perhaps Bayer has grown more cautious: in later appearances, the character began to be referred to as "RM." *ROM Prison Riot* contained the first appearance of Theth, whose significance would grow in time, appearing intermittently in ROM/RM stories as well as the graphic novels *Theth* and *Theth: Tomorrow Forever*. And once again, Bayer cannot resist the self-reflexivity of the medium, producing *Black Star* (2019), a comic whose conceit is that it is the comic Theth reads in *Tomorrow Forever*. The Black Star character bears a strong resemblance to Bayer's use of the Simon the Zombie character in *Birth of Horror* and is another analogue for the supernatural characters of the 1970s.

Despite the use of a semiautobiographical character, and while Bayer uses his own childhood experiences only loosely, the *Theth* narratives fit much more snugly into an autobiographical schema than a confessional one in that they are built around structured sequences of events that build a broader narrative arc (à la Satrapi and Nakazawa) rather than the analytical, first-person ruminations of Crumb and Bechdel. That is not to say Bayer does not occasionally participate in this mode. Bayer's cartoon version, much like Crumb's own, often appears as both a referential version of himself and a cipher for a kind of diaristic ranting, a sort of curmudgeonly self-satire of a grumpy old punk that is stylistically akin to E. C. Segar's Popeye and Frank King's *Gasoline Alley*. Bayer's self-portraiture is merciless in its depiction, the cartoonist's beard rendered in a flurry of scribble, obscuring the mouth (if indeed one was drawn in the first place) from which the avatar's pathos and anxieties utter. Quickly executed, these are modeled on the traditional "gag" strip format of setup, premise, and punch line and regularly appear on Bayer's social media, yet to be collected in physical form. They are rough and fast and often offer deeply, painfully incisive glimpses into the life and anxieties of the cartoonist specifically and the pitfalls of creativity more broadly.

Theth's narratives primarily revolve around the anxieties associated with cartooning, his strained relationships with his family, adolescence, and being a social outcast, a fairly universal series of autobiographical comic tropes. What separates Bayer out, and definitively so, is his insistent adherence to the source material of the comics themselves. The ROM/RM character continually pops up, blurring the line between Bayer's semiautobiographical narrative and those of the comics of his childhood, radically destabilizing

FIGURE 7.8 Bayer, *Theth: Tomorrow Forever*, 10.
Courtesy of the artist.

FIGURE 7.9 Jeff Test, *Black Star* (2019): cover.
Courtesy of the artist.

the usual framework for autobiographical comics. To incorporate a well-known property into a semiautobiographical context offers at once a personalization of and a distancing from its conventions, highlighting the cartoonist's affinity for the source material and the medium more broadly. As Theth draws his comics, his thoughts cohere into something resembling (of course) what the reader will understand as "a Josh Bayer comic," the captions and thought bubbles of which are a commentary on the cartooning process: "Singular characters framed in little boxes. . . . The panel borders will be veins—and also bars. Each page, a cell block—designed to contain monsters. The borders keep them isolated and protected . . . but interconnected—like coiled intestines."[15] As ever, the capitalized lettering lends the text a certain pathos, easily approximating the inner turmoil and need for self-expression of a disillusioned youth.

Bayer's continued and increasingly layered narratives have transcended mere postmodern reference and irony, building a nuanced and visually compelling expression of the dovetailing of art and artist. This increasingly built-up visual composite of word and image gives way to a suppurating anguish and a sincere torment of the cartoonist as commentator to an alienating world where comics provide not only a world within which to escape but a means of expressing oneself in terms commensurate with the protagonist's agonies. This is, of course, highly melodramatic and pathetic, but where would comics be without melodrama and pathos?

8

Nina Bunjevac

• •

One of the now anachronistic words for comics, it will be remembered, is the "funnies." The funnies were the lighthearted relief from the weekend lift-out in the middle of the paper or were placed alongside the crossword, chess puzzle, or mindbender for all the other days. They were benign divertimenti: Dagwood Bumstead, the gormless husband in *Blondie* and his inconceivable large sandwiches for his midnight snacks, or the prisoner of the *Wizard of Id*, with his interminable tallies on the walls of his cell marking the day that would never come. These and others, such as Beetle Bailey and Dick Tracy, were Cold War affairs produced at a time when there scarcely was such a thing as political sensitivity and where the main job of comics was to amuse and appeal. Not so with Nina Bunjevac. Her work is not funny, and its appeal lies well outside the parameters of charm or diversion. For example, *Bezimena* (2018), possibly Bunjevac's most challenging work in a suite of challenging works, uses the myth of Artemis and Siproites to bookend its narrative, a dark allegory for sexual obsession, predatory behavior, and abuse. While the *Bezimena* is not overtly autobiographical, the cartoonist does offer a preface and postscript offering some detail into the events that inspired the work, a dark episode of sexual abuse from her own past, grounding the narrative on literary firmament closer to Surrealism or, perhaps, magic realism.

The former status of comics as the genre of the innocent bystander to the more serious news events recounted in other pages plays a critical role in Bunjevac's work. For when the funnies were not funny, they were heroic with cyborgs and superheroes, and the fact that she diverges from both humor and heroism is key. The informality of comics, the historic "easiness" of the medium—that of giving the images together with words on a plate as opposed to ideational work required of words alone—is at play for the way her works deliver aftershocks. Nothing is delivered as fully formed. The reader is continually haunted by afterimages and nagging questions. While it would be tempting to draw parallels with traditional literature as we have done with other comix authors, it is perhaps less pertinent for the formal and intertextual play with which she engages the medium itself. Using what had long been a kid's medium of zany, cute, cool, gallant, or grand, her works are inexorably cruel and unforgiving.

Featuring an anthropomorphic cat named Zorka, *Heartless* (2012), a collection of short, interlinking stories, may first appear the closest Bunjevac has veered toward any specific genre fare. However, any such insinuations toward the "funny animal" genre of comics are soon dismissed. This anthropomorphic cat works at a brothel, a place that forms an overarching narrative, and is more tragic than comic. The world of *Heartless* is filled with denizens like Zorka, misfits whose place in society tends to be relegated to the periphery: drag queens, strippers, and immigrants. This work is probably the least autobiographical of Bunjevac's oeuvre but does set a formative template for what would come later, including her dense and intricate drawings, a preoccupation with the tensions of cultural diaspora (Bunjevac herself immigrated with her family to Canada from Serbia), and a curious visual tension between Soviet propagandist aesthetics and the symbolism and tonal depth of film noir. This tension is telling and demonstrative of Bunjevac's influences while growing up in a country that has been through considerable social and political change throughout the last century. Serbia split from the Soviet Union in 1948, but such visual influences linger, and film noir was a highly influential cinematic approach of the 1940s and 1950s in both the United States and Europe. Considering both visual modes, Bunjevac's work can be interpreted in a dualistic sense, deploying in turns postmodern literary realist and social realist frameworks in *Fatherland* and the Surrealism and tonal and depth of film noir in *Bezimena*. Film noir itself has literary antecedents in the hard-boiled detective genre and existentialism, often incorporating Surrealist qualities in the form of hallucinations, dreams, and nightmare sequences. Bunjevac's work is a compelling amalgam of these often divergent literary and aesthetic sensibilities, layered as densely and evocatively as her precise knots of cross-hatching.

Literary Realism and Diegesis

Bunjevac's first major work, *Fatherland: A Family History* (2014), is an overtly autobiographical narrative, telling the story of her nationalist father's estrangement from her mother and family and their immigration to Canada, culminating in her father's accidental death in a meeting with other saboteurs to plan a bombing. The history of Serbia in the twentieth century is a complex web of violent international entanglements, of alliances and betrayals, and Bunjevac's father seems to psychically embody the strife of his homeland. The surreal passages that intersperse the more realist and historical elements are intentional interruptions that are far from gratuitous. Although they may not make narrative sense, they are sufficient for adding or building unease in the narrative, reminders that things are neither quite right nor as they seem. In many ways, this technique bears comparison with Goethe's *Faust: The Second Part*, a frankly trippy work written at the end of his life in which Lukács accounts for the nonrealist elements with the more sober term "the fantastical" (*die Phantastische*). The inclusion of fantastical elements, he contends, in no way vitiates the realism of the whole because of the fidelity to other details. Instead, the insertions of fantastical elements such as Walpurgis Night and the witches serve as markers of fear and foreboding while also being metonymic of the religious-magical, the invisible, the imperceptible, the nonempirical. As Lukács remarks, "That is why everything here—with all the historical veracity of content—is saturated with the fantastical: there is no longer any boundary between real and ghostly: a ghostly reality stands before us."[1] Such words have considerable resonance when applied to Bunjevac in light of the many residual ghosts that lay in wait in the wake of the Serbo-Croatian conflict of the 1990s but also well into the many centuries of conflict in this region. As anyone who has lived with trauma knows, the most mundane of the world's surfaces can morph and transmute through the inexorable power of association. Bunjevac's world is one of lost innocence and lurking phantasms and phantoms that periodically break out into the narrative, irrepressible, as if bursting out and then receding again.

Fatherland is bookended and occasionally punctuated with detailed symbolist drawings of eggs and birds, but overall, its narrative sits comfortably alongside the complex literary canon of Serbia. That is to say, the work has a clear parentage in the literary traditions of social realism and Marxist aesthetics, but this is shared with a broader, post–Soviet European worldview.[2] Only in the final passage, upon Bunjevac's mother receiving word of her husband's death, does the narrative diverge from this sense of literary realism, whereupon a sequence depicts her (in silhouette) sinking into a hole and then embracing who we presume is Bunjevac. While the rest of the narrative is rendered in a style that could be conceivably read as an Eastern European take on film noir aesthetics, this sequence alone embraces the genre's penchant for using Surrealist imagery in order to portray the emotional state of characters—in this case, the profound sense of loss, and then release, of Bunjevac's mother.

Perhaps the most notable development in *Fatherland* is its embrace of an overt narrative diegesis. Rather than the mimesis typical of many comics, showing rather than telling, or a middle ground in which plot points are shown but occasionally guided by an omniscient narrator (think of comics' go-to text panel for narrative expediency, "Meanwhile . . ."), *Fatherland* is a story recounted to, rather than experienced by, the reader. The narrative begins with the cartoonist herself drawing eggs (the very eggs that bookend the narrative on the facing page) and being paid a surprise visit by her mother. After some small talk about a photograph of their old house and the way it has changed, the narrative cuts to the recounting of Bunjevac's parents, narrated by the cartoonist. As explored by Deborah James, the narrative of *Fatherland* is built around the shared memories—and therefore a constructed account—between Bunjevac and her mother, family photographs, and the more objective public account, which is drawn from historical accounts, news reports, and photographs.[3] The drawing of the eggs reminds the reader that they are indeed reading a graphic novel, a device that is repeated several times without the story, reemphasizing the diegetic distancing between the author and the narrative, despite its personal and familiar content.

In a powerful sequence of splash pages, we see a camera emanating a graphic "flash," which evokes equal parts advertising and propaganda art, followed by the cartoonist's hand taking a photograph of her and her brother and children from an envelope. This is followed by drawings of another four such photographs, without hands, and then an image of the cartoonist's hand turning the page to reveal the next page, one of the bird images that punctuate the narrative, as if to move on with the story after this brief

FIGURE 8.1 Nina Bunjevac, *Fatherland: A Family History* (London: Jonathan Cape, 2014), 151. Courtesy of the artist.

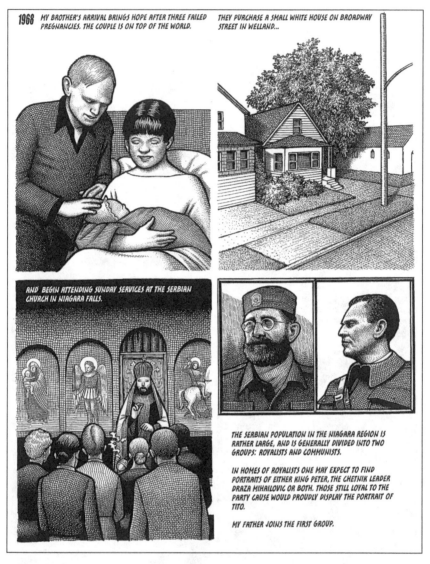

FIGURE 8.2 Bunjevac, *Fatherland*, 135.
Courtesy of the artist.

nostalgic (or melancholic) reverie. Bunjevac's remarkable linear modeling has led some to interpret her work's "allegiance to realistic representation,"[+] but such a distinction overlooks the cartoonist's careful diegetic distancing. These pages include a round-cornered, rectangular-framed motif around each photograph, which is typical of some old-fashioned photo albums. They remind the reader of the stories behind them with the decorative edges of the photographs themselves and construct a truth that appears both factual and subjective.⁵ These images are presented not as naturalistic memories, like the majority of the narrative, but as photographs, vehicles of memory, emphasizing the deliberate distancing of the narrative from both the cartoonist and the reader.

This deliberate skewering of any potential interpretation of the fantastic could be interpreted as a particularly Eastern European approach to cartooning. As Predrag Palavestra describes it, "The radical consciousness of the Slavic world . . . has bred a subversive style: literature of defiance and critical non-acceptance of the ruling ideology and Party culture."⁶ Comparing Bunjevac's Serbian background to her adopted home, Canada, is also revealing in terms of her approach to autobiographical cartooning, a rich tradition in that country, with cartoonists such as Julie Doucet, Michel Rabagliati, Seth (a.k.a. Gregory Gallant), and Chester Brown creating significant works of autobiography. These cartoonists embrace a mode of autobiography more aligned with mimesis yet often resort to the diegetic device of narration. Still, they remain naturalistic in their recounting, free of the deliberate distancing devices of *Fatherland*.

While autobiographical cartooning is a prevalent postmodern tradition in Canada, the embrace of postmodernism is also a distinctive aspect of much post–Soviet Serbian literature,⁷ a line that can certainly be drawn to Bunjevac's oeuvre, whether through osmosis or by design. Authors such as Aleksandar Marčićev and Svetislav Basara often write using unexpected diegetic devices by discursive combinations of contexts and tenses (Basara's *Uspon i pad Parkinsonove bolesti* [*The Rise and Fall of Parkinson's Disease*, 2006]). Another device is a braided, tripartite narrative, written in the styles of "a biographical study carried out by the writer's literature professor at the request of the writer's widow . . . the canonised classics of confessional-autobiographic prose . . . [and] a novel written in the form of an interview"⁸ (Marčićev's *Svi životi Zaharija Neuzinskog* [*All the Lives of Zaharije Neuzinski*, 2008], *Gresi sv. Maxa* [*The Sins of St. Max*, 2007], and *Viktor Ajsberg, Srećan Uprkos Svemu* [*Victor Eisberg, Happy Despite Everything*, 2009], respectively). However, Serbian approaches to such emphasized diegesis are limited to the overtly postmodern. Such distancing devices sometimes appear (albeit in more subtle deployment) in another distinctive contemporary tradition that aligns more with neorealism, closely associated with literary realists of the nineteenth century.⁹ These authors, such as Vladimir Arsenijević and Zoran Ćirić, may appear less overtly postmodern in the sense of formal deconstruction and self-awareness, embracing historical postmodernist qualities in their approximation of the mimesis of neorealism, influenced as they are by nineteenth-century literary giants such as Balzac, Dostoevsky, Zola, Dickens, and Ibsen.[10] Such authors aspire to the (re)construction of a kind of post-Yugoslav and post-Soviet national literature, itself a politically charged and complicated motivation.[11] In Ćirić's novel *Prisluškivanje* (*Eavesdropping*, 1999), a fragmentary approach (not unlike that of Marčićev) is deployed, evoking a sense of the narrator being "replaced by a 'recorder'"[12] rather than that of a traditional third-person omniscience. This more mimetic literary tradition is also notable in relation to Bunjevac's oeuvre in its clipped narration and somber visuals depicting post–Soviet Serbian life, scenes in which the narrator is not explicitly Bunjevac herself. Despite the cartoonist's highly developed artistic skills, *Fatherland* remains sober and objective in its depiction of the world of her childhood and the recent historical context that shaped it. Far more challenging in the context of Serbian postmodern literature is Bunjevac's subsequent work, *Bezimena*, a graphic novel that, while grounded in autobiography, operates more felicitously when considered as a variation of Surrealism, itself highly influential upon Serbian literature.[13]

Bezimena and Surrealism

Film noir may not be an idiom one immediately associates with literary study, but there is much visual and thematic connective tissue to be found in its literary antecedents, particularly Surrealism and the hard-boiled detective genre.[14] The exaggerated graphics and rich, textured tones of film noir are textual echoes of their hard-boiled and Surrealist source material: hyperbolic, melodramatic, nihilistic, plainspoken, yet in the hands of an adept, visually and rhythmically sophisticated.[15] Like many comics, the hard-boiled novel and its cross-media offspring come across as a kind of compelling, operatic trash, an immediately identifiable narrative blueprint from which to mine deep veins of pastiche, irony, self-reflexivity, and compelling visuals. A typical opening salvo from Raymond Chandler's genre-defining 1939 novel *The Big Sleep* reveals his embrace of the inherent visuality of the genre while simultaneously commentating on its construction and theatrical parallels: "She lowered her lashes until they almost cuddled her cheeks and slowly raised them again, like a theater curtain. I was to get to know that trick. That was supposed to make me roll over on my back with all four paws in the air. 'Are you a prize-fighter?' she asked, when I didn't."[16]

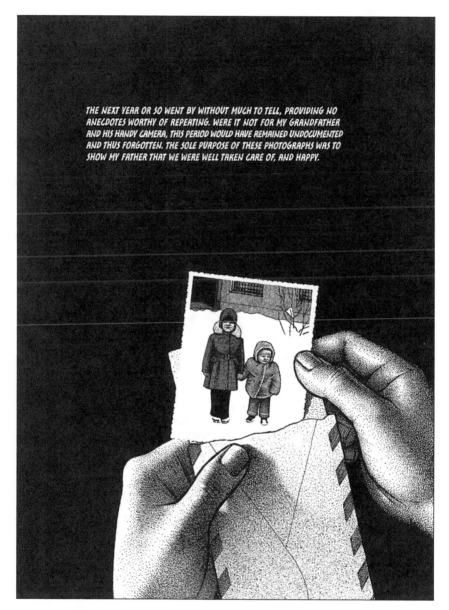

FIGURE 8.3 Bunjevac, *Fatherland*, 38.
Courtesy of the artist.

FIGURE 8.4 Nina Bunjevac, *Bezimena* (Seattle: Fantagraphics, 2018), 14.
Courtesy of the artist.

The noir genre (as it is often referred to in comics) has found renewed popularity since the 1990s with series such as Frank Miller's *Sin City* (1991–2000), Brian Azzarello and Eduardo Risso's *100 Bullets* (1999–2009), and Ed Brubaker and Sean Phillips's *Fatale* (2012–2014) and *The Fade Out* (2014–2016), all of which have enjoyed considerable popularity and critical acclaim. To classify *Bezimena* as noir would not be accurate, as Bunjevac's story deviates from any

FIGURE 8.5 Bunjevac, *Bezimena*, 15.
Courtesy of the artist.

such narrative structure, let alone conventions of genre. However, an understanding of the fringe aspects of noir does provide visual and literary access
points to this complex work, to say nothing of its bold graphic approach.
Beyond the more obvious dream sequences and fanciful, stylized symbolist
production design to be found in much of film noir, there is a recurring strain
of existentialist and nihilistic philosophy and absurdist worldview to be found
in its morally compromised protagonists, which is also strongly associated
with Surrealism.

Bezimena's focus character,[17] Benny, could certainly be characterized as
an outsider, even an alien, in a world he does not seem to completely grasp.
Bunjevac's characterization of Benny borders on sympathetic, a curious distinction for a character charged with rape and murder. As Manea and Precup write of the graphic novel's afterword, "*Bezimena* foregrounds some of
the conditions that may contribute to the emergence of a male perpetrator
capable of committing repeated rapes and murders of young girls, but also,
and perhaps more importantly, focuses on the role of the female accomplice in a manner that is particularly challenging in its formal and ethical
obliqueness."[18] This is an interesting distinction in that such an accomplice
is not incorporated into the narrative, perhaps another example of deliberate distancing, an understandable concession when dealing with such heavy
subject matter. Such a statement is true enough, but whether Benny *actually* stalks White Becky and rapes her friend and her maid is not so clear
cut, thanks in part to the nature of the narrative. Once again operating
as a kind of diegetic recount, *Bezimena* is couched with different modes,
which could suggest that Benny's transgressions are all a fantasy or indeed
that the scene in which he is arrested by the police and interrogated (which
is immediately preceded by fifteen pages of highly Surrealist tableaux) is a
nightmare. The journal he finds that rekindles his schoolroom obsession
with White Becky is full of the very drawings of the narrative depicting him
watching her, raping the nurse, and so on, which brings into question the
nature of authorship, voyeurism, fiction, and even cartooning. When interrogated, the journal contains only children's drawings, suggesting a rupture of realities before and after Benny's arrest. Manea and Precup assume
that Benny is indeed guilty based on Bunjevac's afterword and back-cover
blurb, which alter the experience of reading,[19] categorizing prearrest sex scenes
(which appear consensual) as hallucinations.[20] Further, a literalist reading of the surreal mythological passages bookending the graphic novel as
adaptations of two Artemesian myths referenced in *Bezimena* would seem
to support this theory.[21] However, in the interest of intertextual references

enriching the text, a more open-ended and less black-and-white interpretation may well have been the cartoonist's intent, producing a provocative and morally treacherous literary text.

In the afterword, the cartoonist also notes, "This was a time of pre-war, a period marked by the rise of nationalism and moral darkness, where deception and lies were the currency of the day. The streets and promenades of my hometown were paved with the promises of lucrative supermodel contracts for teenage girls."[22] Such conditional devices, like World War II in much of American noir, serve as a context for strife and moral decay, imbuing protagonists with both a shorthand past and a bulwark for their more antisocial behaviors. Mickey Spillane's Mike Hammer, being one of the noir prototypes across film, literature, and comics, was portrayed as a veteran of World War II. Wallace, the protagonist of Miller's *Sin City: Hell and Back* (1999–2000), is a former soldier and at one stage is drugged, allowing for, like a film noir dream sequence, vivid and Surrealist artistic liberties to be taken, emphasized by the use of full-color art, a first for the series. This is a leitmotif often echoed in more contemporary noir texts: the wars in Vietnam, Iraq, and Afghanistan (also, notably, Brubaker and Phillips's Charlie Parish of *The Fade Out* suffers from PTSD, a decidedly contemporary twist on the World War II veteran).

War forms a backstory to several of Haruki Murakami's novels, most notably *A Wind-Up Bird Chronicle* (1994). Murakami is in many ways a contemporary exponent of hard-boiled fiction, weaving Surrealist passages among his recurring pastiches to the genre. Murakami, who is associated with the magic realism genre, often begins in adherence to the narrative tropes of Chandler and Mickey Spillane: a male protagonist, usually narrating in the first person, is presented with a mystery to be solved, usually taking the form of a missing person. Most of Murakami's novels begin the same way, with the disappearance or death of a cat, the disappearance or death of a wife or lover, or both. It should also be noted that Murakami's protagonists are usually, like those of Spillane and Chandler, a set type, sometimes appearing in multiple stories, though in Murakami's oeuvre, the two-fisted nihilist is replaced with more of a loafing, underachieving everyman. Murakami's work aligns with Bunjevac's in its nuanced approach to eroticism and fetish imagery, of which *Bezimena* is plentiful.[23] Murakami repeatedly returns to the ear, which the majority of his protagonists spend considerable words dwelling upon and describing.[24] Certainly, the ear is a passable object of Surrealist symbolism on par with the eye, which we will return to. In *A Wind-Up Bird Chronicle*, the protagonist is told by Lieutenant Mamiya of horrific

FIGURE 8.6 Bunjevac, *Bezimena*, 78.
Courtesy of the artist.

experiences during World War II serving in the Kwantung Army, which include witnessing a flaying and being left for dead in a well. These recollections are recounted both in person and through letters, a variation of the diegetic approach found in much of Bunjevac's oeuvre.

The horror of war is, of course, one of the core tenets of Surrealism, a critical discourse of outrage and dissociation growing from the charnel house

FIGURE 8.7 Bunjevac, *Bezimena*, 128.
Courtesy of the artist.

of World War I.[25] Stamos Metzidakis characterizes this critique as combining "both the conscious and unconscious realms of experience. . . . In the
eyes of these writers, literature no longer consisted of just a poetic, stylized representation of various concepts or feelings, but instead to become
an authentic presentation of a new, more complete, and, in some regards,
better world."[26] While discussing the Surrealist founder André Breton

and his seminal *Poisson Soluble* (*Soluble Fish*, 1924), Metzidakis makes an observation that is applicable to both the evocative nature of Bunjevac's work and the hybrid form of comics more broadly: "[We] must take into account both the meaning of the words, and the specific shapes and forms these words take on the page. . . . Some of the most rewarding and convincing contemporary readings of such writing have centered precisely around various subliminal narratives and intertextual networks that have been successfully recovered from . . . words and images in automatic texts."[27] This statement applies to the onomatopoeic graphics of sound effects, the mimetic and diegetic narrative representations of reality, and the mechanics of reading the comic book.

George Bataille's *Histoire de l'oeil* (*Story of the Eye*, 1928) is another narrative that explores Surrealist imagery, eroticism, and, notably, rape. Bataille, characterized by some as a "dissident surrealist"[28] due to his rivalry with Breton, invested heavily in Surrealist symbolism, building such ovular metaphors (eyes, eggs, testicles, the sun) and liquid metaphors (milk, semen, urine, blood, tears) into the structure of the narrative itself, forming a recurring visual substructure to the story through the unnamed narrator and his sexual compatriot, Simone, writing extensively of these imagistic fascinations in his own indexical studies.[29] These twin strands of metaphor are notable in their decidedly nonphallic nature, which Barthes categorizes as "round phallicism," a "spherical metaphor: each of its terms is always the significant of another term."[30] The eye, of course, is a staple of Surrealist symbolism and is a recurring motif in *Bezimena*, emphasizing Benny's voyeurism. Notably, he holds a blade close to White Becky's maid's eye (shades of Luis Buñuel and Salvador Dalí's film *Un Chien Andalou* [*An Andalusian Dog*, 1929]) before she strips down to her underwear and high heels and is blindfolded. In the context of the narrative's preoccupation with—though decidedly more subtle than Bataille's approach to—the eye, the blindfold is a pertinent detail in its Surrealist discourse, just as the underwear and high heels are to its fetishism.[31] A notable difference between the two texts is Bataille's direct narrative voice, which, though diverging from Bunjevac's more dietetic, evocative response, does not necessarily fit soundly within the prefectures of realism either.[32]

Bunjevac's innovative approaches to diegetic structure, uncoiling as they do with dreamlike, wordless transitional passages of *Bezimena* and the mimetic and diegetic duality of memory, record, and recount of *Fatherland*, are raised to levels of cinematic melodrama through her strikingly rendered compositions. Such distancing devices are understandable, even necessary,

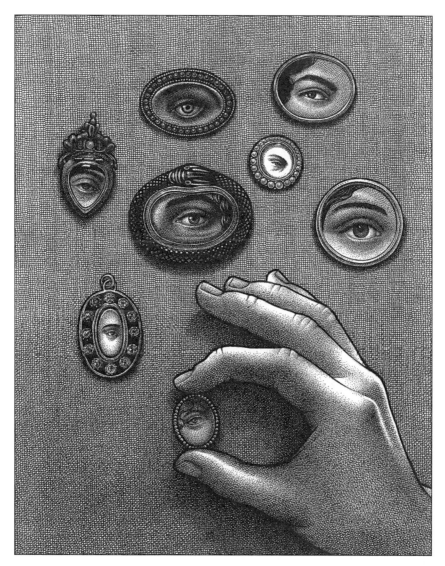

FIGURE 8.8 Bunjevac, *Bezimena*, 42.
Courtesy of the artist.

given the distressing circumstances to which the graphic novel responds. Rape, sexual abuse, and other such traumas are surely difficult topics. To use such sustained narrative effort in part or in full as a meditation on these experiences is a somewhat harrowing proposition but explains the use of allegory in *Bezimena* as opposed to *Fatherland*'s more overtly autobiographical recounting of Bunjevac's experiences. Where *Fatherland* was a closely plotted and observed family drama set against the sweep of history, *Bezimena* is given space for ideas and visual motifs to breathe. Frequently opening out into surreal passages allows the reader to slip into a kind of fugue state with Bunjevac's intricate drawings, drifting in and out of a narrative flow that is more cyclical and self-reflexive than linear, incorporating a filmic and literary base into a visual lexicon of extraordinary sophistication and nuance.

9

Simon Hanselmann

●●●●●●●●●●●●●●●●●●●●●●

The events from 2020 onward caused artists of all kinds to question their process, their content, and their audience. The mass confinements, lockdowns, social constraints, and myriad restrictions, in addition to social unrest and economic crises, reoriented social encounters in a rudely abrupt way. Exhibitions were postponed indefinitely, and social gatherings of all kinds were prohibited. While artists were beginning to reconsider the practices within the virtual realm (and for some yet more virtually than before), writers were inexorably faced with the reconfiguration of what constituted their lifeworld and so-called real life. For the first time in human history, the realities of real life were those that were digitally mediated, where interpersonal contact had shrunk to a minimum, and where human relations were maintained over distances and on flat screens. The vernacular prejudice of reality as a system of physical encounters, of bypassing the artifice of technological intervention, was systematically shattered without any time to adjust or take stock. What also became evident was a tacit rule in art that the more dramatic the crisis, the more it was able to differentiate among artistic aptitudes, since the most inept would always be prone to illustrate, opine, and proselytize. Publications of all ranks and kinds, including the auspicious *New York Review of Books*, *Times Literary Supplement*, and the *New Left Review*, brought out, singly or in series, writers' reflections on the COVID-19 pandemic, with many authors offering their thoughts and fears, often competing in grandiloquence and empathy. And so the lockdown genre was born, or rather reborn. Within a matter of months, for those with the strength to glean them, one memoir blended into another with a self-indulgence that was apparently oblivious to a long and distinguished history. It arguably begins with Giovanni Boccaccio's *Decameron* (1348–1353)—of seven young women and three young men in a villa outside of Florence, taking refuge from the Black Death, recounting stories to lift one another's spirits—and climaxes with Proust housed in his cork-lined room in his apartment on the Boulevard Hausmann, or Camus's *The Plague* (1947), or the grim sequestration of Beckett's characters such as Balacqua or Malone. These examples differ from the contemporary memoir genre in one central respect—namely, that they use allegory and irony to shield from any possibility of self-consciousness or overearnestness.

In many ways, the work and career of Simon Hanselmann can be said to have reached a new level with the coronavirus pandemic, to which he responded with *Crisis Zone*, a serialized daily strip presented on Instagram from March until December 2020, beginning as the cartoonist went into lockdown. The series initially started as a satire of the Netflix documentary *Tiger King* but quickly and nimbly turned into a treatise on COVID-19, lockdowns, TikTok, Trump, the storming of the White House, and, in general, the stupidity of humanity. The strength of Hanselmann's work lay in its resistance to sympathy-mongering reportage and memoir facilitated in large part by the devices that he had already used for some years and had become something of a signature. The characters in his work are not human, or rather they are humans in an animal shape. Using the children's book device of anthropomorphized creatures as a measure for familiarization and displacement, Hanselmann can navigate the absurdities of the modern world without moralizing or overcredulity. By dressing up—or rather, dressing down—events, Hanselmann was able to extract the childishness and hysteria of this time, and while ostensibly making the non-innocent innocent, he was able to allegorize the events to show that they are intrinsic to the human proclivities to oversimplify and demonize, showing the ease with which crisis slides into conspiracy.

Hanselmann is best known for his autobiographical comics, which began as spoofs of the Megg, Mogg and Owl (MM&O) children's book series by Helen Nicoll and illustrated by Jan Pieńkowski. These were a part of the children's book landscape of the 1970s and 1980s (Hanselmann was born in 1981), but the parallels end there. Megg, Mogg, and Owl are housemates, with the first two frequent drug users, often lovers, much to the disdain of straight-man Owl, who plays the structural foil to his slovenly housemates.

FIGURE 9.1 Simon Hanselmann, *Crisis Zone* (Seattle: Fantagraphics, 2021), 34.
Courtesy of the artist.

The Fairy Tale-esque

Like the Kirbyesque, which is an art of homage, pastiche, and structural renewal, the fairy tale–esque works from what Lukács calls the distinct stylization of the fairy tale, with its foregrounding of metaphor and trope and the unquestioning deployment of the unnatural and the coincidental. Hanselmann can be seen to be a prime exponent of the fairy tale–esque for the way that is a conscious slippage between so-called real life and the events recounted in his narratives and who enacts them. It has the air of allegory in which the allegory has dissipated, fallen away, lost or in abeyance.

In his meditation on the distinctiveness of the fairy tale from other genres, Lukács fixes on not only its stylization and the role of chance, coincidence, and happenstance but also its construction of a parallel world that is both independent from yet wholly dependent on our own: "Each fairytale—If I may use this rather strange comparison—is related to all other genres as are non-Euclidian geometries to the Euclidian."[1] It is a comment that is especially felicitous and offers considerable insight into where to situate the work of Hanselmann. Lukács goes on to emphasize that the fairy tale is constructed in such a way that all its conceits, dalliances, and oddities are presented as so many natural and incontrovertible facts—such as an owl that can talk:

> Each fairytale begins in such a way as if it is a real fairytale and not a novel of the fantastical or which ignores some basic fact or some constitutive law of our existence (or adds a new facticity, a new regularity to our reality of which our being is unaware) and on the basis such regrouping of axioms creates a new world that is qualitatively different from our world and strictly governed by laws that are not of our existence, but in which there are just as many "things" and "connections" to things as those that exist for us, only that they are different things and different relationships than those that apply to us.[2]

These factors apply not only to the redistribution of natural (as against unnatural) configurations but to the logistics of life as well, such that we are made to believe that in the fairy tale, things have always been this way.

In the comic genre in general, there is furthermore a different concept of time. It can be a combination of nostalgic past and futuristic present (as in Batman) or a benign limbo in which the unfolding of narration in the story or strip is unsurpassed by a more universal temporal so that the characters exist locked within the strip for all time (Archie, Garfield, Snoopy, etc.).

A similar temporal and formal circumscription occurs in fairy tales, where the "new," the novelty arising in the narrative, as Lukács remarks, is "no longer the current present, but rather something that was never present and, by its very nature, can never become present. This is why there is no contradiction in the concept of the 'new' in fairytales. Every other 'new' arises from time and is posited within a temporal reality, so it is new relative to something else."[3] While this applies to many examples, including several in this book, it is particularly preponderant in Hanselmann's universe, which is poised in its particular space-time that is both paradise and pandemonium.

However, much as we might relate to Hanselmann's characters inasmuch as we do with any narrative we read on paper or indeed watch on screen, theirs is always a displaced reality that is somewhere other than where we live. We feel ourselves observers, and what we share with them is matched as much by how they differ from us. As Lukács affirms, "Every difficulty in life and literature, especially in the true, valuable meaning of the word, results exclusively from the fact that its essence affects us with a binding force. But the fairytale obliges—basically—nothing. We always just watch a fairytale, not live in it. The fairytale creates a new empiricism, but one that differs radically from ours in that it knows no transcendence or transcending: empiricism and metaphysics are thought to be an inseparable unit in the fairytale world itself."[4] No transcendence or transcending—this lies at the crux of Hanselmann's figures in a double sense, wherein they are not in their own complex of time but any triumph can only be measured against the anticipation of a new mishap or misunderstanding. It is a miserabilist loop that is not yet afforded the tragic precisely because of the deferred, or deprived, prospect of this transcendence. It is an eternal return of minor conflict and ultimately inconsequential reconciliation.

These observations are in no way to indicate anything negative, for there are many advantages to us remaining outside and Hanselmann's characters inside. Lukács goes on to remark, "This unity, in another respect, increases the fairytale's ornamental lightness."[5] While we may not compare Hanselmann's work to Disney's Cinderella, it may be compared to many of the Brothers Grimm's fairy tales, particularly in terms of their gruesomeness, in Hanselmann's hands played for laughs rather than moral consequence. Both embrace a world of otherness in which there is always the shadow of grotesquerie and transgression. Hanselmann's characters are at once destabilizing figures, queering agents of change in a heteronormative suburban world and yet completely committed to their own lifestyles, a status quo built around their routines, habits, and vices.

Megg, Mogg, Owl, and Their Noncommittal Queerdom

As well as being a contemporary take on many of the tropes of the Brothers Grimm's fairy tales, Megg, Mogg, and Owl are a decidedly adult addition to the often-overlooked "funny animal" genre of comics, which enjoyed massive popularity in the postwar years. Typically, funny animal comics are usually lighthearted in tone and have varying degrees of anthropomorphism and format (think of Donald Duck or Woody Woodpecker). However, Hanselmann's characters are also highly queer in the most expansive use of the word. This broad categorization applies to not only the comic's inclusion of characters of all manner of gender orientation but its refusal to settle into an in-world "logic" in terms of designations. This may at first appear an arbitrary observation, but consider the in-world logic of Donald Duck and his broader avian-themed home, appropriately called Duckburg. Donald has nephews, an uncle, and a love interest, all ducks. He has avian friends, such as Gyro Gearloose (a chicken, for the record), as well as nonavian enemies, such as the buffoonish dog triplets the Beagle Boys. Not to belabor the point, but the Donald Duck mythos has a certain in-world logic. Hanselmann's world of Megg, Mogg, and Owl begins with its allusions to Nicoll and Pieńkowski's children's books, keeping its vaguely Halloween-themed flavor. A sample of the trio's friend group, as listed at the beginning of *Crisis Zone*, includes "Werewolf Jones (raging id), Booger (transgender boogeywoman), Dracula Junior (gutter philosopher), Mike (passive wizard),"[6] and many of the characters that the gang interact with fit loosely within this framework. Unlike the denizens of Duckburg, however, Megg, Mogg, and Owl interact with real people, albeit on satirical terms. In *Crisis Zone*, artist David Choe is a recurring character, and the MM&O gang is interviewed by Joel McHale after their disastrous reality TV show for Netflix, in the same fashion as he interviewed much of the cast of *Tiger King*. As strange a statement as it is to make, Megg, Mogg, and Owl inhabit a narrative world far more aligned with realism than one might think for a comic about a witch, her pet/lover talking cat, and an anthropomorphic owl. Megg, Mogg, and Owl also belong to a compelling strain of the (typically gag-based) funny animal genre, used for more subversive ends. Edmond-François Calvo's *La Bête est morte!* (*The Beast Is Dead*, 1944–1945) was a satirical excoriation of fascism rendered in lush, bouncy, Disney-style graphics. Crumb's *Fritz the Cat* was a recurring commentary on the sexual revolution of the 1960s. Michelle Perez and Remy Boydell's *The Pervert* (2018) was a graphic novel about a queer sex worker who happens to be an anthropomorphic dog. By using anthropomorphic creatures, which conjure strong associations with fairy tales and childhood cartoons, cartoonists can introduce more overtly sexual, violent, or political content with a puckishly subversive insistence, ironically bringing such narratives more in line with the original grotesque-rie of the Brothers Grimm's fairy tales.

As a trio, Megg, Mogg, and Owl embody Hanselmann's decidedly non-traditional worldview, although the cartoonist rarely gets bogged down in such detail. Rather than designating each character a particular gender orientation, which would be counterintuitive to its own narrative fluidity, the characters and their extended friend group act in unison as agents of disruption in the ordered, straight, White cis world of the status quo. In a world inhabited by witches, vampires, anthropomorphic cyborg bears, and talking cats, to say nothing of "normal" (i.e., non-Halloween-themed) people, race and gender become more normalized. It is important to note that this is not a statement about conformity or assimilation. Cathy J. Cohen highlights the recurring problems of assimilation-based goals in the context of lesbian and gay agendas based on civil rights strategies.[7] Much more aligned with Cohen's argument for a break away from heteronormative categorization and conformity is Hanselmann's work, which, while inherently queer, employs an attitude of noncommitment, embodying multiple and changing identities rather than the oppositional ones that Cohen identifies as counterproductive.[8] Purposeful or not, Hanselmann's characters defy categorization not through overt statement but by a general refusal to remain static. Megg is usually romantically involved with Mogg (ostensibly a male cat, judging from his genitalia, but who are we to assume?) but has dalliances with Booger, a transgender (boogey)woman. Owl, who is largely cast as the straight man in the household, insisting upon cleaning rosters and paying the rent on time, is eventually revealed to be far more promiscuous than assumed, but even he engages (often surreptitiously) in casual queering. At first, Werewolf Jones (WWJ) appears masculine, even butch, and is arguably the most sexually adventurous comic character of all time, which frequently lands him (and his friends) in trouble. This is the core band of misfits (Werewolf Jones appears frequently, despite living elsewhere). Cohen argues that a "politics where the *nonnormative* and *marginal* position of punks, bulldaggers, and welfare queens, for example, is the basis for progressive transformative coalition work. Thus, if there is any truly radical potential to be found in the idea of queerness and the practice of queer politics, it would seem to be located in its ability to create a space in opposition to dominant norms, a space where transformational political work can begin."[9]

FIGURE 9.2 Simon Hanselmann, "Gift for a Baby," in *One More Year* (Seattle: Fantagraphics, 2016), 60.
Courtesy of the artist.

It is interesting to note in this context that Megg is listed in the cast list of *Crisis Zone* as a "welfare witch," clearly referencing the classist and often racist epithet of the welfare queen, which forms a part of Cohen's theoretical queer coalition of destabilizers. Hanselmann often attends public appearances in drag, occasionally sporting a very Megg-like red wig, but in line with Cohen's fluid consideration of queer culture, the cartoonist refuses to be pigeonholed or even elaborate, a "cross-dresser/transvestite, whatever you want to call it. . . . I have no idea [how it affects my writing]. That's for the critics to tell me."[10] Hanselmann's stories are decidedly suburban, and reflect the disaffected Western millennial experience, often drawing from his unconventional upbringing by his biker father and (soon-single) mother, who experienced substance abuse issues.[11] Hanselmann's own resistance to being drawn out over the particularities of queer readings and his fictional gang's own fluidity is likely a personal preference rather than a political or philosophical alignment, but the gang, diverse as it is, incorporates approximations for, as Cohen describes, punks, bulldaggers, and welfare queens, and they are in many ways agents of "destabilisation and even deconstruction."[12] This perspective is not Cohen's (and by virtue of his work, Hanselmann's) alone. Lee Edelman challenges queer people to be "sufficiently oppositional to the structural logic of opposition."[13] Edelman discusses such a position in terms of resituating notions of copulation and childbirth into less heteronormative waters.[14] Werewolf Jones, with his delinquent children (Diesel and Jaxon); his definitive, omnivorous sexual appetites; and his embodiment of jouissance-fueled id, embodies notions of both Cohen and Edelman, at once queer punk destabilizer and procreating agent of non-heteronormativity. Werewolf Jones is a "hot mess" and an agent of chaos that destabilizes the status quo of Megg, Mogg, and Owl frequently (see graphic novels *Megahex* [2014], *Amsterdam* [2016], *One More Year* [2016], and *Bad Gateway* [2019]) and then definitively, in *Crisis Zone* (serialized in 2020, collected in 2021).

Werewolf Jones as Queer "Terrorist"

Perhaps the most jarringly confronting aspect of *Crisis Zone*, and of Hanselmann's MM&O canon in general, are the exploits of the trio's misfit frenemy, Werewolf Jones. For those unfamiliar with the strip, Werewolf Jones is a distillation of the worst aspects of abusive and addictive behavior, cut with moments of generosity and sincerity that serve to keep the character from

FIGURE 9.3 Simon Hanselmann, *Bad Gateway* (Seattle: Fantagraphics, 2019), 33.
Courtesy of the artist.

becoming monstrous, moving him closer to hopelessness. Perhaps the closest literary analogue for Werewolf Jones is to be found in Randle McMurphy of Ken Kesey's *One Flew over the Cuckoo's Nest* (1962). Like McMurphy, Werewolf Jones is a charismatic rabble-rouser intent on disrupting the reigning status quo of his surroundings and has a predisposition toward promiscuity in terms of both stimulants and sex. Both characters are also given multiple chances at redemption through regulation of their behaviors but are ultimately brought low by their inability to temper their thirst for disruption. Werewolf Jones is jailed before reverting to his previously unseen—and not even hinted at—human form, cowed and isolated from the world. Eventually released, he is found dead under a bridge by heroin overdose, unwittingly enabled by Owl giving him cash to leave. McMurphy is lobotomized and subsequently (and sympathetically) smothered by fellow patient and narrator of the novel, Chief Bromden. Like Kesey's novel, *Crisis Zone* is a work of its time and an attempt to make sense of the world in a chaotic period and features characters that choose to either disassociate from or rail against it. In the case of Owl and the Chief, both are morally complicit in—yet ultimately freed by—their part in their friends' destruction.

Once again like McMurphy, Werewolf Jones becomes in *Crisis Zone* the chief antagonist of the narrative, the figure around which the chaos orbits. This is also neatly analogous to the titular *Tiger King* himself (only slightly less impressively known as Joseph Allen Maldonado-Passage). Maldonado-Passage himself is a figure of considerable high camp, completely self-serious in his self-serving quest for notoriety, and as Susan Sontag notes, "One must distinguish between naïve and deliberate Camp. Pure Camp is always naïve. Camp which knows itself to be Camp ('camping') is usually less satisfying."[15] Conversely, Werewolf Jones is acutely self-aware yet completely oblivious to the needs, emotional or otherwise, of those around him, particularly his preteen sons, Diesel and Jaxon. Werewolf Jones's relationship with his sons is also the emotional axis on which *Crisis Zone* finds its structure. One of the many subplots involves Diesel and Jaxon's response to being frequently dismissed and betrayed by their father. While this serves to harden Diesel, encouraging him to lean into the aggression and madness of his father, Jaxon responds to the avuncular warmth and acceptance of Owl. This allows him a sense of agency, and he begins a gender transition, renaming as Desi.

Amid the improvised and reactive daily installments of Hanselmann's tragicomedy, these incremental moments of sincerity serve to ground the pathos of the story, which is in turns bizarre, distasteful, aggressive, darkly comedic, and sharply satirical, intercut with moments of candid and genuine

emotion. It speaks to Hanselmann's skill as a storyteller that moments of resonance can land throughout a graphic novel built around talking animals,
reality television (satirizing the lockdown streaming hit *Tiger King* with
Anus King), and frequent and gleeful vulgarity.

Jasbir K. Puar presents a compelling argument for the post-9/11 establishment deliberately queering the figures of the Islamic terrorist and the suicide
bomber in order to better cast them as nefarious and oppositional adversar-
ies in the eyes of the public.[16] As Puar explains, "Queerness is proffered as a
sexually exceptional form of American national sexuality through a rhetoric
of sexual modernization that is simultaneously able to castigate the other as
homophobic *and* perverse, and construct the imperialist center as 'tolerant'
but sexually, racially, and gendered normal."[17]

While it may seem a leap to view any of Hanselmann's characters through
this framework, the preceding passage is, in many ways, the plight of Hanselmann's gang of misfits writ large. They are considered reprobates, degenerates,
and a symptom of societal malaise, constantly under inspection, judgment, or
attack by the very same society. Certainly, the large cast of *Crisis Zone* comes
up against the authorities on several occasions throughout and are, like ter-
rorists and suicide bombers, castigated as antithetical to the construct of
the "'tolerant' but sexually, racially, and gendered normal" political corpus.[18]
But it is Werewolf Jones that becomes the figurehead—and therefore the
scapegoat—of the gang's "terrorist" actions, finding himself jailed after a siege
at his compound (called "F-cktown," for the record) and, worse, performing
in blackface, all the while being filmed for the reality TV show. Werewolf
Jones is immediately "canceled" and jailed. In a subtle but hilarious creative
decision, Hanselmann did not depict the blackface performance, simply ending the scene after Werewolf Jones slathers three fingers of shoe polish onto
his face. As Puar explains, citing academic José Esteban Muñoz's analysis of a
1990s drag performance by artist Vaginal Davis as a disruptive act, minstrelsy
is inherently a disruptive act in that it embodies "internal terrors around race,
gender, and sexuality."[19] In this way, it is the perfect endpoint for Werewolf
Jones's campaign of terror. The notion of Hanselmann choosing *not* to show
something due to considerations of taste is, with the political and sexual
mayhem of the rest of the narrative, much of which results in death and even
mutilation, is a canny demonstration of self-awareness and a mocking understanding of the fickle nature and hypocrisy of political correctness and woke
culture, something the cartoonist has experienced from both sides. As Puar
explains, the Western construct of the terrorist "is concurrently an unfathomable, unknowable, and hysterical monstrosity."[20]

The Rupture of *Crisis Zone*

Hanselmann differentiates *Crisis Zone* from the many Megg, Mogg, and Owl stories that preceded it, notably through centering the narrative on specific real-world events, a definitive shift away from the comic's status quo. A typical Megg, Mogg, and Owl plot usually revolves around the trio (or often quartet, if WWJ is involved) looking for something to temporarily ease the tedium of everyday life, whether through sex, drugs, TV binges, video games, or occasional visits to the welfare office. Everybody ends up back home, once again bored and possibly stoned.

Using the image-sharing social media platform Instagram to release a daily installment of *Crisis Zone* kept a sense of unpredictability to the narrative, which was immediately divergent from the considered pacing of *Bad Gateway* and the shorter stories of previous volumes. Still drawn with fine lines, Hanselmann this time colored with pencil, likely for the media's speed and with an added benefit of a different aesthetic, not unlike, say, the difference between film and HD cameras in filmmaking so prevalent in reality television. This may appear an arbitrary observation, but as a project and an object, *Crisis Zone* makes frequent references to film and television, including its pulpy, 1980s action movie–themed cover; its closing credits; and an eleven-page "director's commentary" breaking down various plot points, responses to world events, and the creation for the project itself. Indeed, the plot itself becomes highly self-reflexive, with the strip itself building in a reality television show about the chaotic household of Megg, Mogg, and Owl as one of its main plotlines.

Crisis Zone is Hanselmann's longest single work to date. While previous graphic novels often collected material previously serialized elsewhere, they rarely built a continuing story arc beyond ten or so pages. At 176 pages, *Bad Gateway* was by far the cartoonist's lengthiest work to date and still arguably stands as its most visually finished, with Hanselmann's trademark watercolors distinguishing it from most contemporary comics. *Bad Gateway* flags some small but significant deviations from the series' status quo, beginning with Owl moving out and ending with Megg reuniting with her estranged mother. This makes sense considering the narrative momentum needed to carry a longer, self-contained story, but this is also curious in terms of the original, unpredictable reading experience in *Crisis Zone*. However, Hanselmann considers the work noncanonical, if in his typically noncommittal way, mentioning this in *Crisis Zone*'s "director's commentary."[21] This allows for a particularly chaotic rupture from the Megg, Mogg, and Owl status

FIGURE 9.4 Hanselmann, *Crisis Zone*, 212.
Courtesy of the artist.

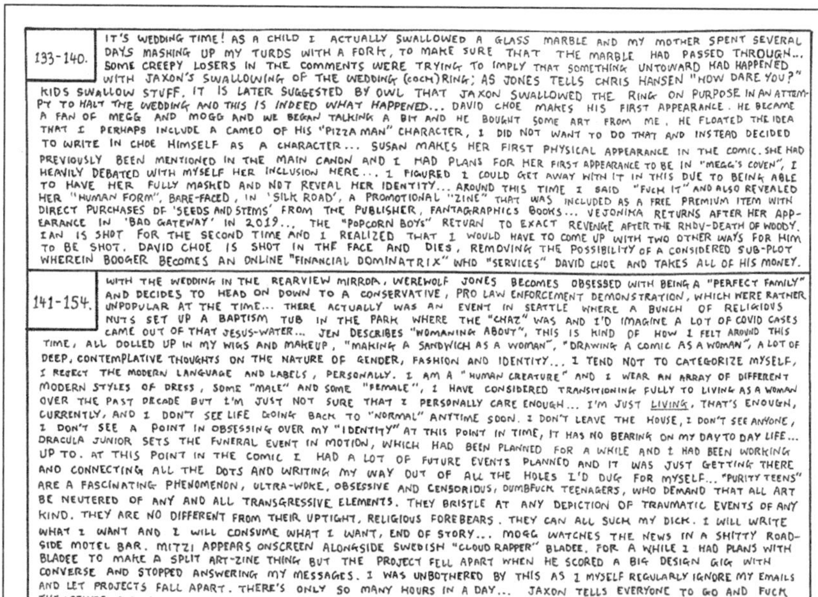

133–140	IT'S WEDDING TIME! AS A CHILD I ACTUALLY SWALLOWED A GLASS MARBLE AND MY MOTHER SPENT SEVERAL DAYS MASHING UP MY TURDS WITH A FORK, TO MAKE SURE THAT THE MARBLE HAD PASSED THROUGH... SOME CREEPY LOSERS IN THE COMMENTS WERE TRYING TO IMPLY THAT SOMETHING UNTOWARD HAD HAPPENED WITH JAXON'S SWALLOWING OF THE WEDDING (cock)RING; AS JONES TELLS CHRIS HANSEN "HOW DARE YOU?" KIDS SWALLOW STUFF. IT IS LATER SUGGESTED BY OWL THAT JAXON SWALLOWED THE RING ON PURPOSE IN AN ATTEMPT TO HALT THE WEDDING AND THIS IS INDEED WHAT HAPPENED... DAVID CHOE MAKES HIS FIRST APPEARANCE. HE BECAME A FAN OF MEGG AND MOGG AND WE BEGAN TALKING A BIT AND HE BOUGHT SOME ART FROM ME. HE FLOATED THE IDEA THAT I PERHAPS INCLUDE A CAMEO OF HIS "PIZZA MAN" CHARACTER, I DID NOT WANT TO DO THAT AND INSTEAD DECIDED TO WRITE IN CHOE HIMSELF AS A CHARACTER... SUSAN MAKES HER FIRST PHYSICAL APPEARANCE IN THE COMIC. SHE HAD PREVIOUSLY BEEN MENTIONED IN THE MAIN CANON AND I HAD PLANS FOR HER FIRST APPEARANCE TO BE IN "MEGG'S COVEN", I HEAVILY DEBATED WITH MYSELF HER INCLUSION HERE... I FIGURED I COULD GET AWAY WITH IT IN THIS DUE TO BEING ABLE TO HAVE HER FULLY MASKED AND MAKEUP, NEVER REVEAL HER IDENTITY... AROUND THIS TIME I SAID "FUCK IT" AND ALSO REVEALED HER "HUMAN FORM", BARE-FACED, IN 'SILK ROAD', A PROMOTIONAL 'ZINE" THAT WAS INCLUDED AS A FREE PREMIUM ITEM WITH DIRECT PURCHASES OF 'SEEDS AND STEMS' FROM THE PUBLISHER, FANTAGRAPHICS BOOKS... VEZONINA RETURNS AFTER HER APPEARANCE IN 'BAD GATEWAY' IN 2019... THE "POPCORN BOYS" RETURN TO EXACT REVENGE AFTER THE RHDV-DEATH OF WOODY. IAN IS SHOT FOR THE SECOND TIME AND I REALIZED THAT I WOULD HAVE TO COME UP WITH TWO OTHER WAYS FOR HIM TO BE SHOT. DAVID CHOE IS SHOT IN THE FACE AND DIES, REMOVING THE POSSIBILITY OF A CONSIDERED SUB-PLOT WHEREIN BOOGER BECOMES AN ONLINE "FINANCIAL DOMINATRIX" WHO "SERVICES" DAVID CHOE AND TAKES ALL OF HIS MONEY.
141–154	WITH THE WEDDING IN THE REARVIEW MIRROR, WEREWOLF JONES BECOMES OBSESSED WITH BEING A "PERFECT FAMILY" AND DECIDES TO HEAD ON DOWN TO A CONSERVATIVE, PRO LAW ENFORCEMENT DEMONSTRATION, WHICH WERE RATHER UNPOPULAR AT THE TIME... THERE ACTUALLY WAS AN EVENT IN SEATTLE WHERE A BUNCH OF RELIGIOUS NUTS SET UP A BAPTISM TUB IN THE PARK WHERE THE "CHAZ" WAS AND I'D IMAGINE A LOT OF COVID CASES CAME OUT OF THAT JESUS-WATER... JEN DESCRIBES "WOMANING ABOUT", THIS IS KIND OF HOW I FELT AROUND THIS TIME, ALL DOLLED UP IN MY WIGS AND MAKEUP, "MAKING A SANDWICH AS A WOMAN", "DRAWING A COMIC AS A WOMAN", A LOT OF DEEP, CONTEMPLATIVE THOUGHTS ON THE NATURE OF GENDER, FASHION AND IDENTITY... I TEND NOT TO CATEGORIZE MYSELF, I REJECT THE MODERN LANGUAGE AND LABELS, PERSONALLY. I AM A "HUMAN CREATURE" AND I WEAR AN ARRAY OF DIFFERENT MODERN STYLES OF DRESS, SOME "MALE" AND SOME "FEMALE", I HAVE CONSIDERED TRANSITIONING FULLY TO LIVING AS A WOMAN OVER THE PAST DECADE BUT I'M JUST NOT SURE THAT I PERSONALLY CARE ENOUGH... I'M JUST LIVING, THAT'S ENOUGH, CURRENTLY, AND I DON'T SEE LIFE GOING BACK TO "NORMAL" ANYTIME SOON. I DON'T LEAVE THE HOUSE, I DON'T SEE ANYONE, I DON'T SEE A POINT IN OBSESSING OVER MY "IDENTITY" AT THIS POINT IN TIME, IT HAS NO BEARING ON MY DAY TO DAY LIFE... DRACULA JUNIOR SETS THE FUNERAL EVENT IN MOTION, WHICH HAD BEEN PLANNED FOR A WHILE AND I HAD BEEN WORKING UP TO. AT THIS POINT IN THE COMIC I HAD A LOT OF FUTURE EVENTS PLANNED AND IT WAS JUST GETTING THERE AND CONNECTING ALL THE DOTS AND WRITING MY WAY OUT OF ALL THE HOLES I'D DUG FOR MYSELF... "PURITY TEENS" ARE A FASCINATING PHENOMENON, ULTRA-WOKE, OBSESSIVE AND CENSORIOUS, DUMBFUCK TEENAGERS, WHO DEMAND THAT ALL ART BE NEUTERED OF ANY AND ALL TRANSGRESSIVE ELEMENTS. THEY BRISTLE AT ANY DEPICTION OF TRAUMATIC EVENTS OF ANY KIND. THEY ARE NO DIFFERENT FROM THEIR UPTIGHT, RELIGIOUS FOREBEARS. THEY CAN ALL SUCK MY DICK. I WILL WRITE WHAT I WANT AND I WILL CONSUME WHAT I WANT, END OF STORY... MOGG WATCHES THE NEWS IN A SHITTY ROADSIDE MOTEL BAR. MITZI APPEARS ONSCREEN ALONGSIDE SWEDISH "CLOUD RAPPER" BLADEE, FOR A WHILE I HAD PLANS WITH BLADEE TO MAKE A SPLIT ART-ZINE THING BUT THE PROJECT FELL APART WHEN HE SCORED A BIG DESIGN GIG WITH CONVERSE AND STOPPED ANSWERING MY MESSAGES. I WAS UNBOTHERED BY THIS AS I MYSELF REGULARLY IGNORE MY EMAILS AND LET PROJECTS FALL APART. THERE'S ONLY SO MANY HOURS IN A DAY... JAXON TELLS EVERYONE TO GO AND FUCK THEMSELVES AND EXTRACTS HIMSELF FROM THE HORRIBLE SITUATION HE FINDS HIMSELF TRAPPED IN. THIS HAD BEEN PLANNED FOR A WHILE BUT I WAS STILL UNSURE OF WHERE EXACTLY HE WOULD END UP AND WHAT WOULD HAPPEN. SOMEHOW JAXON HAS BOUGHT INTO DESI AND IAN'S LIE THAT HE WAS RESPONSIBLE FOR THE TREEHOUSE/MOTEL FIRE AND THE 38 DEATHS. I'M GUESSING THAT HE DID IN FACT KNOCK OVER A CANDLE AROUND THE SAME TIME OF JONES STARTING THE HOT TUB FIRE... I GUESS WE'LL NEVER KNOW... JAXON "TAKES HIS SHIRT OFF IN THE YARD", AS NOTED BY MEGG, THIS IS A REFERENCE TO THE SONG "THE GLOW PT. 2" BY 'THE MICROPHONES' AKA PHIL ELVERUM. THE MICROPHONES/MOUNT EERIE IS MOST LIKELY MY FAVOURITE "BAND" EVER. I'D HAD THE PLEASURE OF HOSTING PHIL AT MY HOME IN HOBART, TASMANIA IN 2004, WHEN I WAS DABBLING IN GIG PROMOTION/ BOOKING. WE HAVE PERIODICALLY KEPT IN TOUCH OVER THE YEARS AND HE IS INDEED A FAN OF THE DISGUSTING ADVENTURES OF MEGG AND MOGG. PHIL IS A VERY FUNNY GUY AND I'M CERTAIN HE COULD BE A CARLIN-LEVEL COMEDIAN IF HE SO CHOSE TO BE. "MICROPHONES IN 2020" IS MY CHOICE FOR RECORD OF THE YEAR IN 2020.
155–177	IT'S FUNERAL TIME! THE "DRACULA JUNIOR JR. FACSIMILE DOLL" SEEMED TO CREEP OUT A BUNCH OF PEOPLE, SO MISSION ACCOMPLISHED. I HAD A LOT OF FUN WRITING THE DOLL'S DIALOGUE THAT IS CLEARLY BEING RECORDED BY AN INEBRIATED WEREWOLF JONES... DESI BARGES IN AND PROCLAIMS SHE IS "SHE-RA", A RACIST LESBIAN". THIS WAS AN INTENSE ONLINE SHITSTORM. I WONT BOTHER ATTEMPTING TO EXPLAIN IT, THIS KIND OF BULLSHIT DESERVES TO BE LOST TO HISTORY. JEN NAMEDROPS "BLAIRE WHITE" WHO IS A RIGHT-LEANING TRANS YOUTUBE "PERSONALITY" WHO IS REVILED BY LEFT-LEANING YOUTUBE "PERSONALITIES". OWL AND VALERIA ARE REVEALED TO BE IN A RELATIONSHIP AND OWL HAS FINALLY BROKEN OUT OF HIS DEPRESSION. A GROUP OF "ANARCHISTS" SHOW UP OUTSIDE THE HOUSE AND BERATE WEREWOLF JONES. THERE WAS A BIT OF A "KERFUFFLE" IN THE COMMENTS, A FEW ANGRY LEFT-LEANING INDIVIDUALS CLAIMING THAT THIS KIND OF BEHAVIOR DID NOT EXIST. A FEW OTHER (MOST LIKELY APOLITICAL SMARTASSES) COMMENTERS POINTED OUT THAT THE DIALOGUE AND ACTIONS OF THE CARTOON ANARCHISTS WAS BASICALLY DIRECTLY LIFTED FROM REAL LIFE, THERE WAS FOOTAGE FREELY CIRCULATING. HERE IN THE PACIFIC NORTHWEST IT WAS NOT UNCOMMON TO HEAR ABOUT ROVING BANDS OF ACTIVISTS WANDERING THE SUBURBS AT NIGHT, SHINING LIGHTS INTO PEOPLE'S WINDOWS AND SHOUTING SLOGANS AND PROFANITIES AT THE SLEEPING ELDERLY, CHILDREN AND EXHAUSTED FRONT LINE WORKERS. THERE WERE MANY INSTANCES OF OUTDOOR DINERS BEING BERATED AND FORCED AT MOB-POINT TO RAISE THEIR FISTS... OR ELSE (?). OFTEN THESE ROVING BANDS WOULD APPEAR TO BE MADE UP OF PREDOMINATELY WHITE INDIVIDUALS. I'VE SEEN NUMEROUS INTERVIEWS WITH ACTUAL BLACK LIVES MATTER PROTESTERS CONDEMNING THIS DUMB SHIT. I THINK IT'S HARD TO ARGUE WITH THE NOTION THAT PERHAPS THIS KIND OF AGGRESSIVE SHIT WAS MUDDYING THE PEACEFUL, INCLUSIVE MESSAGE OF THE BLACK LIVES MATTER PROTESTS... IT'S ALL VERY PLAINLY SPELLED OUT ON PAGE 160 FOR ANY OF THE PREVIOUS EPISODE'S MORONS WHO LACK BASIC READING COMPREHENSION SKILLS... WHILE ALL THIS SHIT WAS GOING DOWN IN THE COMMENTS MY WIFE CAME INTO MY STUDIO WITH A PLASTIC STICK COVERED IN HER URINE AND INFORMED ME THAT SHE WAS PREGNANT WITH OUR CHILD... WE HAD BEEN TRYING FOR A KID EARLIER IN THE YEAR, PUT A HOLD ON IT AT THE BEGINNING OF THE PANDEMIC, BUT HAD RECENTLY RESUMED OUR EFFORTS. WE WERE FUCKING PUMPED! ANY CONCERN OVER PEOPLE WHINING ABOUT POLITICS IN MY "COMMENTS SECTION" FULLY EVAPORATED. MY WIFE FORGOT THAT SHE WAS ANGRY AT ME FOR MAKING A POLITICALLY-CHARGED COMIC THAT SHE HAD WARNED ME NOT TO PRODUCE AND POST, IN THAT MOMENT, EVERYTHING CHANGED, I WAS TO BE A "FATHER", WE WERE STARTING A REAL FAMILY. EVERYBODY CAN SERIOUSLY JUST FUCK OFF, "NEVER TALK TO ME OR MY CHILD AGAIN".

279.

FIGURE 9.5 Hanselmann, *Crisis Zone*, 279.
Courtesy of the artist.

quo, which could have been somewhat difficult to follow, with plot developments that include facial tattoos, a wedding, multiple amputations, and finally Werewolf Jones's unavoidable death.

Hanselmann has never been overly concerned with considerations of taste or decorum. Some of his finest work toes the line between black comedy, stoner jokes, and gonzo character vignettes, a deadpan and self-aware voice unafraid to explore heavy territory, with a register of pathos only accessible through talking cartoon animals. *Crisis Zone* takes Hanselmann's grossout tendencies, his fascination with celebrity and pop culture trash, and the melodrama of friends and lovers and dials it up to a fever pitch. Summarizing the plot would be of no value here. The twists and turns taken over the story's ten months, improvised and released in real time, imbue the narrative with a neurotic and anarchic energy, not unlike the reality television it sought to emulate. The key difference is that while Hanselmann worked daily to release ten panels per day, as to Instagram's format, such a reality show counterpart could only achieve this energy through the editing process. Even in his parody of another medium, Hanselmann's daily approach to *Crisis Zone* could not have been sustained outside of comics. In this way, the rupture of *Crisis Zone* lies in its radical departure from not only its own in-world logic and parameters but serialization and the graphic novel more generally. Where longer story arcs usually play out across planned sequences (whether single issues or graphic novels) over months or years, Hanselmann's twisting, improvised narrative eschews the standard story structures of most mainstream comics, relating more to the elegiac Sunday pages of early strips such as *Little Nemo in Slumberland* and *Prince Valiant* than to contemporary comics. Updating the format of the daily newspaper strip for the Instagram generation may not be Hanselmann's innovation, but certainly his approach to the conceit has injected new life into the conceit of the daily, which has been languishing in the world of diminishing returns of its host medium, the newspaper.

10

The Hernandez Brothers

● ●

In the history of literature, the most famous and infamous pair of siblings is the Goncourt brothers, Jules and Edmond, who in many ways helped shape French literature and culture in the second half of the nineteenth century. Their lives were as peculiar as their work was merciless in its observations of individuals and society. (Lukács numbered them among the detested naturalists, but we are only following his theoretical lead, not reading from a catechism.) Although born eight years apart, they lived as close to one another as two people could, to the point of metaphysical incestuousness, not only writing together but barely spending a day apart, even sharing mistresses. Their copious *Journal*, which they began in 1851 and Edmond continued after Jules's death in 1870, is an eye-opening and often scurrilously frank account of the people and events of the day. Although Edmond, the eldest, outlived Jules by over twenty years—after watching his agonizing death due to syphilis—they are buried in the same grave in Montmartre Cemetery, a fitting conclusion to a relationship that was as macabre as it was endearing. As writers of both novels and histories, they are among those who are credited with the revival of eighteenth-century art and of narrative styles that embraced unconventional formats that were later seen as impressionistic vignettes. In their special case, it is hard to separate the biographical detail of their spiritual, Siamese-twin-like bond from their work, as the pathology that permeates their work can be called more a fusion than a collaboration. (Lukács in his early writing cites them as notable examples of writers who "fuse" into a "new personality."[1])

Hernandez brothers Gilbert (a.k.a. Bert or Beto) and Jaime (a.k.a. Xaime), who are the greatest fraternal team in the history of comics so far, may not have the same luridly obsessive relationship as the Goncourt brothers, and they are closer in age (two years as opposed to eight), but their work, both together and separate, suggests a deep commonality that transcends collaboration. Cofounding *Love and Rockets* with a third brother, Mario, in 1982 was a signal moment in the alternative comics movement. With forays into science fiction, magical realism, and even gag strips, the characters in this series reflect the mixed-race origins of their authors in a way that goes well beyond the tokenistic racial typecasting from art to film. While Mario's contributions became increasingly rare, Gilbert and Jaime's work accumulated into a substantial and dense narrative mass that has only become more robust over the decades. These narratives consist of a cast of characters that move in and out of their respective solo work, the driving element, or thread, being the development of these characters in something of the real time in which they are drawn, which means that some characters move in and out as with a television series, and they visibly age, which is a rarity in comics. Calling to mind William Faulkner's Yoknapatawpha County, a fictional region of the American South where many of his greatest novels are set, the drama of Gilbert's work is in a Central American village, Palomar. Jaime's "Locas" stories are centered on the neighborhood of Hoppers, which is a hybrid of elements of Los Angeles and the brothers' LA-peripheral hometown of Oxnard.

What is continually surprising in the series is the extent to which the relatively discrete elements of each brother cohere with the other, and what is even more intriguing is when they begin to intercalate and merge in a way that—we can only assert speculatively, of course—is only possible by close siblings. The fantastic elements, which are a foil to what can be the bitingly gritty realism of others, are redolent of not only the classic "magic realists" such as Gabriel Garcia Marquez, Italo Calvino, or Jorge Luis Borges but also Goethe's *Faust: The Second Part*. At this point, it is worth returning to Lukács's notion of the "the fantastical" (*die Phantastische*) in regard to Goethe's *Faust: The Second Part*, which we broached in chapter 8: "The fantastical as category (*Gattungsmässigen*), which arises on an illustrative basis, serves to create a real milieu, but free from naturalistic pettiness, insofar as the fantastical situation and the individual characters are raised upward, and by the elevation of the problems to a height and typicality which that category yields in an informal way."² The fantastical and the magical are thus strategic aesthetic portals or stylistic conduits for transmitting complex feelings and states of mind that avoid "naturalistic pettiness"—that is, the reductio ad absurdum to enumerative empirical elements. What the Hernandez brothers give us is a combination of startling—indeed, brutally frank—expressions of human emotional and physical frailty set against the explosive, convulsive expressions of confusions, ambitions, disappointments, and, finally, ecstasies that expand and distort the realistic default only to reassert it. It is a device that is realist in that it delivers us from humdrum life. They are the escape, the promise, and the diversion that make dogged quotidian life both so gratifying and so disappointing. The work of the Hernandez brothers is arguably among the greatest exponents of this narrative combination in comics.

Love and Rockets and Anthology Comics

While in years to come, both Gilbert and Jaime would develop two of the most complex and vast casts of characters in comics, it is important to consider the early stories of *Love and Rockets* as the very sturdy and self-contained launch point, dense with a sense of rich backstory even in its first issue. Although these early stories were far from being as nuanced and masterful as later works would soon be, they created an immediate sense of momentum and interconnectivity, expressed in a manner perhaps only possible by the kind of commonality of vision from which some siblings benefit. From the start, *Love and Rockets* has been an anthology comic, comprising short stories (both self-contained and episodic) by all three brothers. The first (non-self-published) issue of *Love and Rockets* (1982) made its anthology format clear from the outset, with its now iconic cover depicting five women in an incongruous genre grouping, including a superhero, a barbarian, and a woman in curlers and a dressing gown. Many of these early stories consist of enthusiastic homages to silver-age science fiction comics, and while these are artistically notable, they do not benefit from the decades-long character development and world building of the long-term narratives to be found in the "Locas" and "Palomar" stories. The fantastical elements prevalent in the brothers' earliest work, with their strong visual and narrative connectivity—perhaps unavoidable with three comics-obsessed brothers working together and reading each other's work—hint at the cartoonists they would become as their careers developed.

FIGURE 10.1 Jaime Hernandez, "Mechanics," *Love and Rockets* 1 (1982): 37.
Copyright © Jaime Hernandez. Courtesy of Fantagraphics.

Jaime, generally regarded as the fan favorite, took a few years to settle into the urban aesthetics of Hoppers, slowly moving away from the more overt science fiction elements. Rather than rebooting his narrative or relegating early stories to some kind of dream sequence or alternative reality (all three are hallmarks of mainstream comics), the science fiction elements instead have faded into the background, appearing far less frequently, just as they did in Gilbert's work (the science fiction / monster story line "BEM," appearing in early issues, introduced Luba, Gilbert's most complex and well-known creation). Later, in homage to the cover of *Love and Rockets* #1, Jaime drew the cover to the first issue of volume 2 (2001) with six different versions of Maggie, his most beloved character, in the same police lineup, including her early science fiction–themed self. This was not only a wink to the early years of the comic but a more accurate summary of what *Love and Rockets* had evolved into, which is an anthology comic unafraid to destabilize its own structure and self-reflexively poke fun at itself, perhaps the most brotherly thing in the world. For example, an early character of Gilbert's, Errata Stigmata, a sort of Goth dandy who appears intermittently in early issues, is soon revealed to be a comic book character herself, through two of Gilbert's other recurring characters, in "Music for Monsters." To complicate this further, she has appeared in the background of Jaime's stories as well, an exchange that happens periodically in the brothers' work, at once emphasizing *Love and Rockets'* interconnective anthology format and the similarities and differences of the brothers' visual styles. At one stage, Maggie seems to dismiss (or at least poke fun at) her early science fiction self in "The Adventures of Maggie the Mechanic" (1988), a story that rehashes the kind of stories Maggie appeared in early on for two pages, before modern-day Maggie, riding on the bus, throws away the "Maggie the Mechanic" comic in the last panel, blowing a raspberry in exasperation.

While this may sound slightly jarring, and indeed it could well be to a reader used to more recent material, it is a testament to Jaime's storytelling how smooth this transition is, perhaps aided by his occasional narrative forays into professional wrestling, a world of well-established conventions, its own niche terminology, and a narrative self-reflexivity that predates postmodernism by some decades. In the world of pro wrestling, *kayfabe* is a term that has evolved around what was for many years a strict code of professional conduct. Wrestlers, with their constructed "babyface" (good guy) and "heel" (bad guy) personas, were expected to stay in character outside the ring, lest they reveal to the public that wrestling was, indeed, choreographed with predetermined outcomes. In Mexico, this was taken to further heights, with many wrestlers wearing their *luchador* masks in public and even at home, embracing their characters completely. Kayfabe slowly eroded as wrestling began to be televised more frequently, increasing in popularity in the 1980s with the global reach of cable television, and was finally cast aside in the mid- to late 1990s with the so-called attitude era of wrestling, which began incorporating far more elaborate soap opera–style plotlines and backstage reality TV–style content.³ It is telling that Jaime began incorporating wrestling stories into his work years before kayfabe was jettisoned, preempting the backstage irony and roving camera self-reflexivity of postkayfabe pro wrestling. The paradox of wrestling, of being on one level fantastical (planned story lines, predetermined victories and losses) and on another level reflective of life's many drudgeries (a certain physical toll, frequent injuries, and a culture of endless motels and self-medication), is in many respects a reflection of the concerns of *Love and Rockets* in terms of its treatment of realism. The Hernandez brothers' work aspires to linguistic, narrative, and perceptual realism, but in terms of cartooning, they avoid being "realistic"—in the vein of what Lukács would have decried as naturalistic—and load their work (especially in the early years) with the minutiae of a complex comic book metahistory, with references to each other's work (and each other) throughout the many short stories. Both brothers have created works that reference wrestling culture (see Gilbert's compelling five-page "A True Story" [1986] about real-life wrestler Adrian Adonis); however, only Jaime has woven the entertainment into his long-running narratives.

Stylistically, both Gilbert's and Jaime's works draw more from cartoonists such as Alex Toth, Dan DeCarlo, Steve Ditko, and Jack Kirby than from artists of their own generation, and both have a distinctive visual language that favors an efficient cartoonish stylization over the slavish, Hollywood-influenced graphics of many contemporary mainstream comics. Wrestling, a linchpin of Latin American popular culture, is a well that Jaime has drawn from with desultory regularity since the early days of *Love and Rockets*, allowing space for some of the cartoonist's most dynamic and visually audacious visuals and a narrative break from the more internalized of the "Locas" stories. As in his brothers' work, Gilbert's comics have been published predominantly in black and white, and like his brothers, he has developed a dense stylistic shorthand through this framework. Unlike Jaime's work, which consists of a sophisticated interplay of solid positive and negative spaces (Jaime's early cross-hatching and feathering gave way to a visual language increasingly interested in describing form as simply and directly as possible), Gilbert's cartooning reached maturity early on in both narrative and stylistic terms. With its lexicon of hand-rendered midtones, which serve to flatten rather than accentuate form and volume, Gilbert's work often inhabits a gray area in terms of character complexity and depth. Gilbert's characters and narratives operate with a baseline that is somewhat darker than those of his brothers, often connected to a sublimated sense of tension. Gilbert's fictional Palomar is a (relatively) peaceful hamlet situated in the complex political stew of an unspecified country in South America, surrounded by revolution and political upheaval. In this way, it is Palomar that embodies the most fantastical elements of Gilbert's stories. In its poverty, the town has a simplicity of life that at times resembles the conventions of a postapocalypse narrative. Palomar seems to occupy a space that is not of interest to revolutionary types, though its inhabitants are often tested inside and outside of the town's limits. In contrast to Jaime's more urban narrative, Gilbert's "Palomar" stories fit much more comfortably in the literary paradigm of magic realism.[4] Indeed, Gilbert regards Palomar as "mythical," allowing a certain level of strangeness to go unexplained.[5]

While Gilbert and Jaime, having published so much of their work together in *Love and Rockets*, have developed in tandem and have thus established complex narratives that are both separate and related, their work (even when published outside the anthology format of *Love and Rockets*) could not be considered mutually exclusive any more than the Goncourts. Both brothers have occasionally referred to each other's characters as well as drawn their own characters into the other's backgrounds. These puckish visual homages could be considered postmodern but tellingly speak of the brothers' deep knowledge of comic history, particularly conventions of homage and satire. Nowhere have these conventions been explored more thoroughly than in Gilbert's "Hernandez Satyricon" and Jaime's "War Paint," wherein the brothers create short stories about each other's characters. By 1994, when these two stories were published, both cartoonists had settled well into their mature visual styles for over a decade, and to see their "covers" of each other's work was both jarring and visually familiar. While Gilbert explores the crazier science fiction of Jaime's early work with enthusiasm and a satirical edge, playing up on his brother's willingness to explore and abandon narrative threads on a whim, Jaime's more domestic take on Palomar is at turns a somber and nostalgic affair.

FIGURE 10.2 Jaime Hernandez, "Locas 8:01 A.M.," *Love and Rockets* 6 (1984): 15.
Copyright © Jaime Hernandez. Courtesy of Fantagraphics.

Luba and Maggie: Avatars or Objects of Desire

While the Hernandez brothers have created several continuing narratives
over the years, the two that have become linchpins of *Love and Rockets* and its
spin-off graphic novels, the "Locas" and "Palomar" stories, bear further discussion in their own unusual structures. Both narratives, if we are to consider

each a cohesive whole, are centered on a woman. The "Locas" and "Palomar" stories orbit around Maggie and Luba, respectively, but with a cast that slowly expands to such an extent that the characters' presence may be implicit only in the negative space left in their absence. Both characters, having been featured since the very first days of *Love and Rockets*, now have eighty years' worth of development and backstory between them. While Jaime's "Locas" stories tend to feature Maggie in the narrative, at least tangentially, Luba's backstory is expansive to the point where entire narrative sequences have been dedicated to her mother, daughters, half sisters, and even her niece, weaving an elaborate tapestry connecting back to Palomar. Maggie and Luba are to a certain extent avatars for their respective cartoonist, and there remains an unavoidable reading of the characters as objects of desire. Herein lies a dimension of complexity that sits well outside the highly developed character traits and backstories the Hernandez brothers have developed over the past four decades. While the significant casts of "Locas" and "Palomar" characters extend upon these complexities (Jaime's characters Penny Century and Danita Lincoln and Gilbert's characters Fritz, Doralis, Petra, and Maria are all drawn with careful attention to physical attributes), it would be folly to attempt a deconstruction of each, embodying as they do the complicated axis of expression and desire of Luba and Maggie in miniature.

While Gilbert's drawing style is the more overtly sexualized of the brothers (Luba's impressive bustline has been a sticking point for many of the cartoonist's critics), it would be inaccurate to say that Jaime's work eschews such moments completely. The distinction could be that Jaime's work tends toward the "good girl" conventions of *Betty and Veronica*, *Millie the Model*, and Gil Elvgren cheesecake, the big difference being Betty and Veronica are never depicted engaging in a sexual act, least of all with each other. Jaime's sophisticated drawings do betray a highly developed understanding of anatomy and a robust eroticism that is perhaps overshadowed by his brother's propensity for large-breasted women. In many ways, Luba and Maggie are inverse characters: Luba is promiscuous and physically imposing (not only does she have a large bust, high cheekbones, and an ever-present hammer, but her emotive and magnetic presence culminates in her eventual mayorship of Palomar) compared to Maggie's diminutive stature (only her friend and sometime lover, the perpetual second banana Hopey, appears shorter), self-critical nature, and occasionally neurotic tendency toward overthinking. These inversions do not end in the physical and the personal, however, as both Maggie and Luba reflect the scale of their worlds and worldviews. Luba's world is ever expanding, as is her circle of lovers (and, by extension, her sisters' worlds and lovers), anchored in the slowly revealed backstory of the character. Maggie's world is intimate, her list of lovers modest and meaningful, and she pours out her soul as quickly as can be verbalized, usually to Hopey (or whoever fills the negative space she leaves behind).

Both Maggie and Luba gain weight over the course of the years, and while this could be overlooked as mere realism, it is revealed in the respective character's responses to their weight gain. While Maggie frets, particularly about her backside (which is, ironically, coveted by many orbiting characters), Luba seems unphased by such a change, eventually dispensing with her extra weight with as little concern as when she gained it. Even in Luba's teenage years, as depicted in "Poison River," wherein she spirals into a complex marriage and copious drug use, the character maintains a detached equanimity, as if observing events rather than experiencing them. As such, the repercussions are largely borne by other characters, with Luba simply moving forward, seemingly unaffected. This is the opposite of Maggie, whose commentary of her own narrative jams often forms the momentum (gentle though it is) of her stories. Jaime has commented that the Hopey-Maggie connection was his Mexican American equivalent of the Betty and Veronica nexus in the *Archie* comics. The added exceptions are that their obsession with one another becomes sexually consummated and that Hopey and Maggie do grow old, though whether they "end up together," as in most romance comics, remains to be seen. Thus they can also be interpreted as avatar figures of temporality against the atemporality of "classic" comics, from *Peanuts* to *Archie* to *Richie Rich*, where comfortingly—and, it would have to be admitted, somewhat grotesquely—the characters do not grow old, locked in a time warp of the land of milk and honey, the economic post–World War II boom of the United States, an age of exceptionalism and entitlement that is now experiencing the many aftershocks of realization that the dream is not eternal. Hopey and Maggie are the nonprivileged versions of this dream. As Dan Nadel comments, "Maggie and Hopey have gradually aged perhaps twenty years since their introduction nearly forty years ago—they were punks, 'it' girls of their scene, and then continued growing into complicated adults, allowing Hernandez and his earliest readers to explore their own lives through and alongside their characters, as with, say, François Truffaut's Antoine Doinel or Philip Roth's Nathan Zuckerman."[6] Or the recurring characters of Balzac or Agatha Christie's Hercule Poirot and Miss Marple. Luba, even as her past is slowly revealed in subsequent stories, always appears to be a woman with a past and a complex inner world. This is emphasized by Gilbert's far less frequent deployment of thought balloons.

While they do appear, it is most often in the stories of particular characters, such as Luba's niece, Venus, whose own adventures are structured as a variation of the shorter setup and punch line stories à la *Archie* and *Betty and Veronica*. Luba herself rarely emits thought balloons, emphasizing both her inner strength and her mystery. Maggie, on the other hand, is perhaps the character who has emitted the most in the vast *Love and Rockets* cast, with Jaime revealing her thoughts and emotions by way of a running commentary on the story beats of the comic. Thus, Maggie's internal monologues (and Luba's lack thereof) operate in tandem with the broader narrative structure of the comic, stretching and compacting time and chronology with remarkable sophistication.

Referring these characters back to *Archie* helps elaborate the extent to which they are, in Lukács's parlance, "types." Each of them represents a particular position within the fabric of the narratives, each responsible for the push and pull of the encounters between different forms of human awareness of worldviews. Lukács's types are not stereotypes, however, but are character formations that stand in dialectical relation to one another. Their purpose and meaning are not only according to their immanent inner nature but according to the ways their subjectivity shapes the situations into which they are thrown. Lukács observes that "in art where more and more concrete people in concrete situations create concrete objects that convey them, and concrete feelings that express them, there comes a need to focus on symbolizing the typical in people and situations."[7] Taking Luba as an example, a central aspect of her typicality is her reticence and taciturnity. What she does not say speaks to the relative presence of that trait in all of us when faced with overbearing or overexpressive people or confronted with challenges that do not invite simple answers. As implied in the word itself, the type is invested in a little distortion and exaggeration, but only to the end of extracting an aspect of reality that is not available to us through systematic or "scientific" representation or analysis.[8]

Technique

Nadel elaborates on Jaime's draftsmanship, which he extols as among the most "graceful" in the history of comics: "His refined lines, made with a Hunt Extra Fine No. 22 pen, distill multiple strains of cartooning and commercial art into a handmade (no rulers allowed) language of structural and emotional perfection. Lines move from thick to thin, they are uneven—there

FIGURE 10.3 Gilbert Hernandez, "Luba Conquers the World," *Love and Rockets* 14 (1985): 5. Copyright © Gilbert Hernandez. Courtesy of Fantagraphics.

is life in them."⁹ There are many unspoken canons and ways of proceeding within the world of comics and graphic novels that resemble something like the laws of medieval guilds. Although they are not inscribed in law, there are tacit protocols and codes of honor that have developed out of the medium that are based on skill and experience but also on an intuitive knowledge of what is most effective in bringing the events to life—the generation of realism. In essence, these unspoken laws boil down to one: don't cheat, but let your skill and experience and invention speak for themselves, to stand on their own proverbial two legs. ("Don't cheat" is the equivalent of the mobster's prescription "Don't snitch.") "Narrative cartooning," of which Jaime as Nadel contends is one of the great exemplars, "is based on shorthand drawings of place, space, emotions—things that would consume pages of prose or occupy a Félix Valatton canvas." Jaime achieves a rare balance between image-making skill and narrative depth, tending to expose the extent to which graphic novels with excellent drawings can often carry vapid plots or where bracing stories are incommensurate to the drabness of the drawing.¹⁰

By 1988, Jaime had established the stylistic groundwork that has since come to be understood as his mature work in terms of both drawing and storytelling sophistication; however, it was a relatively short story wherein both of these aspects cohered into a greater narrative whole of remarkable power and economy: "Flies on the Ceiling" (1988–1989), a fifteen-page story about supporting character Izzy, a writer, and her troubled past. In a wordless, nine-panel tour de force, Jaime establishes in the first page Izzy's occupation, explosive family life, broken marriage, abortion, and attempted suicide. The story, whereby Izzy moves to Mexico, finds love, and ultimately realizes that she cannot stay, is loaded with Christian iconography and is Jaime's most surreal work, with a number of visual metaphors creeping at the periphery of the panels wherein Izzy is suffering what could be a psychotic break after an implied rape. She has conversations with an unseen Satan; vomits dark, reptilian creatures; and may or may not give birth. Condensed, as the story is, to a mere fifteen pages, it maintains a remarkable sense of momentum, not unlike Gilbert's often-compressed narratives (perhaps the reason for a Gilbert-drawn appearance of a young Maria, Luba's mother, in one panel, to say nothing of the story's young boy with whom he shares a nickname). The story would be a high watermark for *Love and Rockets* and a clear demonstration of Jaime's command over the medium.

Conversely, Gilbert's visual style and narrative sophistication would mature in a more slowly burning fashion. While Jaime's stories were always fairly self-contained, even while forming episodic segments of longer narratives, Gilbert's

FIGURE 10.4 Jaime Hernandez, "Flies on the Ceiling," *Love and Rockets* 29 (1989): 1.
Copyright © Jaime Hernandez. Courtesy of Fantagraphics.

stories often insisted on a greater commitment from the reader. While Jaime's
visual and narrative accessibility may explain his initial popularity among the
three brothers, it would be a mistake to overlook Gilbert's artistic powers,
which form another inversion. Like Jaime, Gilbert makes use of large areas
of black; however, unlike the visual lexicon of Jaime's "Locas" stories (domi-
nated with a deep consideration of spatial design and composition), his is a

world of midtones and textures. Gilbert's mature visual lexicon is indexical and direct, and unlike Jaime's, the surface of which has not changed dramatically since the 1990s, his linear economy and sense of design have continued to evolve. Comparing a 1990 drawing of Luba to a 2020 one, for example, reveals a surprising evolution. Gone are the deep shadows and suggested curvature of her form (not unlike Jaime's early work), replaced with a pristine and consistent line, a stylization far more consistent with the *bande dessinée* than the American comics of Gilbert's youth. One of Gilbert's early masterpieces, "Human Diastrophism" (1987–1988), stands as a fascinating example of the cartoonist presenting the world of Palomar as a compelling graphic whole and establishing the evocative visual lexicon that he would develop for years to come. The narrative, which revolves around a serial killer coming to Palomar, changes the status quo of Gilbert's stories dramatically and is rendered with lush midtones and rich blacks, heightening the atmosphere and tension of the Central American village. Compared to Jaime's "Flies on the Ceiling," it is a slowly unfolding mystery but no less effective in its existential and metaphorical power. While the two stories, like the two brothers in question, have differing visual approaches, it is their narrative approaches to time that perhaps most noticeably differentiate them.

Love and Rockets and Time

Both Gilbert's and particularly Jaime's works are frequently and understandably praised for their graphic sensibility and nuanced portrayal of complex women, but their relationship to time is an important aspect of their work, which is barely discussed. Like their mature graphic styles, their approaches to time as a narrative device differentiate Gilbert's and Jaime's work substantially yet affirm a sense of commonality between them. As in other media, particularly film and television, the flashback is used extensively by both Gilbert and Jaime. These can be interspersed in small quantities or extended for entire chapters and further serve to flesh out the characters. In an interesting deviation from film and television, however, the characters age. This is much more akin to the "slower" medium of the novel than film in terms of the mechanics of the Hernandezes' storytelling. Despite comics' expedient formal ambidexterity, the Hernandez brothers maneuver a level of narrative density rare to the medium, particularly in the anthology format. While many anthology comics tend toward narrative momentum in order to quickly take hold of and then maintain the reader's attention in the span of only a few pages, with a conveniently placed cliff-hanger to bring them back (a formula developed to perfection by the British especially, whose comics have historically gravitated toward the weekly anthology format), the Hernandez brothers, and especially Gilbert, reverse the formula in terms of sheer narrative density. Gilbert's "Poison River" (1989–1993) takes the cartoonist's highly compressed narrative to its limits. The story makes use of jump cuts between panels that create a sense of forward chronological momentum, allowing the cartoonist to move frictionlessly forward in time weeks or even months within a matter of panels. These temporal jumps allow for an incredibly dense narrative in terms of chronology and the events therein, often contained within a strict page count. Fleshing out Luba's pre-Palomar backstory is a bravura demonstration of economy, weaving a vast and highly detailed narrative with numerous characters over a significant period of time in a mere 184 pages.

Conversely, Jaime tends toward decompression, with an entire episode or story taking place exploring one scene instead of many. Where other cartoonists might focus on a party scene, Jaime would just as likely explore the decision to go to the party and then present getting to the party as the party itself. In this way, Maggie (sometimes literally) stumbles through life and relationships, narrating through her thoughts. Time moves forward in a naturalistic fashion in "Locas" stories, which are then augmented with flashback sequences. Maggie has aged in time, though not forty years' worth. She appears to be in her early twenties in early stories and in her forties in recent stories. Jaime does, however, incorporate significant jumps in time, often between stories. Given the often-transitory nature of Jaime's characters' share-house living and relationship status, a jump forward in time brings with it a useful tension revolving around what has happened to specific characters over intervening years.

Luba, like the "Palomar" stories in general, has a more complex timeline. To begin with, when Luba first appears in Palomar, she is very much a woman with a past, and while her age is somewhat mysterious and indeterminate, she appears to be around her early thirties. Luba is aged and de-aged for entire narratives, and in some stories, she does appear to have aged in real time. This ricocheting across different temporalities calls to mind Joseph Conrad's *The Secret Agent* (1907), in which details recur from earlier scenes about which the reader already knows the outcome with the effect of stirring uneasiness in the reader, prompting suspicion that earlier events require deeper scrutiny or inspection from a different angle. The reprising of events suggests an insufficiency in the nature and order of their presentation in the first place, with the net effect of creating an uncertainty over the accuracy of

FIGURE 10.5 Gilbert Hernandez, *Love and Rockets: Poison River* (Seattle: Fantagraphics, 1994), 128. Copyright © Gilbert Hernandez. Courtesy of Fantagraphics.

both instances. Another notable example is Margaret Atwood's *Blind Assassin* (2000), which engages the novel-within-a-novel form whose partitioning within the main narrative becomes increasingly more unstable and porous as the novel unfolds. (One of the most famous temporal warps of this kind is of course *Swann in Love*, the novel within a novel following the first volume of Proust's *À la recherche*.) This is not unlike Jaime's aforementioned backstage examination of the invented narratives and personae of pro wrestling. Gilbert has also explored stories within stories, with Luba's older cousin Ofelia writing a work of autobiography that forecasts her sister, Fritz, later starring in a B movie about Palomar. This is in part commentary upon the brothers' own experiences with the frustrating optioning process of Hollywood.[11]

Among the most prescient and lasting odd couples of literature is the bumbling upper-class toff Bertie Wooster and his soberly insightful valet, Jeeves, crafted by P. G. Wodehouse. Although their literary life is finite, they come to us episodically, as if their many contretemps and imbroglios (and their corrections thanks to Jeeves) could go on indefinitely. Seen against one another, each story has the status of both concrete events and parable. Similarly, while the figures in *Love and Rockets* do age and change according to the inexorable ebb and flow of life, they also occupy dual realms. One is of the distinctly real and gritty world of "real life," while the other is the suspended perenniality of the serial comic, at once modern utopia and limbo. Unlike *Archie* comics, which represent a kind of timeless Asgard to White U.S. suburbia, the legacy of the Hernandez brothers is to stir up the parallel realms of realist literature with the presumption of innocence that underscores the serial comic. The tension is evident and deliberate. Their world is one that has stepped out of the timeless realm into time, but it is precisely having done this that allows the rhetoric of immortality to be retained, not as triumph, but as a nagging and often melancholy reminder of time passed and lost.

FIGURE 10.6 Gilbert Hernandez, "Hector," in *Ofelia: A Love and Rockets Book* (Seattle: Fantagraphics, 2015), 183.
Copyright © Gilbert Hernandez. Courtesy of Fantagraphics.

11

Tommi Parrish

• •

The "everyday" is a concept that is far more troubled than it seems. This is something that Lukács signaled in repeatedly pouring scorn on what he believed were degradations of realism in naturalism and socialist realism, which he would also call "photographic"[1] for the former and "illustrative"[2] for the latter. Both assumed for themselves their own pieties. Socialist realism is more explicit. It is easy to sniff out and discredit because of its liturgical adherence to ideology and party doctrine. "Photographic" naturalism was a little more deceptive given its ostensibly omnivorous and unjudgmental deployment of information. It represses the way information is ordered by consciousness through all kinds of processes, some traceable, some not. The "everyday" also comes to us through the writings of Henri Lefebvre and has since been simplified as a valorization of humble over momentous things. Unfortunately, many things get lost in such simplifications, especially in appreciating the level of judiciousness and skill required for the representation of the everyday, a truism that, since the shift in art from the sacred to the secular, artists of every generation fail to grasp. The fabric of perception let alone a realist work of art is through selection and exaggeration. The work of Tommi Parrish is dedicated to this approach; its everydayness is always intentioned and never succumbs to slavish literalness. Her drawing calls to mind Alois Riegl's concept of the haptic in the art of ancient Egypt and before, where the size of limbs of people was based on their role in the action or hierarchy. In this regard, Parrish's art is eminently transactional; it is embedded in human reactions and exchanges with one another or the objects and spaces around them.

Thus, Parrish makes use of "real" situations based on the everyday, but an everyday that is never made banal or righteous in its reluctance to deliver anything bigger. Her characters go to parties, have conversations, and eat meals together, and these occurrences are conveyed with conversational dialogue that is still closely observed. In an interview for the *Comics Journal*, Parrish describes her characters as "just people living their lives, trying to work it out, and [f-cking] it up sometimes, and not [f-cking] it up other times." It is a comment that is unremarkable for artists and writers devoted to the everyday, but then she follows with a remarkable statement: "They're the stories that I find really interesting because they make up everything."[3] Notwithstanding the ambiguity lost in the double use of the collective pronoun, Parrish's emphasis on invention is critical here in her own creative process but also in the assembly, performance, and representation of the everyday itself, not only for her as overseer and puppet master, but for the characters themselves.

As if to divert the reader from any simplistic understanding of realism, Parrish's drawings drive one compellingly to different conclusions, toward an emphasis on narration over description (to allude to Lukács's distinction). Perhaps of all the artist-writers examined in this book, Parrish veers most stridently away from cleverness and artistry. Her figures are stylized into large, cartoonish slabs, volumetrically rendered in gouache and watercolor, accentuating their smooth forms. Faces are blank, small, expressionless, uttering statements completely contravening their visual near anonymity or interchangeability. The primary visual cue toward expression—at least in the more normalized sense of contemporary cartooning, which is rooted in an index of rote faces—is conversational gesture, once again closely observed and directly linked with the dialogue. With these blank near ciphers comes a sense of dissociation, disconnected need, or even alienation, paradoxically delivering very human conversations about the dramas of urban life: anxiety, dating, sexuality, gender, relationships, and so forth. However, Parrish's deskilled technique—which has its origins in the German Expressionists such as Emile Nolde and Ludwig Kirchner of the early twentieth century—should not be construed as facile subjectivism (which was, incidentally, Lukács's complaint of both artistic and literary Expressionism). Rather, it is a technique that generates an informality for the reader. The economy of visual frills and the pared dialogue allow for a psychological

FIGURE 11.1 Tommi Parrish, "Sasha," *Now* 7 (2019): 11.
Courtesy of the artist.

space that is freed of grandiloquence to make the encounters of humble people relevant and penetrating, for the aesthetic aim is to maintain such encounters without the interference of condescension, remorse, pity, or unwanted concern.

The Alienation of the Everyday

Things just are as they are. Unlike many cartoonists who favor a conversational narrative and closely observed (and closely drawn) characters, Parrish's characters are often devoid of facial expressions and, even more strikingly at times, specific gender. Sometimes her characters are rendered with a small, spherical nub for a head, no face, hair, anything, as if a toy factory line had malfunctioned, forgetting to add those last parts. As Parrish comments, "It feels stressful deciding what—it feels stressful unnecessarily gendering a character."[4] And yet the characters teeter between being ciphers and individual beings with a specific history and experience. The many instances of blankness in facial expression (and gender) establish a different set of parameters between text and expression (facial or gestural) than we are used to, in a similar way as a silent film may be "read" by a contemporary viewer: dialogue and expression both exist, but the mechanics of their narrative are functionally different from what we are used to. In silent film, this resulted in the heightened importance of slapstick and other visual heavy lifting. In Parrish's work, this results in a closer sense of the dialogue's emotional heft and an anonymous universality to the characters.

If there are equivalents in literature, it may be some of Brecht's or Ionesco's characters, who exist as lever points to create a mood or make a statement but who scarcely exist in and for themselves. The same could be said of many of Beckett's characters, who are reduced to but owe their being to a set of basic functions, like Molloy's stone sucking or Watt's dizzyingly interminable running up and down the stairs. It is also the emphasis on these acts and the unadorned things that preoccupy them that render them faceless. Yet Parrish departs from modernist authors in her instinctual resistance to nihilism. There is a point to life for Parrish that lies in the people who are living it. This sounds like a banal statement, but it is fundamental to the notion of the everyday, in which the challenge is always to avoid lapsing into redundancy and irrelevance. In Parrish's work, this never occurs. Despite their strange anonymity and their gender agnosticism, Parrish's characters are never caricatures or ciphers because they are invested with internal life and are aware of the messiness of life and the consequences of their actions. Our intimacy with them is their absence of the heroic. The unnaturalistic bent of her methods of depiction does not, however, deprive them of functionality and engagement. The many elements of abstraction serve yet to underscore that they are very much of this world and at the mercy of it.

Furthermore, the interchangeability of Parrish's characters is also an important consideration in the context of autobiography. While there are many instances where the reader may surmise that elements of Parrish's narratives might be drawn from experience, there is no clear avatar for the cartoonist and therefore no clear vehicle for autobiography. At best, the reader can suppose certain elements as autobiographical, but unlike cartoonists who make use of loosely self-representational avatars, Parrish's avatars would seem to be situational, recounting moments or conversations rather than telling a story in the first person. Instead, the entire cast can at times be read as an analogue for the cartoonist, obscured by the blank anonymity of the actors in Parrish's drama. This both resists clear readings of Parrish's work as autobiographical and cements their effectiveness as confessional.

Parrish's slablike forms are usually of indeterminate gender, even when depicted with genitalia. This approach to the figure suggests Plasticine models, rendered in a three-dimensional space, perhaps a remnant of the cartoonist's interest in sculpture.[5] A compelling example of this fluidity is "Generic Love Story," a four-page comic collected in *Perfect Hair* (2016) that depicts two characters of indeterminate sex or gender embracing. Both have heads consisting only of a sphere with a single dot for an eye and, in some panels, a cylindrical, marionette-like nose. They are referred to as Figure 1 and Figure 2, and their movements are commentated with insights such as "Figure 2 is currently 'only a bit gay sometimes' which is confusing and a source of anxiety" and "Figure 1 is an artist of mounting acclaim. At 36 Figure 1 will say to their therapist that they have always used art to disassociate from life." This plastic approach to characters allows a universalist access to identity that is based on words and actions rather than the few (indexical) physical traits that are offered, making Parrish's works a kind of anticaricature.

As David Carrier notes, caricature relies on exaggeration and, like comics, deformation.[6] This is a noteworthy distinction in the context of Parrish's body of work, for the characters are so often devoid, or close to it, of distinguishing facial features beyond (perhaps) a hairstyle or a pair of spectacles, if indeed they are presented with faces. In this way, they are anticaricatures, characters whose substance is built from the background detail and very little of the subject's visual description, let alone exaggeration, as we

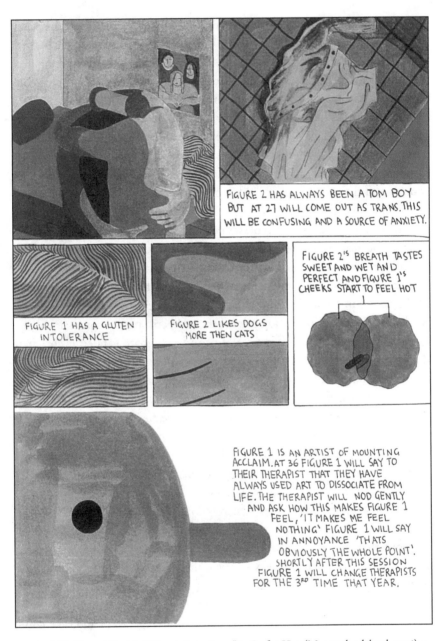

FIGURE 11.2 Tommi Parrish, "Generic Love Story," in *Perfect Hair* (Montreal: 2dcloud, 2016), 3. Courtesy of the artist.

have grown accustomed. Carrier cites Ernst Gombrich, who has discussed the subject at length in both *Art and Illusion* (1960) and *Meditations on a Hobby Horse* (1963) and notes that the tradition of caricature had its origins in the academy and the ruling class.[7] This aspect contrasts greatly with Parrish's more Marxist approach to comics as an accessible art form, just as it contrasts her nondescript plastic representation of the human figure and, particularly, the face. In an arresting concession, Carrier suggests that caricatures and comic characters "are never ideal enough to be beautiful."[8] Certainly this claim would have validity in the context of Parrish's work, if only because her characters are near identical in face and proportion, placing a greater emphasis on a character's words and actions than their appearance. Explicit indication of the character's beauty would be needed, such as dialogue supporting this idea or perhaps an act of generosity or demonstration of ideological heroism, to indicate beauty in a Parrish comic. This Plasticine ambiguity further established Parrish as a cartoonist whose approach is far more literary than filmic in execution.

Roland Barthes discusses the material of plastic, and applying its thrust to Parrish's approach to the human figure is revealing: "[Plastic's] constitution is negative: neither hard nor deep, it must content itself with a neutral substantial quality despite its utilitarian advantages: *resistance*, a state which signifies no more than the simple suspension of yielding."[9] Barthes describes plastic as both magical and domestic, "a spectacle to be deciphered."[10] Parrish's characters are nothing if not domestic, everyday participants and spectators in the urban lives they pass through, but magic is to be found, or at least hinted at, in their interactions. One such narrative, a short story called "I Was Just Trying to Be Alive" (2015), is a vignette centering on two of Parrish's ungendered slab people in a small apartment. One is pacing, anxious, and pronounces, "I don't like this anymore," reaching for words that cannot be articulated. Asked *what* they don't like, the character responds "Everything / anything / I don't know" before abruptly going outside. In terms of Parrish's approach to perspective, "outside" in this case is depicted as a flattened plane of cloudlike shrubs suggesting an enforced approximation of depth. The cartoonist's flattened perspectives emphasize the faceless or near faceless characters' solidly and physicality, rendered richly as they are in gouache and watercolor. This visual paradox of flatness and volume is not unlike that of the magical and the domestic.

FIGURE 11.3   Tommi Parrish, "I Was Just Trying to Be Alive," *Sissy Blvd* (2015): 2.
Courtesy of the artist.

Representations of the Real

Returning briefly to Cathy J. Cohen's calls for a more nuanced approach to queer political strategies that are based outside of an assimilationist framework, Parrish's comics quietly and articulately hew to the personal. Unlike Hanselmann's *Crisis Zone* in particular, which jibes with much of Cohen's specificity by virtue of its large, evolving, and largely gender-fluid cast, Parrish's is less easily deconstructed by this framework because of its comparatively intimate scale and general resistance to being overly specific in terms of its own gendering. While *Crisis Zone* could be seen as perhaps the first great artistic response to COVID-19, released in real time, Parrish has also been working on such a response. As one might expect, Parrish's work is one of considerable introspection, carefully staged and plotted, different from Hanselmann's response in form as well as content. What the two cartoonists do share is a loyalty to the grid, using it as a system of storytelling, very rarely deviating from its insistent divisions of linear time. Parrish lets scenes unravel over time, sometimes stretching out conversations for entire graphic novels. *The Lie and How We Told It* (2017) is a bravura demonstration of Parrish's mastery over narrative time. Beginning with a chance meeting in a supermarket of Cleary and Tim, two old friends decide to catch up in a park. Their conversation meanders from the lighthearted to the melancholic, punctuated by a forty-three-page interlude as Cleary reads a book and Tim buys wine. The conversation then resumes until the characters part ways after a more awkward (and inebriated) series of moments at a bar. The narrative of the interlude thus resumes for another sixteen pages while Cleary reads on the train home, ending with her finishing the book and leaving it on the train for somebody to find. Such a structure serves to anchor the narrative visually and to create a clear delineation between Cleary's interactions and the book she is reading.

Aside from the occasional establishing shot, *Lie* stays within the six-panel grid for the entire narrative, save the interludes, which have their own format (full-page, single-panel images facing full-page, single-panel text). This consistent grid layout establishes a kind of metronomic logic to the narrative. Each panel marks an increment of time, and with the everyday moments of Parrish's stories, this is a highly effective device—pauses, pregnant silences, and drags of a cigarette all play out in their own time—a radical and effective inversion to the usually condensed storytelling of comics. The book within a book (or more specifically comic within a comic) further exaggerates this manipulation of time. Rendered in an unadorned black-and-white line, a

marked departure from Parrish's usual gouache work and the broad varia-
tions of opacity the medium enables, the book also marks a rhythmic shift,
composed of single panels. It also features a repeated motif of a street scene
comprising seemingly identical rooftops receding into the distance, which
is used to bookend these two sequences. This device emphasizes the change
of perspective, but its function as such only becomes apparent upon repeti-
tion. Such a nuanced, elastic, and understatedly deliberate approach to time
aligns more comfortably to the novel or the play than to film, the rapid pace
of which seems to be increasingly imitated in contemporary mainstream
comics. Parrish's work is not of a piece with what has increasingly become
a formal, medium-oriented, and commercial collaboration between comics
and film. Instead, the works insist upon the irregularity of time in the individual made yet more irregular when compounded with multiple points
of view.

When attempting to represent the plurality of experience and consciousness, the causal-diachronic flow of representation inevitably falls short. To
characterize the difference in approach, Lukács ventures several binaries in
some of his best-known essays, such as "Narration or Description?" ("Erzählen
oder beschreiben?," 1936) and "Reportage or Portrayal?" ("Reportage oder
Gestaltung?," 1932). In the former, he lays out in considerable detail the two
approaches of rendering events according to a unified causal frame on one
hand and as an agglomeration of facts and circumstances on the other. In
one of the numerous onslaughts against literary naturalism—with Émile
Zola suffering the lion's share of blame—Lukács discusses the way that naturalism traduces the aims of realism with an overearnest and pseudoscientific
approach to representation that is overly literal. Through excessive description and an unnecessarily rigid acceptance of linear time, naturalism ends
in capturing the world in the most uncompelling and vapid way. Whereas
"narration organizes, description homogenizes [*das Erzählen gliedert, die
Beschriebung nivelliert*],"[11] "dehumanizing" human relations to material
ones.[12] On the other hand, the narratological approach is far more compositional, availing of multiple points of view, acknowledging that the writer's
worldview is one amid many: "For the deeper, the more differentiated, the
more fed by lived experience a worldview, the more diverse and varied its
compositional expression can become."[13] Translating such an observation to
Parrish's work, the frequently divergent and idiosyncratic worldviews of the
characters, seen discretely or imbricated one over the other, make for a scene
of representation in which personalities are in a tense and stimulating state of
continual negotiation: divergence and convergence.

FIGURE 11.4 Tommi Parrish, *The Lie and How We Told It* (Seattle: Fantagraphics, 2017), 14. Courtesy of the artist.

Thus, Parrish employs a similar narrative device to differentiate two con-current scenes in the eight-page *Untitled* (2018), making full use of the pos-sibilities of both the comic grid and the comic page as structural devices. Once again, the cartoonist sticks to a self-imposed grid structure consisting of an upper square grid, rendered in full color, depicting one scene, and a lower strip, executed in linear black and white. As both narratives—or more accurately, both narrative strands—progress, we realize that the upper fol-lows the past and the lower follows the present. Notably, this is a Parrish work in which the sex and gender of the characters are insinuated through visual indicators, such as the male character's stubble and baldness and the female character's braided hair and breasts. There is, of course, room for variation within these parameters, but in the context of Parrish's work, such details stand out. The upper grids depict the relationship as it was, and the lower strips depict the solitary male character detailing complicated feelings after the couple has parted ways. The narrative is entirely domestic, suggest-ing moments of emotional profundity of both despondence (frustration at a pedestal fan's inability to cool a bedroom) and ecstatic rapture (kissing naked in the rain) in equal measure, tempered by the context of everyday life.

Opacity and Trace

While readers are greeted with Parrish's immediately recognizable approach to figures and perspective and on a deeper level the cartoonist's varied strate-gies to representing the movement of time, some of the more subtle visual subtleties deserve attention. In particular, Parrish often deploys the use of varying states of opacity in painted work, which allows for evidence of visual groundwork, traces of the process of creation. This is a divergence from the norm in comics. Comics, as a medium whose final form is dependent upon mechanical reproduction, have been home to a certain division between original drawings and the finished product. This is largely predicated on the grounds of "finish"—that is, delivering original art (originally constitut-ing inked and lettered drawings on Bristol board) ready for the subsequent processes of coloring and printing. This has been open to variation in recent years with the advent of digital technologies, which allow the execution of any of these roles to be carried out without a physical component. In the case of comics published online only, this potential to create comics com-pletely virtually from beginning to end is a possibility, but typically there remains some connection to the physical, whether it be original drawings or, in the case of the numerous comics now drawn on tablets, the final, printed work. This digital slickness offers potential for speeding up the assembly-line creation process of mainstream comics considerably and so has been largely adopted. However, driven by such commercial considerations, digital rendering has shifted comics as a whole toward the Hollywood blockbuster aesthetic. Heavy-handed color grading; rounded, photoshopped figures; and a dubious presumption of "reality" have become hallmarks of the contemporary mainstream comic. However, the rupture in comics between finished and unfinished lies not in the digital but in reproduction.

From the beginning, original comic art made use of the limitations of print technology, or more specifically, a knowledge of which marks would and would not reproduce. Obviously, the intense black inks of the comics would translate legibly, as would dot screens and gray washes. Additional plates could be used for color, masterfully when budget and technology allowed (compare the Sunday pages of Alex Raymond's *Flash Gordon* and Hal Foster's *Prince Valiant* to the subsequent and comparatively crude pigmentation of early issues of *Superman* and *Captain America*), but white correction fluid and nonphoto blue pencil were always key tools in the cartoonist's arsenal. These tools allowed cartoonists the freedom to self-edit without beginning from scratch or risking an inferior product.

Unlike the early days of the medium, original comic pages and strips are today highly sought-after art objects, largely because of these traces of the creative process. While opaque white is often used as a method of cutting back into solid-black areas (see the work of Josh Bayer or Frank Miller's *Sin City* series for exemplary examples), it is most revealing when covering up mistakes or more often as an editing device. The opaque white of many original pages reveals personal preference more so than artistic shortcomings. For instance, opaque white may reveal a decision to reduce detail in a surface as ostentatious, superfluous, or distracting to the composition overall.[14] Its use signifies not a devaluing of the original piece either but rather lingering, tantalizing evidence of the artistic presence of the cartoonist. For example, surviving original pages reveal Will Eisner, who often inked his own material, as a profligate user of opaque white in the same way as they reveal Milton Caniff as frugal in its use.[15]

Certainly, such objects are subject to discourse over what constitutes finish, especially in light of a completely virtual assembly line that can lack a physical object completely. The attraction and collectability of the original comic page as a phenomenon would be well suited to analysis within a Benjaminian framework: "In even the most perfect reproduction, *one* thing is

FIGURE 11.5 Tommi Parrish, "Untitled," *Now* 4 (2018): 42.
Courtesy of the artist.

lacking: the here and now of the work of art—its unique existence in a particular place. It is this unique existence—and nothing else—that bears the mark of history to which the work has been subject. This history includes the changes in ownership. Traces of the former can only be chemical or physical analyses (which cannot be performed on a reproduction), while changes of ownership are part of a tradition which can be traced only from the stand-point of the original in its present location."[16] The changes of ownership Benjamin notes refer to the owners of the art objects themselves, but the fact that many comics are made by small teams of cartoonists, each with his or her own task, could be considered in this sense, particularly the penciller's and inker's "ownership" of each page. Parrish, who works alone writing, drawing, painting, and lettering, has no such split authorship, yet a trace of the cartoonist's hand is often in evidence. Watercolor and gouache, Parrish's primary media, are of course highly variable in their opacity and ideal for building layers and texture and allowing (when desired) underlying pencil or ink marks to show through. The greatest exponent of this technique is of course Henri Matisse, who in many of his ambitious finished works would ensure that the process of resolving the line was retained along with the "finished" line itself, with the effect of both undermining and emphasizing the impression of finish by emphasizing the struggle to do so. This could come in the form of several lines around the principal contour or a region of paint that was plainly different from other passages, suggesting a correction or revision. The similarity to these effects with motion blurs or regressive staccato line iterations beyond a form to suggest movement is no mistake at all, building in the viewer the feeling of the process of drawing and painting as embedded within the "final" work itself.

An often-overlooked aspect of comics in general is the lettering. Most often executed by a specialist distinct from the cartoonist (though there are, of course, exceptions, particularly in European comics), the speech bubbles, sound effects, and text panels can have a strong influence on the effectiveness of the overall medium. Comics as a hybrid art form operate on a complex visual axiom that, due to its use of multiple visual elements, relies heavily upon a formal and mechanical smoothness. Text panels and speech bubbles are used to guide the reader just as explicitly as image, and so the considered treatment of these conventions is vital. Parrish takes an approach that is as adaptable as the panels themselves, weaving around figures and suggesting the movement and rhythm of conversation with see-through speech bubbles, visual annotations that exist outside of the onomatopoeia of traditional comic sound effects. As Groensteen observes, "When comics are in color the balloons are most often presented as white. . . . The whiteness of the balloon, which is that of the paper, attests to its indifference to the illusionist conventions that govern the image."[17] Further, the balloon does not designate a natural cavity in the space that is depicted; it inscribes a zone of opacity within the "transparent plane" that we identify as the panel.[18] This is a highly nuanced distinction and a convention that Parrish often subverts. Frequently using text unanchored by speech balloons, thought bubbles, or text captions, which could be interpreted as inner monologues, Parrish often employs a stance of ambiguity as to the status of certain text, suggesting an interior or internalized aspect to characters and more generally to the narratives created.

There is nothing superficial about Parrish's works. They eschew a world easily rendered or described. Instead, her world is one of many individuals, not atomized but defined according to the ways in which they are trying to get things right and that such interaction is essential to a definition of society. In the words of Lukács, the accomplished realist "knows how thinking and feeling grow from social being, how experiences and sensations are parts of an overall complex of reality."[19] Parrish's work is very much a testimonial of the "complex": the real constituted through the "not quite right" and the "getting it right," as it were, and when things go well, it only does so for a finite period, which then necessitates a new call to action, which in her case is a new story, a new strip, more drawings.

FIGURE 11.6 Parrish, *Lie and How We Told It*, 78.
Courtesy of the artist.

12

Yoshihiro Tatsumi

• •

The work of Yoshihiro Tatsumi is frank and often harsh in its depiction of reality. Even lighter stories often contain undercurrents of despair, as if the lightness will end or is but brief consolation for a deeper foreboding. While early in his career Tatsumi embarked upon the kind of episodic genre fare pioneered by cartoonists such as Osamu Tezuka, his later work turned toward darker concerns in self-contained stories, which he called *gekiga*. Many artists, designers, and writers who identify as Japanese—from Kenzaburō Ōe to Rei Kawakubo—in some respects are inclined to resist the "post-Hiroshima" label, not as a matter of repressive disavowal but more because of the extraordinary strain such an event exerts on any artist's work, threatening to overshadow any other aspects. Yet with this grim but inescapable cultural inheritance in mind, Tatsumi cannot escape the label. The drained, almost dissociative lack of drama and the shying away from histrionics are endemic to a condition that has been reduced, personally and as a group, to degree zero. The dialogue is always sparing, and although there is evident autobiographical content, it is usually displaced through pseudonyms and avatars. One consistent aspect is the encounter between beings shorn of transcendence. In one short story, "Sewer" (1969), a sanitation worker brings the aborted fetus of his lover wrapped in a cloth to work to abandon it in the muck. It is later discovered by his coworker, unwrapped and once again abandoned to the muck. "That's a shame, no gold or silver on this one," he says. This is by far the bleakest of Tatsumi's works but speaks to how uncompromising, how implacably brutal, his work often is.

For most reading this book, and for the present writers as well, it is difficult if impossible to try to begin to understand the atmosphere of devastation, confusion, mixed feelings, and guilt inherited by the devastation of Japan after World War II. In his introduction to his translation of Saiichi Maruya's *Grass for My Pillow* (*Sasamakura*, 1966), Dennis Keene draws attention to the considerable lag in consideration given to the experiences of the war, with only some voices beginning to emerge a decade or more later, as testified by Maruya's novel about the tribulations of a man, Shokichi Hamada, who had been an active draft dodger during the war. As Keene explains, under the Meiji constitution, conscientious objection had no space for activity as it had in the West, carrying far more than opprobrium, and was considered a serious offense.[1] Hamada, an active outsider, is therefore a symbol of Japan's alienation from the world both before the Meiji Restoration and after the war, beset by doubt and with a past he is compelled to hide. In the mid-1960s, when the novel is set, Japan was still a very divided country with a brittle sense of itself. Despite the economic miracle of the 1960s, as it was called, Keene remarks, "it was still common for them to refer to Japan as only a poor country, and this was not a piece of assumed social modesty but felt to be a statement of fact. The great effort of hosting the Olympic Games of 1964, with all the upheaval they caused in Tokyo, was presented abroad as a joyful awareness of the country's reacceptance into the family of nations, whereas most people in Japan saw it as an example of overreaching, of putting a bold façade upon something not all that impressive in itself."[2] In short, many Japanese of the postwar years, with the country's heady changes, found themselves occupying multiple psychological and social positions wrought by the contradiction between the grisly past and the rebuilt present, traumatic memory and optimistic projections into the future. Many for whom memories were still fresh found themselves having a quizzical attitude and to be in the bitter situation of being observers of their own lives, having been compelled by circumstances well beyond their control to adopt a detached attitude to their existence, if only for self-protection.

Perhaps the most read detached observer of life is Albert Camus's Meursault in *L'Étranger* (*The Outsider*, 1947), with whom Tatsumi's often nameless avatar shares the demeanor of the disillusioned—but perhaps more appositely, it is the protagonist in Imre Kertész's first and best-known book, *Fateless* (*Sorstalanság*, 1975). (Camus had a considerable influence on Japanese postwar fiction; Kertész would come later and is still hard to find in Japanese translation.) Writing about himself but in the third person, *Fateless* tells of Kertész's experience as a youth in the Nazi death camp of Auschwitz, which he survived because he was interned there toward the end of the war. When it was published, and still to this day, the novel drew quizzical and sometimes unsympathetic responses from its audience, particularly Jewish readers. The principal objection was that the narrative was too pared down, too matter-of-fact, which had a normalizing effect in its depiction of the horrors of the Holocaust. Most controversial of all is the ending, where the protagonist, having escaped, finds himself back in Budapest at the same time when the city is being liberated from Nazi control. He is met by a stranger who expresses his jubilation, a response that is not shared and perhaps cannot be shared. Instead, he responds with a gnawing feeling of remorse for what he had left behind, as if that had been the only source of his survival. The subtlety and realism of this conclusion were lost on many readers who believed it to be a betrayal and a trivialization. Yet it was precisely his identification with the situation set before him and his embracing of it that allowed him to cope, a disassociation that was effectively a sublimation on a grand scale. It is a realization that is as brutal as it is startling in its honesty and astonishing because it falls outside of responses expected by those not forced to undergo such dehumanizing experiences. Not for nothing that Kertész decried Spielberg's *Schindler's List* (1993) as kitsch, a distinctly Hollywood Holocaust. Kertész would not have had the same response to Tatsumi's work, which is framed by the unerring awareness of what we can and have done to ourselves and that humanity is stalked by inhumanity. To authors such as Kertész or Tatsumi, such a realization is not pessimism per se but rather reflects a need to see the world in the starkest terms. Tatsumi's work is therefore directly or indirectly an analysis of the postwar condition in Japan, which experienced huge social, cultural, political, and economic shifts. Where Tatsumi's mentor and contemporary Osamu Tezuka's work is often considered a commentary on the broader historical strokes of these shifts—a renewed national sense of purpose and identity, a shift toward technological innovation (*Tetsuwan-Atomu*, or Astro Boy, as he is known in the West, being the most obvious corollary)—Tatsumi's work is indicative of the tarnished side of this shining coin.

While contemporary scholarship upon the work of Tatsumi may at first appear belated—the cartoonist died in 2015, and much of his oeuvre was

FIGURE 12.1 Yoshihiro Tatsumi, "Black Smoke," in *The Push Man and Other Stories* (Montreal: Drawn & Quarterly, 2012), 38.
Copyright © Yoshihiro Tatsumi. Used with Permission of Drawn & Quarterly.

created in the 1950s, 1960s, and 1970s—his reputation in the West as an innovator and forerunner of the preponderance of autobiographical comics we have today has solidified in recent years in tandem with the increase in Western popularity and scholarship of manga and the translation of several key works. Key among these is *A Drifting Life* (2008), a monumental 834-page graphic novel that documents the cartoonist's youth in postwar Japan. Eleven years in the making, *A Drifting Life* is a late entry in Tatsumi's canon, applying his narrative instincts to a much broader canvas than the short stories he is otherwise known for. Where Tatsumi's contemporaries have acquired a quaint sense of cultural nostalgia in their ubiquity (Tezuka in particular), Tatsumi's currency has only grown and bears further study in a contemporary context.

Gekiga and Postwar Tokyo

Gekiga (meaning "dramatic pictures"), which Tatsumi, among several other cartoonists, innovated, was a more cinematic and adult-oriented form of manga that emerged in the postwar era. Like their French and American counterparts, this generation of *mangaka* took cues from the increasingly sophisticated visual language of film, a medium that enjoyed an incalculably large artistic, commercial, and critical resurgence in 1950s Japan. With its darker aesthetic, *gekiga* reflected the grim realities of Japan's postwar recession. Tatsumi's work in particular can be read as a testamentary portrait of postwar Tokyo in the same way that much of Dickens's oeuvre could be considered a portrait of Victorian London or Dostoevsky's work of nineteenth-century Russia. Within the work of these authors, place and its sociopolitical context form an inextricable reality that the protagonist must struggle against. Both present cities as complete worlds, vast and rapidly changing constructs that characters can only traverse and never escape. This is Tatsumi's postwar Tokyo, a heaving and monstrous dystopia built on human misery. Like many in the work of Dickens, Tatsumi's characters are everymen, distinguished not by their morals, heroism, or nobility but rather by their capacity to endure life's hardships. While, in terms of serialization, the two could not be more different (Dickens with his episodic cliff-hangers, Tatsumi preferring to end stories with a detached, existential whimper), their cities are inextricable from their narratives. (Incidentally, such inextricability is what Lukács sees as an essential aspect of realism as opposed to naturalism, in which the protagonists are reduced to deracinated actors against a backdrop from which they are inexorably separate or indeed dispensable.) Tokyo is as much a character in Tatsumi's *gekiga* as London is in Dickens's novels and short stories, as much a state of being as a place to suffer through, a context broadening the extremities of the modern human experience: "Suffering comes from three quarters: from our own body, which is destined to decay and dissolution, and cannot even dispense with anxiety and pain as danger-signals; from the outer world, which can rage against us with the most powerful and pitiful forces of destruction; and finally from our relations with other men."[3]

Raskolnikov of *Crime and Punishment* (1866) is perhaps Dostoevsky's most notorious and memorable protagonist (among a list of memorables), presented with a full and complex gamut of human emotions, including positive and negative traits, all of which are raked over in the character's lengthy internal monologues. However, and this is crucial in consideration of Tatsumi's work, Raskolnikov is not entirely presented as an everyman—far from it. He is a highly complex and conflicted being torn between many different standpoints. Like Dostoevsky, the character is educated and blessed (or cursed) with a very definite societal perception, setting Raskolnikov apart from the social context in which he finds himself. Raskolnikov's passion and willingness to subvert the status quo contrasts with many of Tatsumi's characters, who often possess no visible talents or particular intelligence. Rather than railing against the world within which they find themselves trapped (à la Raskolnikov), Tatsumi's everymen meander from one situation to the next, accepting their lot with a calm detachment.[4] They work, often in the face of intolerable cruelty or social horrors; spend their downtime in unsatisfying domestic situations; and repeat, usually with no recourse. Even the most radical of Tatsumi's everymen can only deviate by way of inaction. Kin-San, the protagonist of "Black Smoke" (1969), a furnace worker, endures a repetitive and thankless job, cuckolded by his taunting, drunken wife in silence. After a car accident, he is informed that he will no longer be able to father children, which is counterbalanced by one of his grimmer menial tasks—collecting small bundles from a nearby abortion clinic to be shoveled into the furnace. On the final page of the short story, his wife falls asleep while doing the ironing in front of the television. Kin-San leaves his wife and the smoking iron, finds a view of the city, and watches the smoke billow into the sky. Such pages speak to Tatsumi's narrative economy and the nihilistic poetry of his version of Tokyo.

Unlike Raskolnikov, a student manqué who exhibits an albeit scattered intellectual curiosity, the characters of Hans Fallada's *Jeder stirbt für sich allein* (*Alone in Berlin*, 1947) are, like those of Tatsumi's *gekiga*, largely plain, working-class people of modest aspiration and relatively narrow outlook. Fallada's protagonists, Otto and Anna Quangel, find their means of resistance to the repressive Nazi government through the act of writing postcards attacking the government and surreptitiously leaving them around the city. Populated with a diverse cast that includes petty criminals, an estranged postmistress, a family of Nazi sympathizers, a retired judge, an elderly Jewess, and the detective searching for whoever is behind the dissident messages, Fallada's Berlin is sketched in a series of ostensibly unrelated vignettes. (It is tempting to digress into a discussion of Georges Perec's cryptically episodic *Life: A User's Manual* [*Vie: La mode d'emploi*, 1978] here, but that would veer us too off-course.) Connections between characters are slowly revealed throughout the course of the braided narrative until the Quangels are finally arrested and put to death. In another parallel with Tatsumi, the protagonists are potentially the simplest characters of the entire narrative. Powerless and heartbroken at the loss of their children, they seek action through the only conceivable avenue, the modest postcard. Where the personalities of the more devious characters (the scheming Borkhausen and the licentious, groveling Kluge) are sketched in lascivious detail, the Quangels are far less malleable, constructed as hardworking, upstanding citizens. Like Tatsumi's protagonists, the Quangels do not have the luxury of the eccentricities of personality beyond those afforded to them through work—in Otto's case, in a factory. While the novel is based on the true story of Otto and Elise Hampel,[5] Fallada also incorporated some autobiographical elements, which extend beyond the author's profound sense of alienation into his tendency toward heavy drinking (striking because this is attributed to the reprobate, Kluge, who is portrayed as a stooge rather than a villain) and an episode of attempted repossession of the author's house at the hands of a Nazi sympathizer.[6] Dispossession is a recurring theme of the novel and is a fear that haunts several of its characters.

Fallada's paranoid, inhuman Berlin is in many ways a literary cousin of Dickens's oeuvre, built around a literary London that was in turns dirty, crushing, hopeful, and melancholic but always a winding, labyrinthine stage for the examination of humanity. Dickens's relationship with London has been examined at length in an effort to understand the man, the city, and his work. Walter Benjamin, writing in comparison to authors of Paris (including himself), noted that the author *needed* London.[7] However, Dickensian London was not unlike postwar Tokyo in its heaving expansion, widespread

FIGURE 12.2 Tatsumi, "Black Smoke," 40.
Copyright © Yoshihiro Tatsumi. Used with Permission of Drawn & Quarterly.

poverty, and embrace of technology as a catalyzing agent of unprecedented change. Jeremy Tambling, who wrote extensively about Dickens's relationship with London in his erudite *Going Astray: Dickens and London* (2009), characterizes the city as the author's "obsession."[8] Breaking the author's oeuvre down into thematic chapters framed by different literary approaches to the city is a sharp way of digesting an intimidating life's work and underscores London's pivotal role in Dickens's work. Just as Dickens's vision of London can now act as a time capsule for the city over the author's lifetime, so too does Tatsumi's vision of postwar Tokyo. Where Dickens's descriptive passages of the people and places of London have their beginnings in his career as a journalist, Tatsumi's depictions of Tokyo are remarkably concrete in their melancholic clarity, capturing the decay and grime of a city yet to reinvent itself.

In his introduction to an interview with Tatsumi, publisher and comic scholar Gary Groth makes some critical remarks that are revealing in their incisive particularity: "I was troubled by a number of tics that comprised the backbone of Tatsumi's aesthetic: the narrowness, aridity and sameness of the vision; the dramatic implausibility and jerry-rigged mechanics of many of the stories; characters who are either stereotypes or ciphers (albeit powerful ciphers); and a tendency toward heavy-handed, literal-minded metaphors (the rat in 'My Hitler,' the piranhas in 'Piranha')."[9] These "tics," as Groth characterizes them, are notable in that they form the foundation for the cartoonist's distinctive visual and literary approaches and account for much of the power and universality of the stories. Although Groth partially acknowledges the postwar context of the cartoonist's darker works ("clearly a sincere expression of Tatsumi's convictions, and his artistic choices, whatever my reservations, took courage and tenacity"[10]), it seems that such a context is not to be considered axiomatic in such works. This is a surprising admission from Groth, who has interviewed many of the great cartoonists at length as editor in chief of the *Comics Journal*, which has been publishing new issues, through the prestigious Fantagraphics, for many years. Couching the interview as he does with several caveats—he had looked through but not read Tatsumi's work, commenting, "I usually only interview artists whose work I like, and I didn't feel entirely comfortable interviewing Tatsumi," and then noting the artist's "surprising" sense of humor[11]—Groth gives the impression of somewhere between confusion and distaste, despite discussing the background of some of the more disturbing themes before embarking on what reads as a perfectly amicable interview.

FIGURE 12.3 Yoshihiro Tatsumi, "Beloved Monkey," in *Abandon the Old in Tokyo* (Montreal: Drawn & Quarterly, 2012), 104.
Copyright © Yoshihiro Tatsumi. Used with Permission of Drawn & Quarterly.

TATSUMI: I lived only about 10 minutes away from Itami Airport. The airport was a target, so my house actually had a couple of bullet holes going through the walls. One of the things that was most unforgettable was the scent of the rotting corpses on the streets. That they would be left there for days on end, and to this day, I can't forget that, the smell of rotting flesh.

GROTH: I assume that that was a pretty deeply etched part of that experience. Did that affect your later aesthetic sensibility?

TATSUMI: Well, what really was ingrained in my mind was the juxtaposition between ugliness and beauty, wealth and poverty, and this idea of the outside and inside and the discrepancy between the two. And so even when Japan started to enjoy economic growth—

GROTH: —Prosperity?

TATSUMI: —prosperity, I was still unable to shake the feeling that this was only a façade and right beneath the surface was all this kind of ugliness still.

GROTH: Do you think that that is empirically true, or merely your perception? Have you investigated this?

TATSUMI: It was true to my own experience, and for me, I started really writing comics in my 20s, and I've always targeted my work to readers of my own generation. So, for my intended readers, I think that this was a certain kind of truth, but perhaps for younger generations of readers, they may have felt some discomfort or alienation from this kind of depiction.[12]

Perhaps this exchange speaks to the differences in perspective between the prosperous years of postwar United States (Groth was born in 1954) and the comparatively difficult years (in both economic and psychic terms) of postwar Japan. Tatsumi was nineteen years older than Groth; World War II ended when he was ten, and it became a recurring narrative backbone for many of the cartoonist's stories.[13] This aligns with Mark Williams's view that "the neglect of artistic works by historians, political scientists, economists, journalists, etc. may help explain (though only partly) why so many constitutive elements of the Asia-Pacific War . . . remain controversial."[14] Notably, the interview took place in the context of the three existing English translations of Tatsumi's *gekiga* being published rather than his autobiographical *A Drifting Life*, a dense but far less aggressively critical and disturbing affair. As Williams explores, the trauma of the postwar experience is particularly present in the literature of Japan.[15] To separate this context from a body of work as singular as that of Tatsumi would seem to be erroneous.

Tatsumi and Autobiography

While contemporary analysis of Tatsumi's work may appear out of place beside other selected case studies, consideration must be given to its growing influence. Tatsumi's work has until recently been obscure in the West next to household names such as Katsuhiro Otomo, Masamune Shirow, and Akira Toriyama and has only recently been translated—and thus "discovered"—by American and European audiences. In many respects, Western comics have now caught up to the autobiographical strategies and narrative economy of Tatsumi's postwar canon, which remains startlingly fresh. Indeed, over the intervening years, few cartoonists (East or West) have attempted to convey such a sober and cynical perspective in their media. As Charles Hatfield puts it, such deliberate approaches to one's own context can be manipulated by the "fundamental tension between the verbal and visual codes. This tension enables the graphic enactment, on the picture plane, of the critical estrangement or distancing between the autobiographer and his/her 'past self' as depicted in the work."[16] However, standing well outside of Tatsumi's genre or *gekiga* fare is *A Drifting Life*, a narrative much more closely based on Tatsumi's life rather than his *gekiga*, which draws more from his postwar context. The usual observational stance of Tatsumi's avatars is not unlike the author's own nature, as his double (here called Hiroshi Katsumi) could easily be several of those found in short stories, to say nothing of their visual similarities (strangely, the other seemingly recurring avatar resembles the old man Tatsumi would eventually become). He experiences surges of energy and optimism, but these are mostly confined to the act of cartooning, something not to be seen in Tatsumi's short stories. Otherwise, Tatsumi's avatar does indeed lead a meandering existence, observing as much as participating. A drifting life, indeed.

As previously mentioned, Camus's character Meursault from *The Outsider* is a comparable literary analogue for many protagonists of Tatsumi's *Gekiga*. However, in the instance of *A Drifting Life*, Camus's *Le Premier Homme* (*The First Man*), incomplete at the time of Camus's 1960 death but posthumously published in its incomplete form in 1994, is a far more suitable comparison as a largely autobiographical—yet partly fictionalized—account of the author's life. Like Tatsumi's (anagrammatical) *Drifting Life* avatar, *The First Man* features an avatar for the author, Jacques Cormery; however, it is the sweep of history that defines both characters, a quality both Tatsumi's and Camus's characters tend to possess. Where the adult Meursault wandered passively, refusing to engage

FIGURE 12.4 Yoshihiro Tatsumi, *A Drifting Life* (Montreal: Drawn & Quarterly, 2008), 366.
Copyright © Yoshihiro Tatsumi. Used with Permission of Drawn & Quarterly.

even after he took a life, the youthful Cormery is portrayed as passionate and adventurous—quite unlike Meursault in this way—but undercut with a sense of melancholy, springing from the character's impoverished yet happy childhood[17] and the absence of the dead father he cannot remember, growing up into a figure closer in temperament to the author himself. Even Camus's notes, which are included as footnotes to help flesh out the narrative in its unfinished form, reveal the character's sense of alienation.[18] *The First Man*, like much of Tatsumi's work, is set in relief to the aftermath of war, though in the case of Camus, this is embodied not in the moral decay of Tatsumi's Tokyo but as a profound personal *lack* in many of the characters, created by the void left by departed loved ones in the wake of World War I. Cormery's visit as an adult to the grave of his father frames the subsequent passages outlining his youth with this familial absence while simultaneously building the world of his childhood: "Then he read the two dates, '1845–1914,' and automatically did the arithmetic: twenty-nine years. Suddenly he was struck by an idea that shook his very body. He was forty years old. The man buried under that slab, who had been his father, was younger than he. . . . He looked at the other inscriptions in that section and realized from the dates that this soil was strewn with children who had been the fathers of greying men who thought they were living in the present time."[19]

Tatsumi's *gekiga* is largely devoid of familial units, depicting solitary workers toiling in obscurity in an uncaring city. When a family does appear, it is usually in grotesque parody, as in Kenichi Nakamura's elderly, incontinent mother in *Abandon the Old in Tokyo* or the chiding wife and girlfriends who appear in several narratives. In these stories, the family is more often than not a burden, reiterating the emphatic role of the worker in postwar Tokyo, as is Nakamura's mother, who is a living, though ailing, example of the cost of a lifetime of hard work and perhaps of what is to come. However, family is depicted in a far more positive light in *A Drifting Life*. The Tatsumi avatar, Hiroshi, has encouraging parents despite their own problems and hardships. Hiroshi's brother Okimasa is perhaps his most challenging family member, in turns jealous and generous, a complicated and angry figure who suffers from pleurisy and is confined to bed for much of the narrative. Okimasa's lot improves, and he eventually joins Hiroshi in his burgeoning career as a *mangaka*.

Roman Rosenbaum characterizes *gekiga* cartoonists such as Tatsumi and Shirato Sanpei as instrumental in the broader "precarious proletariat" ("precariat") movement in postwar Japan.[20] While much of Tatsumi's oeuvre fits within Rosenbaum's analysis of the massive sociopolitical changes

FIGURE 12.5 Tatsumi, *A Drifting Life*, 224.
Copyright © Yoshihiro Tatsumi. Used with Permission of Drawn & Quarterly.

in Tatsumi's lifetime, it would be a mistake to limit the cartoonist's entire body of work within this context. Many of Tatsumi's *gekiga* characters are deeply flawed, which may begin to account for the decades-long gap between Japanese- and English-language publications of his work.[21] Tatsumi's "The Washer," "Beloved Monkey," "Unpaid," and "The Hole," all collected within *Abandon the Old in Tokyo*, rate among the cartoonist's darkest and most elliptical work. While these stories certainly explore the Marxist concerns outlined by Rosenbaum, Tatsumi's character studies veer into profoundly unnerving images and territory, including voyeurism and a fetish for cleanliness, self-amputation and pack mentality, bestiality and deformity, and imprisonment. Perhaps Tatsumi's own typically concise self-characterization in relation to his work is the most telling: "I myself am a very normal person. Please do not interpret these stories as representative of the author's personality."[22] Questioned by Tomine in regard to the many characters appearing throughout the cartoonist's work, Tatsumi's response is in turns circumspect and tongue in cheek: "The character that looks identical throughout my work is, of course, different in each story, but he essentially represents my view. You could say I projected my anger about the discrimination and inequality rampant in our society through him. Do you see why my protagonists couldn't possibly be handsome?"[23] Anger seems to be at the root of much of Tatsumi's most notable work. *A Drifting Life* concludes in 1960 with Hiroshi attending a seven-thousand-strong student demonstration after the death of student Michiko Kanba at the hands of riot police. This, alongside the New Treaty of Mutual Cooperation and Security between Japan and the United States, signed the same year, symbolically marked the end of the postwar period in Japan and neatly bookends the massive work, as the first page depicted the 1945 surrender, marking the end of World War II. Reinvigorated by the demonstration, Hiroshi is moved to tears, realizing the forgotten element of *gekiga*, anger, and vowing, "I'll never be done with gekiga!"[24] The epilogue brings the narrative back to the personal, the 1995 seven-year memorial ceremony of Osamu Tezuka's death. While Tezuka had not been mentioned in the narrative for some time, the scene depicts Tatsumi's avatar leaving the service and lamenting the death of his mentor and the loneliness of the world he left.[25]

This is a fascinating coda to what is a retelling of Tatsumi's life story. Rather than summarize an artistic mission statement or conclude with a poetic moment, the graphic novel ends as so much of Tatsumi's work ended: with a narrative ellipsis, once again contextualized in the shadow of Tezuka,

FIGURE 12.6 Yoshihiro Tatsumi, "The Washer," in *Abandon the Old in Tokyo*, 73.
Copyright © Yoshihiro Tatsumi. Used with Permission of Drawn & Quarterly.

once again ending with dissonance. This may seem to reflect a rather grim worldview. However, it is useful to remember that in lives disturbed by cataclysm and perennial disappointment, it is a far better consolation to be offered a frank summation of the circumstances rather than be offered spurious optimism whose aftereffects will only be a perpetuation of the events that prompted such false escapism in the first place.

Conclusion

• •

Our New Urizens

In his commentary on William Blake in his documentary on the romantics, Simon Schama comments that the poet-painter was the inventor of the first superheroes, singling out his Urizen, the embodiment and upholder of reason and law. It is an observation that is meant to be more than just tactical bathos for a lay audience; it lies in how Blake devised characters independent of both classical and biblical precedents. Moreover, Blake was both an artist and a writer, with text and image always closely imbricated, to the extent that one can scarcely be separated from the other when considering his work and contribution. And his contribution was indeed immeasurable, his standing being preeminent in British art and letters, for many on par with Shakespeare and Milton. As such, although he died in relative obscurity, there is no want of literature on Blake's importance nor the complex and rich interplay between text and image. It remains only to say that the work for which he is best known is largely that on paper, more graphic than painterly. Was Blake the inventor of the first superheroes? Perhaps, but it does not matter. What matters more are the many family resemblances with comics and graphic novels, thereby describing a lineage far deeper and older than that of the decades after World War I. There are many comics and graphic novels that deserve—no, need—to be treated with the seriousness of so-called proper literature. While such a consideration twenty years ago may have been considered heinous, it is now arguably exigent.

Using the philosophical and critical framework of Lukács's extensive literary theory to help advance this claim is something of an audacious conceit; however, hopefully, it appears to have had some justification, for as we have seen, Lukács's conception of realism was far from one of slavish mimetic replication but rather based on a nuanced acknowledgment of the individual's relationship to the collective in forms that grasped that for art to succeed, to be more than just a bad copy, it must enact a transformation of selection and concentration. It was only through such a process that the work of art could circle back to have any purchase on the world whence it came, where it would be viewed, read, and judged. Although Lukács was not unique in the view that people turn to art for more than consolation, at his best (when not fighting strawmen enemies ranging from the expressionists to the existentialists), he was a fierce and tireless defender of the capacity of art to cut through the forces of rationalization and objectification—that is, reification—on which capitalism depends. To ask what Lukács would have thought of the artist-writers we have examined here leads nowhere, but suffice to say that comics and graphic novels are a product of capitalism, just as the Lukács acknowledged the novel was around the eighteenth and nineteenth centuries. A bourgeois medium that explored the vicissitudes and fault lines of the bourgeois condition in the interminable conflicts between self and society, the realist novel had the potential, Lukács believed, to be a formidable way of bringing the reasons for these conflicts, especially those according to socioeconomic material conditions, into sharper relief.

Graphic novels, too, have that potential, whether they are grounded in everyday lives or they take recourse to the fantastical and "fairy tale–esque," as we have attempted to characterize it. True, there is always an escapist element to the garden-variety comic (although we would be loath to want to define what that actually is), but the shallow escapism quickly wears thin. It would be naïve and short-sighted—also patronizing—to relegate graphic literature to light entertainment. We have already pointed out that many critics of the early nineteenth century, when the novel was on the cusp of its full blooming, said the same, and to their peril. It is not for nothing that Batman continues to be one of the most popular superheroes: this is because he has some elements of plausibility in being human. He is also not all virtuous but is driven and constrained by his own anger and emotional limitations. The Joker is in many ways his Janus double, the Mr. Hyde to his Dr. Jekyll. Both are embodiments of what Lukács in his early critical work explored in terms of the demonic. Batman as a metonym of the mainstream genre that dates to the origins of commercial comics is also a figure that lurks in the background, if ever so remotely, of not only the dark and violent graphic literature (of the *Sin City* genre) but, indeed, the more mundane work that deals with the human struggle for heroism marred by the civil war within.

It may still be uncomfortable for graphic novels to be inserted into academic curricula but less so for reasons that may have been used "in the old days," when high art was far more easily separable from low. It may be because there is still a dearth of material that offers a methodology for evaluative critical practice. With this book, we hope to join the growing critical literature that has set about to address this.

Acknowledgments

Adam Geczy would like to thank the University of Sydney.

Jonathan would like to thank the Rockhampton Museum of Art and the Rockhampton Regional Council for their support of this project.

The authors are grateful to those that have created the many works cited and discussed within this book, especially to the cartoonists who generously allowed us to reproduce their wonderful work, including Josh Bayer, Gabrielle Bell, Nina Bunjevac, Eddie Campbell, Simon Hanselmann, Gilbert Hernandez, Jaime Hernandez, Shaky Kane, Erik Larsen, Tommy Parrish, Jeff Test, and Lale Westvind. Thank you also to Dona Corben for allowing us to reproduce her late husband's extraordinary work and to Drawn & Quarterly for allowing us to reproduce that of Yoshihiro Tatsumi. Thanks also to David Carrier, Ed Luce, Christopher Sperandio, and Stanley Wany for their spirited and valued correspondence around this wonderful art form.

Notes

Introduction

1   Adam Geczy and Vicki Karaminas, *Gaga Aesthetics: Art, Fashion, and the Up-Ending of Tradition* (London: Bloomsbury, 2021); David Carrier and Joachim Pissarro, *Aesthetics of the Margins / The Margins of Aesthetics: Wild Art Explained* (Pennsylvania: Penn State University Press, 2019).
2   See Geczy's introduction to Adam Geczy and Jacqueline Millner, *Fashionable Art* (London: Bloomsbury, 2015).
3   Adam Geczy and Vicki Karaminas, *Critical Fashion Practice: From Westwood to Van Beirendonck* (London: Bloomsbury, 2017).
4   Carrier and Pissarro, *Aesthetics of the Margins*, 7.
5   Carrier and Pissarro, 167–179.
6   Carrier and Pissarro, 188.
7   Terry Eagleton, *Literary Theory: An Introduction* (1983; repr., Minneapolis: University of Minnesota Press, 1996), 22.
8   In his influential but controversial work *The Great Tradition* (1948), Leavis traced a genealogy through Jane Austen, George Eliot, Henry James, and Joseph Conrad. Dickens, Sterne, and Hardy were conspicuously omitted. While Leavis would later revise his position on Dickens, whom he previously dismissed as an "entertainer," he stayed firm about Hardy, which may have cast his own theory and authority into discredit. Leavis would also fall out with Eliot, but what left a lasting mark on the literary establishment—inciting both detractors and defenders—was the apostolic zeal of his standards.
9   Eagleton, *Literary Theory*, 28.
10 Eagleton, 28.
11 Eagleton, 28.
12 Lukács's *The Historical Novel* and *Studies in European Realism* are, however, cited in his bibliography under "Marxism." Eagleton, 223.
13 Theodor Adorno, "Reconciliation under Duress," in *Aesthetics and Politics*, trans. and ed. Ronald Taylor (1977; repr., London: Verso, 1995), 151.

14 Georg Lukács, "Erzählen oder beschreiben?," in *Essays über Realismus, Werke* (Berlin: Hermann Lichterhand, 1971), 4:210; all translations are my own unless specified.

15 Thierry Groensteen, *The System of Comics*, trans. Bart Beaty and Nick Nguyen (Jackson: University Press of Mississippi, 1999), 12–13.

16 David Carrier, *The Aesthetics of Comics* (Pennsylvania: Penn State University Press, 2000), 68.

17 Carrier, 71.

18 Bradford W. Wright, *Comic Book Nation: The Transformation of Youth Culture in America* (London: Johns Hopkins University Press, 2001), 95.

19 Robert Crumb, Noah Van Sciver, Chris Ware, and Daniel Clowes, some of the most influential American cartoonists of the last half century, have written and drawn dozens of screeds about their perceived marginalization at the hand of the art world; some are more successful than others.

Chapter 1   Literary Theory

1 Bernard Williams, *Marxism and Literature* (New York: Oxford University Press, 1977), 47.

2 Williams, 48.

3 Williams, 51.

4 Lukács, "Schriftsteller und Kritiker," *Werke*, 4:402.

5 Scott McCloud, *Understanding Comics: The Invisible Art* (New York: William Morrow, 1994), 9.

6 John Holbo, "Redefining Comics," in *The Art of Comics: A Philosophical Approach*, ed. Aaron Meskin and Roy Cook (Sussex: Wiley Blackwell, 2014), 4.

7 Holbo, 5.

8 Holbo, 6.

9 Holbo, 15; emphasis in the original.

10 Holbo, 21.

11 Holbo, 25.

12 Lukács, *Die Gegenwartsbedeutung des kristischen Realismus, Werke*, 4:510.

13 Lukács, "Vorwort," in *Balzac und der französische Realismus, Werke*, 6:437.

14 Lukács, 435.

15 Lukács, "Tolstoi und die westliche Literatur," *Werke*, 5:275.

16 Lukács, "Maxim Gorki: Der Befreier," *Werke*, 5:292.

17 Fredric Jameson, "The Case for Georg Lukács," *Salmagundi*, no. 13 (Summer 1970): 3.

18 Jameson, 4.

19 Lukács, "Friedrich Engels als Literaturtheoretiker und Literaturkritiker," *Werke*, 10:506.

20 Friedrich Engels, quoted in Lukács, 531.

21 Lukács, 529.

22 Lukács, 531.

23 John Golding, *Cubism: A History and an Analysis 1907–1914* (1959; repr., London: Faber and Faber, 1988), 33.

Chapter 2   Recuperating Realism

1 Adorno, "Reconciliation under Duress," 152.

2 Jameson, "Case for Georg Lukács," 5.

3 Jameson, 35.
4 Bertolt Brecht, "Against Georg Lukács," in Taylor, *Aesthetics and Politics*, 80.
5 Brecht, 80; emphasis in the original.
6 Brecht, 80.
7 Brecht, 81.
8 Brecht, 81.
9 Brecht, 81.
10 Brecht, 82.
11 Lukács, "Vorwort," 435.
12 Brecht, "Against Georg Lukács," 82.
13 Eugene Lunn, "Marxism and Art in the Era of Stalin and Hitler: A Comparison of Brecht and Lukács," *New German Critique*, no. 3 (Autumn 1974): 22.
14 Lukács, *Die Gegenwartsbedeutung*, 469–470.
15 Lukács, 500.
16 Adorno, "Reconciliation under Duress," 151.
17 Lukács, "Es geht um den Realismus," *Werke*, 4:3334.
18 Lukács, "Erzählen oder beschreiben?," 213.
19 Georg Lukács, *Die Theorie des Romans* (Berlin: Paul Cassirer, 1920), 44.
20 Jameson, "Case for Georg Lukács," 11; emphasis ours.
21 Lukács, *Die Theorie des Romans*, 50.
22 Lukács, 50.
23 Lukács, 55.
24 Lukács, 87.
25 Lukács, 88.
26 Lukács, 99.
27 Lukács, 99–100.
28 Lukács, 107.
29 Lukács, 111.
30 Lukács, 119.
31 Lukács, 122.
32 Lukács, 132.
33 Lukács, 132–133.
34 Lukács, 133.
35 Paul de Man, "Georg Lukács's *Theory of the Novel*," *MLN* 81, no. 5 (December 1966): 533.
36 De Man, 534.
37 Lukács, *Die Theorie des Romans*, 167.
38 De Man, "Georg Lukács's *Theory of the Novel*," 168.
39 Lukács, *Werke*, 10:530.
40 Béla Királyfalvi, *The Aesthetics of György Lukács* (Princeton: Princeton University Press, 1975), 77.
41 Lukács, *Über die Besonderheit als Kategorie der Ästhetik*, *Werke*, 10:758.
42 Lukács, 767.
43 Királyfalvi, *Aesthetics of György Lukács*, 82.
44 Lukács, *Werke*, 10:769–770.

Chapter 3 Classic Novels, Classic Comics

1 Lukács, "Erzählen oder beschreiben?," 223–224.
2 Lukács, 226.

3   Lukács, "Es geht um den Realismus," 323–324.
4   See also David Carrier, "Proust's *In Search of Lost Time*: The Comics Version," in Meskin and Cook, *Art of Comics*, 188: "Nowadays, however, film has its canons and numerous highly sophisticated academic interpretations. Comics, by contrast, although widely read, are as yet of marginal interest."
5   Marcel Proust, *Contre Sanite-Beuve* (Paris: Pléïade, 1954), 657–658.
6   Marcel Proust, *Textes retrouvés*, ed. Pierre Kolb and Larkin Price (Urbana: Illinois University Press, 1968), 223.
7   A sculptor known as "Ski" makes a peripheral appearance.
8   Carrier, "Proust's *In Search of Lost Time*," 188–201.
9   Gérard Genette, *Palimpsestes: La littérature au second degré* (Paris: Seuil, 1992).
10 Carrier, "Proust's *In Search of Lost Time*," 198.
11 Carrier, 201.
12 Henry James, *The Turn of the Screw* [graphic comic] (West Haven, Conn.: Academic Industries, 1984), accessed February 19, 2021, https://archive.org/details/TheTurnOfTheScrew-GraphicComic/page/n1/mode/2up.
13 Martin Rowson, Charlotte Lindemann, and Gabriel Roth, "*Tristram Shandy*: The Comic Book: Graphic Novelist Martin Rowson on How He Adapted Sterne's Unadaptable Masterpiece," *Slate*, February 18, 2016, accessed February 1, 2021, https://slate.com/culture/2016/02/martin-rowson-on-his-tristram-shandy-graphic-novel-adaptation.html; Martin Rowson, *The Life and Opinions of Tristram Shandy, Gentleman* (London: Picador, 1996).

Chapter 4   Was Wertham Right?

1   Bart Beaty, *Fredric Wertham and the Critique of Mass Culture* (Jackson: University Press of Mississippi, 2005), 113.
2   Beaty, 201.
3   Carol L. Tilley, "Seducing the Innocent: Fredric Wertham and the Falsifications That Helped Condemn Comics," *Information & Culture* 47, no. 4 (2012): 388.
4   Beaty, *Fredric Wertham*, 157.
5   Christopher Pizzino, "On Violation: Comic Books, Delinquency, Phenomenology," in *Critical Directions in Comics Studies*, ed. Thomas Giddens (New Orleans: University Press of Mississippi, 2020), 13.
6   Pizzino, 30–32.
7   Graham Robb, *Balzac* (London: Picador, 1994), 62.
8   Robb, 81.
9   Robb, 83.
10 Robb, 84.
11 Charles Augustin Sainte-Beuve, *Mes Poisons*, ed. V. Giraud (Paris: Plon, 1926), 109.
12 Kathryn Sutherland, "'Events . . . Have Made Us a World of Readers': Reader Relations 1780–1830," in *The Romantic Period*, ed. David Pirie (London: Penguin, 1994), 11–12.
13 Sutherland, 12.
14 Quoted in Sutherland, 13; emphasis in the original.
15 Fredric Wertham, *Seduction of the Innocent: The Influence of Comic Books on Today's Youth* (New York: Rinehart, 1954), 118.
16 Beaty, *Fredric Wertham*, 16.
17 Fredric Wertham, quoted in Wright, *Comic Book Nation*, 94.

18 Tilley, "Seducing the Innocent," 385.

19 Beaty, *Fredric Wertham*, 46.

20 Wertham, *Seduction of the Innocent*, 25.

21 Wertham, 79.

22 Beaty, *Fredric Wertham*, 201.

23 Tilley, "Seducing the Innocent," 383–413.

24 Tilley, 402.

25 Tilley, 402–403.

26 Gerard Jones, *Men of Tomorrow: Geeks, Gangsters, and the Birth of the Comic Book* (Sydney: Random House, 2004), 256.

27 Amy Kiste Nyberg, *Seal of Approval: The History of the Comics Code* (Jackson: University Press of Mississippi, 1998), 167.

28 Nyberg, 168.

29 Nyberg, 167–168.

30 Beaty, *Fredric Wertham*, 104.

31 Wertham, *Seduction of the Innocent*, 33.

32 "Brokebat Mountain: 'Batman Is Gay,' Says George Clooney," PinkNews, March 3, 2006, https://www.pinknews.co.uk/2006/03/03/brokebat-mountain-batman-is-gay -says-george-clooney/.

33 Les Daniels, *DC Comics: Sixty Years of the World's Favorite Comic Book Heroes* (London: Virgin Books, 1995), 114.

34 Beaty, *Fredric Wertham*, 201.

35 Glen Weldon, *The Caped Crusade: Batman and the Rise of Nerd Culture* (New York: Simon & Schuster, 2016), 50.

36 Mark Cotta Vaz, *Tales of the Dark Knight: Batman's First Fifty Years: 1939–1989* (New York: Ballantine Books, 1989), 44.

37 Vaz, 125.

38 Morrison's affinity for Batman and his multivalence is well documented and is actively explored throughout the writer's various stabs at the character, ranging from 1989 right up until 2013.

39 Grant Morrison and Dave McKean, *Arkham Asylum: A Serious House on Serious Earth* (New York: DC Comics, 1989), 20.

40 Marc Singer, *Grant Morrison: Combining the Worlds of Contemporary Comics* (Jackson: University Press of Mississippi, 2012), 66.

41 Wertham, *Seduction of the Innocent*, 31.

42 David M. Halperin, "How to Do the History of Male Homosexuality?," in *The Routledge Queer Studies Reader*, ed. David Hall, Annamarie Jagose, Andrea Bebell, and Susan Potter (London: Routledge, 2013), 267.

43 Wertham, *Seduction of the Innocent*, 15.

44 Wertham, 34.

45 Grant Morrison, *Supergods* (New York: Spiegel & Grau, 2011), 55.

46 Tilley, "Seducing the Innocent," 401.

47 Jones, *Men of Tomorrow*, 270.

48 Gershon Legman, *Love and Death: A Study in Censorship*, partially reproduced in Jeet Heer and Kent Worcester, eds., *Arguing Comics: Literary Masters on a Popular Medium* (Jackson: University Press of Mississippi, 2004), 119.

49 Jones, *Men of Tomorrow*, 274.

50 Craig Yoe, *Secret Identity: The Fetish Art of Superman's Co-creator, Joe Shuster* (New York: Abrams, 2009), 17.

51 Yoe, 21.
52 Yoe, 26.

Chapter 5   The Balzac of Comics

1 Sean Howe, *Marvel Comics: The Untold Story* (New York: Harper, 2012), 360–361.
2 Bart Beaty, *Comics versus Art* (Toronto: University of Toronto Press, 2013), 88.
3 Mark Evanier, *Kirby: King of Comics* (New York: Abrams, 2008), 150.
4 Beaty, *Comics versus Art*, 89.
5 Charles Hatfield, *Hand of Fire: The Comics Art of Jack Kirby* (Jackson: University Press of Mississippi, 2012), 173–174.
6 Lukács, "Balzac und der französische Realismus," *Werke*, 6:469.
7 Beaty, *Comics versus Art*, 56–57.
8 Beaty, 55.
9 Andre Molotiu, "Permanent Ink: Comic Book and Comic Strip Art as Aesthetic Object," in *Comic Art in Museums*, ed. Kim A. Munson (Jackson: University Press of Mississippi, 2020), 50.
10 Beaty, *Comics versus Art*, 29.
11 Leslie Jones, "Cracking the Comics Canon," in Munson, *Comic Art in Museums*, 259.
12 Christopher Couch, *Jerry Robinson: Ambassador of Comics* (New York: Abrams, 2010), 184–185.
13 Evanier, *Kirby*, 203–205.
14 Beaty, *Comics versus Art*, 56–57.
15 In a marvelous series of examples of the swipe's artistic currency, sections of cartoonist Charles Burns's "swipe files" are reproduced alongside some of the work made in reference to them in Todd Hignite, *In the Studio: Visits with Contemporary Cartoonists* (New Haven: Yale University Press, 2006), 113.
16 Sam Adams, Noel Murray, Keith Phipps, and Leonard Pierce, "Reinventing the Pencil: 21 Artists Who Changed Mainstream Comics (for Better or Worse)," A.V. Club, July 20, 2009, accessed March 5, 2021, https://avclub.com/reinventimg-the-pencil-21-artists-who-changed-mainstre-1798218160.
17 John Carlin, "Masters of American Comics: An Art History of Twentieth-Century American Comic Strips and Books," in *Masters of American Comics*, ed. John Carlin, Paul Karasik, and Brian Walker (Los Angeles: Hammer Museum; New Haven: Yale University Press, 2005), 148.
18 Groensteen, *System of Comics*, 24.
19 Evanier, *Kirby*, 147.
20 Morrison, *Supergods*, 122.
21 Hatfield, *Hand of Fire*, 175–176.
22 Hatfield, 226–227.
23 Grant Morrison, quoted in Hatfield, 180.
24 Glen David Gold, "Lo, from the Demon Shall Come—the Public Dreamer!!!," in Carlin, Karasik, and Walker, *Masters of American Comics*, 259.
25 Hatfield, *Hand of Fire*, 153.
26 Hatfield, 182. It is worth noting that Colletta, one of Kirby's most frequently used inkers, rates only one brief mention in Evanier's *Kirby* monograph.
27 Perhaps not such an unusual notion: in the 1980s, Kirby did extensive toy and animation concept work.

28 Randy Duncan, Matthew J. Smith, and Paul Levitz, *The Power of Comics: History, Form and Culture* (London: Bloomsbury, 2015), 221.

29 Howe, *Marvel Comics*, 345–346.

30 Howe, 336.

Chapter 6 Figurative Pseudonyms

1 Lukács, "Der historische Roman des demokratischen Humanismus," *Werke*, 6:279.

2 Arnold Hauser, *The Social History of Art*, vol. 3 (London: Routledge, 1999), 65.

3 Hauser, 369–370.

4 Hauser, 370; emphasis ours.

5 Hauser, 371.

6 Lukács, *Goethe und seine Zeit, Werke*, 7:79.

7 "Aber abgesehen von jenen grundlegenden Veränderungen, deren Character wir soeben, gelegentlich des 'Werther,' analysiert haben, nimmt Goethe noch eine weitere entscheidende Korrektur an der Figur seines Helden vor: er nimmt ihm die Goethesche *Genialität*. Und ebenso macht es Gottfried Keller in seinem noch Stärker autobiographischem Roman, im Grünen Heinrich. Warum? Weil beide grossen Erzähler—Goethe und Keller—klar gesehen haben, dass die biographische Gestaltung der Genialität, die in der Biographie gegebene Entstehungsgeschichte eines genialen Meschen und seiner genialen Leistungen, den Ausdrucksmitteln der epischen Kunst widerstreitet"; Lukács, 6:371.

8 Lukács, 6:371; emphasis in the original.

9 Lukács, 6:372; emphasis in the original.

10 Beaty, *Comics versus Art*, 201.

11 Beaty, 215.

12 Beaty, 214–215.

13 Beaty, 215.

14 Bart Beaty, "Autobiography as Authenticity," in *A Comic Studies Reader*, ed. Jeet Heer and Kent Worcester (Jackson: University Press of Mississippi, 2008), 228.

15 Jacob Brogan, "Masked Fathers: *Jimmy Corrigan* and the Superheroic Legacy," in *The Comics of Chris Ware: Drawing Is a Way of Thinking*, ed. David M. Ball and Martha B. Kuhlman (Jackson: University Press of Mississippi, 2010), 20.

16 *Shonen*: literally, "few years," one of the five primary categories of manga, aimed at boys up to the age of fifteen.

Chapter 7 Josh Bayer

1 Gérard Genette, *Palimpsestes: Literature in the Second Degree*, trans. Channa Newman and Claude Doubinsky (Lincoln: Nebraska University Press, 1997), 125.

2 Genette, 127.

3 Genette, 128.

4 M. Thomas Inge, "Form and Function in Metacomics: Self-Reflexivity in the Comic Strips," *Studies in Popular Culture* 13, no. 2 (1991): 8.

5 Inge, 10–12.

6 Inge, 10.

7 Marshall McLuhan, "Comics: *Mad* Vestibule to TV," in Heer and Worcester, *Arguing Comics*, 110–111.

8 Inge, "Form and Function," 2.

9 Roy Cook, "Why Comics Are Not Films: Metacomics and Medium-Specific Conventions," in Meskin and Cook, *Art of Comics*, 173.

10 Cook, 174.

11 Cook, 175.

12 Lukács, *Über die Besonderheit*, 736–737.

13 Lukács, 82.

14 Destroyer Duck was a character created by Kirby and Gerber to help fund Gerber's lawsuit against Marvel Comics over the ownership of Howard the Duck, another of his creations.

15 Josh Bayer, *Theth: Tomorrow Forever* (Denver: Tinto, 2019), 97–98.

Chapter 8   Nina Bunjevac

1 Lukács, *Faust-Studien*, *Werke*, 6:551–552.

2 Predrag Palavestra, "Before 1989: Literature as a Criticism of Ideology in the Slavic World and Serbian Literature," *Serbian Studies* 18, no. 2 (2004): 371, accessed November 13, 2021, https://link.gale.com/apps/doc/A251858388/AONE?u=usyd&sid=bookmark-AONE&xid=7c3cdec8.

3 Deborah James, "Drawn Out of the Gutters: Nina Bunjevac's *Fatherland*, a Collaborative Memory," *Feminist Media Studies* 15, no. 3 (2015): 529–530.

4 M. Precup, "To Dream of Birds: The Father as Potential Perpetrator in Nina Bunjevac's 'August, 1977' and *Fatherland*," in *The Graphic Lives of Fathers: Memory, Representation and Fatherhood in North American Autobiographical Comics*, ed. Roger Sabin, Palgrave Studies in Comics and Graphic Novels (London: Palgrave Macmillan, 2017), 109.

5 Precup, 122.

6 Palavestra, "Before 1989," 371–372.

7 For a concise yet comprehensive overview of the complexities of postwar and then post-Soviet development of Serbian literature, see Milan Orlić's "Post-Yugoslav Serbian Literature and Its Roots in the Social and Political Changes," *Transcultural Studies* 14 (2018): 101–118. Orlić, himself a writer and publisher, has a nuanced and incisive understanding of the dense literary and political landscape of Serbia.

8 Orlić, 103.

9 Slobodan Vladušić, "Neorealism in Serbian Prose of the 1990s: Its Development and Transformations," *Serbian Studies* 20 (2006): 151.

10 Vladimir Gvozden, "The Serbian Novel after the End of Utopia," in *Primerjalna Književnost* [*Comparative Literature and Literary Theory*] 43, no. 2 (2020): 43.

11 Gvozden, 46, 56–57.

12 Vladušić, "Neorealism in Serbian Prose of the 1990s," 153.

13 For a thorough historical account of the influence of French and German literature on Serbia and the generational split between Serbian modernists and Surrealists, see Anton Kadić's extraordinary "Surrealists versus Modernists in Serbian Literature," in *From Croatian Renaissance to Yugoslav Socialism*, ed. C. H. Van Schooneveld (The Hague: Mouton, 1969), 192–227.

14 Jeremy Stubbs makes a convincing argument for the influence of Surrealist literature upon modernist depictions of Paris in popular culture and by extension internationally, including the masked antihero Fantômas, who first appeared in 1911, a considerable precursor to the superhero (the Shadow did not appear in the pulps and on radio until 1931 and likewise the Phantom in comic strips until 1936). See Stubbs's

"Surrealist Literature and Urban Crime," in *The Cambridge Companion to the Literature of Paris*, ed. Anna-Louise Milne (Cambridge: Cambridge University Press, 2013), 161–188.

15 For a crash course in Surrealist dream sequences and symbolist production design in Hollywood film noir, see Boris Ingster's *Stranger on the Third Floor* (1940), Edward Dmytryk's *Murder My Sweet* (1944), Alfred Hitchcock's *Spellbound* (1945), Orson Welles's *The Lady from Shanghai* (1947) and *Touch of Evil* (1958), and Robert Aldrich's *Kiss Me Deadly* (1955), the latter five of which are adapted from literary sources. While Welles's highly innovative approach to cinematography and production design can be traced back to his groundbreaking on- and offstage theater career and abiding love for the pulps and hard-boiled novels (as biographed in Simon Cowell's *Orson Welles: Road to Xanadu* [London: Jonathan Cape, 1995]), Hitchcock went as far as to recruit Salvador Dalí to work on the dream sequence of his film, which, somewhat tragically, was edited down from twenty minutes of screen time to just two. The sequence remains a high watermark of cinematic production design.

16 Raymond Chandler, *The Big Sleep* (London: Penguin, 1970), 3.

17 Terms such as *protagonist* and *antagonist* seem ill-equipped to describe Bunjevac's treatment of Benny, a cipher upon whom is projected the many social, sexual, and psychological complexities of the narrative.

18 Dragoş Manea and Mihaela Precup, "'Who Were You Crying For?' Empathy, Fantasy and the Framing Device of the Perpetrator in Nina Bunjevac's *Bezimena*," *Studies in Comics* 11, no. 2 (2020): 375.

19 Manea and Precup, 379–380.

20 Manea and Precup, 382.

21 Manea and Precup, 380.

22 Nina Bunjevac, "Author's Afterword," in *Bezimena* (Seattle: Fantagraphics, 2018), iii.

23 Manea and Precup, "'Who Were You Crying For?,'" 375.

24 If Chandler appears to be a "leg man" and Spillane a "breast man," Murakami would appear to be an inveterate "ear man."

25 Stamos Metzidakis, "Graphemic Gymnastics in Surrealist Literature," *Romanic Review* 81, no. 2 (1990): 211.

26 Metzidakis, 212.

27 Metzidakis, 212–213.

28 Elza Adamowicz, "Exquisite Excrement: The Bataille-Breton Polemic" (paper presented at Polemics, Queen Mary / Goldsmiths University of London, London, 2005), accessed November 17, 2021, https://www.researchgate.net/publication/333950028_Exquisite_excrement_the_Bataille-Breton_polemic.

29 Of particular relevance to George Bataille's *Story of the Eye* (trans. Joachim Neugroschel [London: Penguin, 2001]) is his *L'Erotisme* ([Eroticism], 1957) and *Visions of Excess: Selected Writings, 1927–1939* (trans. Allan Stoekl, Carl R. Lovitt, and Donald M. Leslie Jr. [Minneapolis: University of Minnesota Press, 1985]), both of which include sustained analyses of many of the themes and symbols of the novel and outline Bataille's use of transgression as an agent of critique.

30 Roland Barthes, "The Metaphor of the Eye," in Bataille, *Story of the Eye*, 121–122.

31 Emily Apter, "Female Fetishism on the Fin de Siècle," in *Eroticism and the Body Politic*, ed. Lynn Hunt (Baltimore: John Hopkins University Press, 1991), 168.

32 Susan Sontag, "The Pornographic Imagination," in Bataille, *Story of the Eye*, 88.

Chapter 9   Simon Hanselmann

1   Lukács, "Bela Balázs und die ihn nicht mögen," *Werke*, 1:740.
2   Lukács, 1:740.
3   Lukács, 1:743.
4   Lukács, 1:743–744.
5   Lukács, 1:744.
6   Simon Hanselmann, *Crisis Zone* (Seattle: Fantagraphics, 2021), iii.
7   Cathy J. Cohen, "Punks, Bulldaggers, and Welfare Queens: The Radical Potential of Queer Politics?," in Hall et al., *Routledge Queer Studies Reader*, 75.
8   Cohen, 76.
9   Cohen, 75.
10   James Reith, "Simon Hanselmann: I Hate Twee Art. Life Is Not Nice," *Guardian*, April 14, 2016, accessed October 13, 2021, https://www.theguardian.com/books/2016/apr/14/simon-hanselmann-interview-megg-mogg-and-owl.
11   Richie Pope, "Simon Hanselmann Interview," *Forge*, April 25, 2019, accessed October 13, 2021, https://issuu.com/forgeartmag/docs/issuu22/s/122384.
12   Cohen, "Punks, Bulldaggers, and Welfare Queens," 77.
13   Lee Edelman, "Queer Theory, Disidentification, and the Death Drive," in Hall et al., *Routledge Queer Studies Reader*, 294.
14   Edelman, 290.
15   Susan Sontag, "Notes on Camp," in *Against Interpretation and Other Essays* (London: Penguin, 1961), 282.
16   Jasbir K. Puar, "Queer Times, Queer Assemblages," in Hall et al., *Routledge Queer Studies Reader*, 515.
17   Puar, 516.
18   Puar, 516–517.
19   José Esteban Muñoz, quoted in Puar, 519.
20   Puar, 520.
21   Hanselmann, *Crisis Zone*, 271.

Chapter 10   The Hernandez Brothers

1   Lukács, *Heidelberger Philosophie der Kunst (1912–1914)*, *Werke*, 16:57.
2   Lukács, *Faust-Studien*, 548.
3   Rather than destroying pro wrestling's credibility, dismissing Kayfabe actually propelled the entertainment to new heights of popularity and paradoxically returned it to its continental American (rather than Grecian) roots—that is, a traveling show more akin to theater or vaudeville than sport.
4   Derek Parker Royal, "Palomar and Beyond: An Interview with Gilbert Hernandez," *MELUS* 32, no. 3 (Fall 2007): 221–246.
5   Royal, 228.
6   Dan Nadel, "Clean Lines, Messy Lives," *New York Review of Books*, July 23, 2020, 47.
7   Lukács, *Über die Besonderheit*, 757.
8   Lukács, 757.
9   Lukács, 48.
10   Lukács, 48.
11   Sam Adams, "*Love and Rockets*' Hernandez Brothers on 30 Years in Comics," A.V. Club, October 19, 2012, accessed June 6, 2021, https://www.avclub.com/love-and-rockets-hernandez-brothers-on-30-years-in-com-1798234102.

Chapter 11   Tommi Parrish

1   Lukács, *Werke*, 2:40.
2   Lukács, 5:549.
3   Rachel Davies, "'That's Just What My Life Looks Like': A Tommi Parrish Interview," *Comics Journal* 12 (February 2018), accessed July 7, 2021, http://www.tcj.com/thats -just-what-my-life-looks-like-a-tommi-parrish-interview/.
4   Davies.
5   Davies.
6   Carrier, *Aesthetics*, 16.
7   E. H. Gombrich, *Meditations on a Hobby Horse* (London: Phaidon, 1963), 134–135.
8   Carrier, *Aesthetics*, 16.
9   Roland Barthes, "Plastic," in *Mythologies*, trans. Richard Howard and Annette Lavers (New York: Hill and Wang, 1972), 194.
10   Barthes, 193.
11   Lukács, "Erzählen oder beschreiben?," 214.
12   Lukács, 226.
13   Lukács, 228.
14   It must also be noted that in the case of a penciller/inker team, as in so many main-stream comics, this lies firmly the purview of the inker, that figure whose role is so heavily contested yet so vital in shaping, editing, and clarifying the finished product.
15   Original pages by cartoonists such as Eisner and Caniff are hotly collected and can be prohibitively expensive. For high-quality reproductions of original pages, see books such as Carlin, Karasik, and Walker's *Masters of American Comics*, Evanier's *Kirby*, and Hignite's *In the Studio*, all of which place an emphasis on the original page as an art object and sometimes compare it with the printed work. Interest in such material is perhaps best reflected in Jack Kirby, *Jack Kirby: Pencils and Inks* (San Diego: IDW, 2016), which features reproductions of penciled and inked pages side by side for comparison.
16   Walter Benjamin, "The Work of Art in the Age of Reproducibility (Third Version)," in *Walter Benjamin: Selected Writings*, vol. 4, *1938–1940*, trans. Edmund Jephcott et al. (Cambridge, Mass.: Harvard University Press, 2003), 253.
17   Groensteen, *System of Comics*, 70.
18   Groensteen, 71.
19   Lukács, "Es geht um den Realismus," 321.

Chapter 12   Yoshihiro Tatsumi

1   Dennis Keene, "Translator's Introduction," in *Grass for My Pillow*, by Saiichi Maruya, trans. Dennis Keene (New York: Columbia University Press, 2002), 2.
2   Keene, 12.
3   Sigmund Freud, *Civilization and Its Discontents*, trans. Joan Riviere (New York: Jonathan Cape & Harrison Smith, 1930), 28.
4   Adrian Tomine, "Q & A with Yoshihiro Tatsumi," in *The Push Man and Other Stories* (Montreal: Drawn & Quarterly, 2012), 205.
5   See Hans Fallada, "The True Story of *Alone in Berlin*," in *Alone in Berlin* (London: Penguin, 2009), 599–602.
6   Geoff Wilks, afterword to *Alone in Berlin*, 573.
7   Walter Benjamin, quoted in Jeremy Tambling, *Going Astray: Dickens and London* (London: Routledge, 2009), 7.

8   Tambling, 1.
9   Gary Groth, "Yoshihiro Tatsumi Interview," *Comics Journal* 281 (February 2007), accessed July 30, 2021, http://www.tcj.com/yoshihiro-tatsumi-interview/.
10 Groth.
11 Groth.
12 Groth. Note Groth's questioning about the "empirical" truth of Tatsumi's perception of ugliness.
13 Tomine, "Q & A," 209.
14 Mark Williams, "Life after Death? Writing the Alienated Self in Post-War Japan," *International Academic Forum Journal of Literature and Librarianship* 2, no. 2 (Autumn 2013): 11.
15 Williams, 10.
16 Charles Hatfield, *Alternative Comics* (Jackson: University Press of Mississippi, 2005), 131.
17 Alice Kaplan, foreword to *Personal Writings*, by Albert Camus, trans. Justin O'Brian (London: Penguin, 2020), xiv.
18 Albert Camus, *The First Man* (London: Penguin, 1996), 16.
19 Camus, 20–21.
20 Roman Rosenbaum, "Graphic Representation of the Precariat in Popular Culture," in *Visions of Precarity in Japanese Popular Culture and Literature*, ed. Kristina Iwata-Weickgenannt and Roman Rosenbaum (London: Routledge, 2015), 134.
21 Adrian Tomine, introduction to *Push Man and Other Stories*, i–ii. Tomine, an auto-biographical cartoonist of considerable repute, was instrumental in having Tatsumi's work translated and released in the West. Tomine's interview with Tatsumi is reproduced across all three of Drawn & Quarterly's published volumes of Tatsumi's *gekiga*.
22 Tomine, "Q & A," 206.
23 Adrian Tomine, "Q & A with Yoshihiro Tatsumi," in *Abandon the Old in Tokyo* (Montreal: Drawn & Quarterly, 2012), 196.
24 Yoshihiro Tatsumi, *A Drifting Life* (Montreal: Drawn & Quarterly, 2009), 827–828.
25 Tatsumi, 833.

Index

Page numbers in *italics* refer to figures.

Milton, John, 233
Minerva Press and Library, 69–70; *Children of the Abbey*, 70; *The Philosophic Kidnapper, a Novel, altered from the French*, 70; *Vicissitudes Abroad, or the Ghost of my Father*, 70. *See also* Lane, William
modernism, modernist, 4, 88
Moebius, 15
Montesquiou, Comte Robert de, 54
Monty Python's Flying Circus (TV show), 76
Moore, Alan, 111; *From Hell*, 56–57, *58, 59*; *Watchmen*, 76. *See also* Campbell, Eddie; Gibbons, Dave
Morrison, Bill, *Radioactive Man*, 96. *See also* Vance, Steve
Morrison, Grant, 79. *See also* Batman (character)
Motion Picture Production Code. *See* Hays Code
Muños, José Esteban, 172
Murakami, Haruki, *A Wind-Up Bird Chronicle*, 155–156
Museum of Modern Art (New York), 13

Nabokov, Vladimir, 124; *King, Queen, Knave*, 27
Nadel, Dan, 186, 189
Nakamura, Kenichi, *Abandon the Old in Tokyo*, 228
Nakazawa, Keiji, 109, 114, 139; *Barefoot Gen*, 117, 119
Nazi, Nazism, 63, 66, 80, 81, 217, 221; SS, 80
Nerval, Géard de: *Les Filles du feu*, 53; *Sylvie*, 44, 53–54
Netflix, 162
New Left Review, 161
New York Review of Books, 2, 161
Nicoll, Helen: Megg, Mogg, and Owl (children's books), 163. *See also* Hanselmann, Simon; Piénkowski, Jan
Nietzsche, Friedrich, 80; *Übermensch*, 80
Nightmare on Elm Street, A (film franchise), 56
Nolde, Emile, 198
Nordau, Max, *Degeneration*, 72
Norse mythology, 100

Oe, Kenzaburo, 215
Olympic Games, 216

O'Neil, Dennis, 137
opera, 51–52
Orlic, Milan, 246n7
Ormston, Dean, *Black Hammer*, 96. *See also* Lemire, Jeff
Others, The (film), 57
Otomo, Katsuhiro, 226
Outcault, Richard F.: *Hogan's Alley*, 129; Yellow Kid, 129

Painter, George, 54
Palavestra, Predrag, 149
Palazzo Medici-Riccardi, Florence, 52
Panter, Gary, 94, 127; *Dal Tokyo*, 94
paracomics, 27
Parker Brothers (toys), 139
Parrish, Tommi, 197–212; everyday, 200–203; and expressionism, 198; "Generic Love Story," 201, *202*; "I Was Just Trying to Be Alive," *204*; *The Lie and How We Told It*, 205–206, *207, 213*; *Perfect Hair*, 201; "Sasha," *199*; *Untitled*, 208; "Untitled," *Now 4*, *210*
Peanuts (comic), 186
Peckinpah, Sam, 76
Pekar, Harvey, 109
Perec, Georges, *Life a User's Manual*, 221
Perez, Michelle, *The Pervert*, 166. *See also* Boydell, Remy
Petronius, *The Satyricon*, 67
Pettibon, Raymond, 131
Phantom, the (character), 87, 137
Phillips, Sean: *The Fade Out*, 152; *Fatale*, 152. *See also* Brubaker, Ed
Photoshop (software), 15–16, 93
Piave, Francesco Maria, 51
Piénkowski, Jan: Megg, Mogg, and Owl (children's books), 163. *See also* Hanselmann, Simon; Nicoll, Helen
Pinterest, 92
Pissarro, Joachim, 2–4, 14. *See also* wild art
Pizzino, Christopher, 66
Poe, Edgar Allan, 1, 49, 60; "The Fall of the House of Usher," 57, *61, 62*; "The Murders in the Rue Morgue," 77. *See also* Corben, Richard
Poggioli, Renato, 30
Popeye (character), 137
popular music, 2